Thy Will Be Done

COMBONI INTERNATIONAL SCHOLASTICATE
ELSTREE

David K. Glenday FSCJ

Dawson Place: 21/1/1978

THY WILL BE DONE

Praying the Our Father as Subversive Activity

Michael H. Crosby, O.F.M. CAP.

ORBIS BOOKS
Maryknoll, New York 10545

The Catholic Foreign Mission Society of America (Maryknoll) recruits and trains people for overseas missionary service. Through Orbis Books Maryknoll aims to foster the international dialogue which is essential to mission. The books published, however, reflect the opinions of their authors and are not meant to represent the official position of the Society.

Imprimi Potest:
Lloyd Theil, O.F.M. Cap.
Minister Provincial
Midwest Province, O.F.M. Cap.

Nihil Obstat:
Francis Dombrowski, O.F.M. Cap.
Richard J. Sklba, S.S.L., S.T.D.

Imprimatur:
Most Reverend William E. Cousins
Archbishop of Milwaukee

May 14, 1977

The *Nihil obstat* and *Imprimatur* are a declaration that a book or pamphlet is considered to be free from doctrinal or moral error. It is not implied that those who have granted the *Nihil obstat* and *Imprimatur* agree with the contents, opinions, or statements expressed.

LIBRARY OF CONGRESS CATALOGING IN PUBLICATION DATA

Crosby, Michael, 1940–
          Thy will be done.

          Includes bibliographical references.
                    1.   Lord's prayer.   I.   Title.
BV230.C76   226'.96'066   77-5118
ISBN 0-88344-496-8
ISBN 0-88344-497-6 pbk.

Contents

PREFACE   vii

INTRODUCTION: NOT ANOTHER BOOK ON THE OUR FATHER!   1

1. LORD, TEACH US TO PRAY   5

   Spirituality Within Our Institutional Reality   7
   Adapting to the Gaps   10
   Spirituality in a World of Alienation   14
   Pathology and the Ministerial Dimension of Human Life   17

2. OUR FATHER WHO ART IN HEAVEN   21

   Being-in-Participative Community   22
   God's Concerns for the Earth   27
   Spirituality as Participating in God's Concerns   33

3. MAY YOUR NAME BE HOLY ON EARTH AS IN HEAVEN   37

   Liberation: The Revelation of the Name   39
   Jesus Revealing God's Name   48
   Baptized in the Name   50
   Liberation as Naming Reality   53

4. MAY YOUR KINGDOM COME ON EARTH AS IN HEAVEN   59

   The Nation as God's Kingdom   62
   The Church as God's Kingdom   66
   Pilgrims and Strangers in This World   68
   The Cross: Sign of Conflict Among Kingdoms in This World   70

5. SIGNS OF THE KINGDOM COME ON EARTH AS IN HEAVEN   77

   Truth: Nonparticipation in Lies   79
   Justice: Knowing God and Being Known by God   86
   Peace: Sharing Resources and Rights   92

v

6. Thy Will Be Done on Earth as in Heaven   97

   God's Will as Mission in the World   101
   The Will of the Powers and the Principalities   103
   The Cross: Reconciliation and Resistance   110

7. Give Us This Day Our Daily Bread   117

   Worship: The Sign of Having Done Justice   118
   Eating the Bread and Recognizing the Body   124
   Ritual Without Reality   131

8. Forgive Us Our Debts as We Forgive Those Indebted to
   Us   136

   Cancellation of Debts   138
   Freeing the Enslaved   144
   Returning the Land   150
   Abstention from Work   158

9. Lead Us Not into Temptation. . .   163

   Institutions and Social Sin   167
   Isms in Institutions and Ideologies   170
   Ideology as Reinforcing Institutions and Isms   176

10. . . . Deliver Us from Evil   186

   Community: The Gathering of Gifts   188
   Conscientization: Reading Reality to Write History   193
   Conversion: Intellectual, Moral, and Religious Reform   197

11. Amen   212

Notes   219

Acknowledgements   231

Scriptural Index   236

Celano Index   239

General Index   240

Preface

This book resulted from many factors, primarily from a retreat given to Franciscan Friars at Holy Name College in Washington, D.C. Outlines and tapes used there have served as the basis for this book.

The book is dedicated to the members of the Midwest Capuchin Province—past and present. I have lived all of my adult life in communities with these men who have tried and are trying to put teeth into the Franciscan vision of life. It has been out of the mutual sharing of life and opportunity and discouragement and hope with them—those who have died, who have left, and who remain—that this book is written.

It has resulted from a good education provided me by the Order in its own institutions and beyond, as well as from ministerial possibilities in the black community and in the Milwaukee Justice and Peace Center. Sharing with people in these ministries has helped shape the reflections contained here.

Two members of the province helped immeasurably in the remote and immediate writing. One has left and the other remains. Dale Olen helped me in many ways to develop models for presentation; the tenth chapter would be much weaker without his insights. Dan Crosby, my brother, helped me in background on prayer and a better understanding of the individual and interpersonal levels of life. He also helped me clarify material by his editing. In this he was joined by Sr. Florence Shigo and Lisa McGaw.

I would also like to thank Joelyn Olen and Steve Erceg for the innumerable drafts they prepared, and Irene Brown for her painstaking care in arranging final details.

While I have tried to refrain from sexism in language as far as possible, the book suffers from the fact that the majority of quotations used reflect an overly-male ideology. Because our language has yet to provide adequate words that can refer to God that do not reflect this terminology, I have used these as part of the limited expression of our times. All direct biblical quotations are from the *New American Bible*.

Introduction
Not Another Book on the Our Father!

Maybe they said the same thing about Origen's exposition of the Lord's Prayer, or Tertullian's. Maybe, after the Pax Romana settled into the community, they said the same of Gregory of Nyssa and Cyril of Jerusalem. At any rate, this book is an attempt to do for our age what they, as well as writers throughout the centuries, attempted to do for theirs: to make prayer and living harmonious.

If we investigate the many authors who have been led to write treatises on the Our Father or have been inspired by the words of the Our Father, we find they often were trying to understand it in light of their own surrounding realities. Thus, when late Hellenistic philosophy and culture arose, Origen saw the need to view the Lord's Prayer in its light. Tertullian and Cyprian offered the African church an interpretation of the prayer they could pray in their reality. As a distinctive Latin Christianity took shape toward the end of the fourth century, Augustine offered a fresh vision of the Our Father for the Latin West, which remained until the Middle Ages and beyond, with Thomas Aquinas, Meister Eckhart, and Martin Luther using it as a base for new ways to live the faith in their environmental contexts.

Before going further, let me say that I am not trying to put myself in the categories of such doctors as those mentioned above. Yet, reflecting on our world today—which has been defined by the 1971 Synod of Bishops of the Catholic church as environmentally "marked with the grave sin of social injustice"—it does seem that if one is to pray the Our Father and work for its realization on earth as in heaven, it must be interpreted in light of the reality in which we make our address to God and as members of a faith community.

While this understanding led indirectly to this book, the im-

1

mediate cause resulted from three things that happened to me in the past ten years. The first occurred in a corner classroom of a theologate nestled in the safe and secure woods of northern Wisconsin where I was a student. Here I learned that the Our Father was part of the *disciplina arcana*, the secret that was handed on to those entering the Christian community. The second occurred on the expressways of the United States and at parties and in the homes of average people. Here I heard the Our Father sung by Sr. Janet Mead, openly proclaimed over the airways, in corner bars, and via family-room stereos. The third occurred in Washington, D.C., with First Order Franciscans from the Holy Name Province. Here I gave a retreat with the theme, "For a Franciscan to pray the Our Father in a world marked by the grave sin of social injustice, there are equally grave economic, political, and social consequences."

How do these three "immediate causes" relate to the purpose in publishing this work on the Our Father? Perhaps a quick background on each of the causes might help.

1. The "discipline of the secret" required that certain sacred rites and formulae, especially the Creed, the Lord's Prayer, and the words of consecration, should be kept hidden from those who were not baptized; these should not be committed to writing but communicated only by word of mouth among those accepted as believers. While there were pedagogical reasons for this discipline to become part of the liturgical formation of the third and fourth centuries, an analysis of the words of the Our Father as interpreted by the pagan environment surrounding the early community also reveals a practical reason for its secrecy: It represented a viewpoint and ideology counter to that which legitimized the institutions of that day.

In the first and second centuries, as documents such as the communications between Pliny and Trajan attest, allegiance to the empire was determined by proclaiming the kingship of the emperors, the holiness of their name, and submission to their will. To declare otherwise, as demanded by praying the Our Father, was to act subversively toward those powers and principalities. Thus, there was a practical reason for the *disciplina arcana* (as is true of most liturgical practices). The author of *Christian Antiquities* wrote as early as 1841: "The reason which led to the introduction of this discipline probably was the persecution to which the early Christians were subject. Under these circumstances, they very naturally would conceal their worship as far as practicable from the observation of their enemies, by whom they were surrounded. This precaution is distinctly indicated in the . . . letter of Pliny."[1]

I believe that the reasons for the *disciplina arcana* were influenced by the infrastructures of the world that persecuted those publicly attesting to other realities—given Herod's fear about the possibility of another kind of peace on earth coming from another king (cf. Matt. 2:1–8, 16–18) and Pilate's fear about the possibility of another king besides Caesar (cf. John 19:12–16). Without entering into the dispute over these reasons, it is safe to say that most, if not all, of the phrases of the Our Father called for the creation of conditions on earth that would be considered counter to those of first- and second-century environments.

Looking at those times and reflecting on the presence of Jesus in history, I can only conclude that the Our Father was a subversive prayer. Even though it was a declaration that summarized praise and petition, for those without faith it summarized a threat and delegitimation. Just as God's will for peace was interpreted as a threat, so the faith that inspired a community to pray and live out these words in its history could not achieve credibility in society.

2. In 1974 "The Lord's Prayer" approached the top of the pop music charts across the nation. Realizing that this same "top secret" prayer had now come to such legitimation by society that society would use it to make money created dissonant notes in my psyche. Somehow there seemed a contradiction about having the Our Father accommodated so well into North American production-consumption patterns when, in another world marked by the sin of the beast (cf. Rev. 13ff.), it was transmitted in secret. In addition, the fact that some could enjoy the Lord's Prayer over the airwaves as they jostled freeway traffic or sat in parked cars, while still others rejoiced in the fact that with such a record there might be another chance to show how relevant religion can be for the young, seemed to indicate the extent to which we have forsaken our biblical roots.

Hearing that record made me ask, "What has brought us to the point where we find people who profess Christianity making money from the very prayer Jesus taught? How can we get excited about hearing the Lord's Prayer played over the airwaves sandwiched between a sexist remark by a chauvinist male disc jockey and an ad for Preparation H? Isn't there some contradiction when we hear the prayer played at a football game by a marching band as it forms itself into a cross before the thousands assembled for the great American liturgy of sport—the hawkers, the statisticians, the drunks, the enthusiasts, the odds makers?" Such questions indicated to me that it just didn't make sense. And what made even less sense was the realization that few people would be able to make sense out of what I was thinking!

I could only conclude that if it is now acceptable for the system literally to capitalize on what once de-legitimated society, then we must consider how the Our Father evolved to this state from its origins of prayer and ministry.

3. Having ministered in a central city for five years before working with religious congregations in their effort to live and promote justice, I began to see how divorced a ministry that tried to include a call to individual, group, and systemic conversion was from traditional forms of prayer—even though the words of the psalms and the rest of Scripture reflected a reality that once united prayer and daily life. Not only did mysticism and ministry seem to be opposed; the two-story approach to spirituality, which stressed such things as prayer and community before apostolate and world, spoke of a spirituality no longer relevant to my present environment.

With all this uneasiness within me, and after being asked to give a retreat at the House of Theology for the Holy Name Franciscans in Washington, I ran across a statement (no. 33), in *The Vocation of the Order Today*, which was addressed to all the Friars Minor of the World by the 1973 General Chapter of the Franciscans:

> Our desire to create, in the very heart of the city, a fraternal community, where men of diverse types and background share life, goods, work; a fraternity which renounces all dominion in order to serve, which chooses a life style that brings it close to the poor and makes it sensitive to the lot of all who are oppressed, creates, whether we wish it or not, both social and political repercussions.[2]

Such a statement—especially the phrase "whether we wish it or not"—seemed to be saying for our era what Jesus was for his. "Whether he wished it or not," his good news was bad news for the powers and principalities of his world; his reconciliation was resistance to them; his peace resulted in their violence; his being conquered by them conquered them. "Whether we wish it or not," he had said, "they will harry you as they harried me" (John 15:20). Just our effort to create a community on earth reflective of that kingdom in heaven would "create, whether we wish it or not, both social and political repercussions," as he promised:

> If you find that the world hates you,
> know it has hated me before you.
> If you belonged to the world,
> it would love you as its own;
> the reason it hates you
> is that you do not belong to the world.
> But I chose you out of the world (John 15:18–19).

For me all this came together in the scene where Francis accepted the fact of being chosen from the world. He divested himself of its way of interpreting reality, which he had previously reinforced by his whole life, and stood naked before that same reality, declaring, "From now on I can freely say *Our Father who art in Heaven. . . .*"[3]

With apologies to Origen, Augustine, Thomas Aquinas, and Martin Luther *et alii* and *aliae*, I have tried to show, by reflection on the Our Father, how prayer and living might harmonize. Reflecting on our total reality, as Jesus and Francis did on theirs, and publicly professing what the Lord's Prayer means according to God's plan for the world offer the possibility of uniting a mystical and ministerial dimension to our spirituality.

This book develops a spirituality for American society in the last quarter of the twentieth century. It does not purport to reflect a perfect science or a pure exegesis; yet, at the same time, it does not want to be invalidated by either. The assumption undergirding this book is that God's revelation in both Jewish and Christian Scriptures occurs in a total environment that includes individuals, groups, and structures. The involvement of God's revelation in such a setting has its effect on our lives in our particular reality. Revelation and reality cannot be separated. Such an approach or methodology may be considered too ideological. Yet, as Avery Dulles has shown regarding the church and its various models, it is difficult if not impossible to escape ideological persuasions. Even the generally accepted view that exegesis (especially scriptural exegesis) is neutral reveals, upon further analysis, a subtle but nonetheless effective control by an ideology. If it is accepted that all interpretation reflects and sustains particular ideologies, judgment of this book should determine if the particular ideology presented herein represents a valid approach to spirituality or not, especially insofar as spirituality cannot be separated from a reality context.

As with any new way of looking at something familiar, this work will be criticized for not having said enough. It doesn't stand as *the* answer for all reality. It doesn't purport to be a work of scholarly sociology or refined scriptural exegesis. It has arisen from a firm conviction that I must let God's Word become planted in my life in a world that is quite alien to that Word. It is, in summary, my attempt—the attempt of one person in one environmental setting—to let God's revelation say something to me and by my words here (coupled with my prayer and ministry) possibly have something to say to my society.

This book is meant for people in today's society who are concerned about spirituality and justice, about exercising their charisms in prayer, healing, and prophecy. If I have been successful in uniting these aspects and whether the Our Father should be prayed as subversive activity in our society can be determined only by the individuals and communities who reflect on the book's contents. Such a determination will come not merely from intellectual agreement or disagreement with what I write. The real determination will come from whether or not individuals and communities are challenged to deeper conversion by what is said here (and, even more, by praying the Our Father more authentically). If this happens, then this book will be contributing something to the creation of his kingdom here on earth as it is in heaven—and we will have succeeded by being faithful to the process.

1

Lord, Teach Us to Pray

SPIRITUALITY WITHIN OUR INSTITUTIONAL REALITY

When the disciples approached Jesus, asking him to teach them to pray, he taught them words whose real meaning they discovered only later. In the concrete experience of their living, they found that it was not enough for Jesus to offer them certain words which, when placed together, might be considered prayer. The only way those words could become prayer would be if they were offered in the context of their world and the environment about them. The disciples had to undergo a whole relearning process about prayer as well as their world. This reconditioning would be based on their growing realization that prayer means relating words to reality.

For us to pray in the manner of the first disciples, we too must be prepared to go through a relearning process. If Jesus is to have an impact on us and our world with the meaning of the Our Father's words, they must be understood and addressed within our environment—which has attempted to "word" us out of reality. Thus, an analysis of our present world, which evidences a culture that tries to control us by manipulation of words (and, thereby, of reality itself), is essential if we are to pray as Jesus would have us pray—by our lives.

Such an analysis of this reality demands critical reflection. This will help us determine how far we have traveled from our origins, which once led to Jerusalem. Such an investigation might show us what relearning we must undergo and what conversion we must make if we are to return to those biblical roots that must be continually nourished for effective growth and renewal.

When a person's current interpretation of reality no longer holds credibility as a way to salvation, he or she seeks a new way, a more credible vision. Often, on finding that vision, one closely identifies with the person (founder) from whom it was received: "Lord, to whom shall we go? You have the words of eternal life. We have come to believe; we are convinced that you are God's holy one" (John 6:68–69). A new faith is discovered and professed, not just in the person, but in the *values* and *ideals* concretized in the lifestyle and attitudes of the one to be followed. The leader has reflected an approach or an answer for some of the problems that gnaw at the heart of the person's human needs. The profession of faith in the leader by others creates a movement and gives inspiration. The thoughts, words, and style of the leader create the foundation for the kind of presence the followers are to mirror to society. The manner of this presence in society reflects a basic stance that differs from the existing modes of operating in the society.

In this light, we can better appreciate why the first disciples, used to traditional ways of praying, asked Jesus to teach them a new way to pray that would correspond to their new way of living. In "The Pater Noster as an Eschatological Prayer," Raymond Brown notes:

> What is interesting is the fact that the disciples felt the need of asking Jesus how to pray, or that Jesus gave them a model of prayer. This indicates a realization that the traditional Jewish prayer formulae were no longer adequate for the followers of Jesus. From the time of His introduction by John the Baptist, Jesus had stood for a certain newness in religion. When His observances were compared to those of the Pharisees, He had said that one should not put new wine into old wineskins (Mk. 2:22). In the very Sermon on the Mount which frames the PN, He had shown His freedom with regard to the Torah by repeating over and over, "You have heard it said, but I say." Now, if Jesus presented Himself as the representative (and, indeed, the incarnation) of a new way of approaching God, it was only logical that He would have a new way to pray to God. Thus, while many phrases of the PN may be found in contemporary Jewish prayers, there is a new spirit that invests the

"Lord's Prayer." The Jewish prayer formulae, depending heavily on the Old Testament, were for the community of Israel, which regarded God's manifestation of Himself to their father as the definitive way of approaching God. The PN is a prayer for the Christian community, for those who believe that Jesus is the way to God and that the new and final dispensation has come.[1]

Today, while we profess gospel values and ideals, their practice in many of our traditions and norms, including prayer itself, indicates an emptiness in our profession of "faith." And because there seems to be such a difference between what we profess as values and ideals and what we practice in our norms and traditions, we face a true credibility gap, especially among critical thinkers. Often we have to admit that we have little to offer when the world comes to us, saying, "Are you the ones who are to come, or shall we look for another?" (cf. Matt. 11:4).

A recent Harris poll surveying the degree of people's confidence in key U.S. institutions revealed that organized religion evoked confidence, trust, or credibility from only 36 percent of those polled—four percentage points behind the military, eight points behind local police, eighteen points behind local trash collection, and twenty-one points behind the medical profession.[2] In mid-1977, leading Americans in many fields were asked to rate institutions, organizations, and activities (on a scale rising from 1 to 7) in regard to their influence "on decisions or actions affecting the nation as a whole." Results published in *U.S. News & World Report*[3] showed how little organized religion has to say in this country (and how much it isn't even heard as it talks to itself?)—just a fraction above the movies and almost three points behind television (see the table on p. 11).

Twenty-five other institutions in the United States are seen as having more influence on people than the institution many of us are part of—even as "professionals"! What will our response to these findings be? Will we argue the statistics? Or will we say the gospel we profess isn't meant to have influence in the world? "You are the salt of the earth. But what if the salt goes flat? How can you restore its flavor? Then it is good for nothing but to be thrown out and trampled underfoot" (Matt. 5:13).

With lack of confidence in institutional organized religion, its ability to bring about the concerns of the Lord in other institutions, especially in political and economic fields, will be minimal. The same was true in Jesus' time. Even though Jesus viewed his mission specifically toward his own institution (cf. Matt. 15:24), he found that because it was so interlinked politically and economically with other institutions, it had little real influence, except to reinforce the existing reality as it had come to be defined by them.

Why is there this confidence and credibility gap? Why, in light of the conditions of the world (which are hardly approaching God's plan for it), does the church's call to conversion have so little influence on other key institutions? Conservatives have their reasons. Liberals have their reasons. And none of these reasons is satisfactory.

None of the reasons seems realistic. Somehow all of us seem to be locked into the present situation as it is interpreted *for* us. Even our vision for the future, for justice in the world, seems to be controlled by our situation in the church, our place in society. Thus we offer little hope, little credibility to anybody.

ADAPTING TO THE GAPS

To be hopeful persons whose reasons and actions offer credible solutions to people's questions must become our goal. We have to show by word and deed that, through the Word by which we have been formed, we are that community signifying "Our Father who art in heaven." If, in order to be such a sign of hope, we find ourselves being critical as members of our various institutions, it might be beneficial to recall the words of the Vatican Council's Decree on Ecumenism:

> Christ summons the Church as she goes her pilgrim way to that continual reformation of which she always has need, insofar as she is an institution of men here on earth, for, if the influence of events or of the times has led to deficiencies in conduct, in Church discipline, or even in the formulation of doctrine (which must be carefully distinguished from the deposit itself of faith), these should be appropriately rectified at the proper moment. [4]

THE BIG TEN

AVERAGE
RATING

1. White House...6.64
2. Television 6.05
3. Labor unions...5.85
4. Supreme Court...5.76
5. Big business..5.70
6. U.S. Senate...5.53
7. Federal bureaucracy..5.42
8. U.S. House of Representatives..............................5.30
9. Banks...5.17
10. Newspapers...5.00

OTHER RANKINGS

11. Lobbies and pressure groups................................4.97
12. Cabinet..4.83
13. Wall Street..4.59
14. Democratic Party..4.50
15. Educational institutions 4.32
16. Public-opinion polls...4.26
17. Family..4.23
18. Legal profession..4.16
19. Radio 4.13
20. Advertising agencies 4.07
21. State and local government...................................4.06
22. Magazines 4.05
23. Civil-rights organizations 3.87
24. Military 3.83
25. Medical profession...3.47
26. Organized religion..3.40
27. Cinema 3.11
28. Small business...2.84
29. Republican Party 2.70

Through its own words, the church recognizes (more than many other institutions, whose realities are enslaved by their articulations) the need of a continual critique that is life-giving. If you do not critique, you are not converted; if you are not converted, you do not grow; if you do not grow, you cannot have life. You are dead, whether person, group, or institution. You serve no purpose (cf. Luke 14:35).

This understanding of the need for a critique of the world, on the levels of the individual, the group, and the institution (or structure), now brings us to the next element we need to analyze if we are to say "Our Father" in the way Jesus and the early Christians prayed it. Such a critique is mandatory if we are to bridge the gap between what we profess (say and pray) and what we practice (do and minister).

The very fact that the church has institutionalized the values and ideals of Jesus into a systemic network of traditions and norms (largely controlled by one class—the white, male clerics) has brought about large-scale fragmentation within various local communities. These communities or institutions often define the needs of their members (and, therefore, their "need" to be obedient to the way they should view and live in reality). Yet the result often appears to be as many levels of "obedience" as there are members.

As the schema below shows, there are five main ways people adapt to their conditions of alienation in order to survive. Using

RESPONSE TO INSTITUTIONALIZATION[5]

INDIVIDUAL MODES OF ADAPTATION	VALUES/IDEALS	TRADITION/NORMS
I. Conformity	+	+
II. Innovation	+	−
III. Ritualism	−	+
IV. Retreatism	−	−
V. Rebellion	±	±

values and ideals (what we profess) as one area, and norms and traditions (what we practice) as another, we find members of the church responding quite differently to the institutional realities of which they are a part. One person may even adapt in several different ways: for example, as a conformist in one area, such as prayer, while a rebel in another, such as sexuality.

Some may say that the way to deal with problems is to demand "obedience," as "in the good old days." Others may say such a situation calls for people to form new communities. It seems to me, however, that both approaches beg the question. If it can be accepted by all that no present forms of adapting to our reality have been as healthy as had been hoped, we might be spared conformists arguing with ritualists and innovators, and rebels arguing with both, while retreatists are off "doing their thing." If all of us could rise above our individual forms of adaptation to look at the bigger world-reality, and with a contemplative vision perceive its underlying infrastructures and recognize those incompatible with God's plan and kingdom, we might find grounds for a new beginning, for a *communal* renewal of the church. Only by looking at our world *in toto*—at that which underlies our own individualism and group isolationism—can we hope to begin dealing with the "sin of the world" that helps to create our environment.

Because the major institutions are interdependent, a systemic relationship among various key institutions (economic, political, and religious) creates a need for institutional survival that is beyond the simple control of any one individual or group. Thus, an infrastructure is created in which these and other institutions reinforce each other's basic goals through their norms and traditions. By definition, these infrastructures become the underlying system that enables the whole structure composed of individuals, groups, and institutions to survive.

Perhaps it is precisely because we have failed to incorporate into our worldview this third level of reality, which has a high degree of influence on individuals and interpersonal relationships, that we find individual Christians adapting to renewal isolated from each other. Local churches and groups are becoming equally isolated. Caught up in so many forms of alienation, we have little or nothing to say to the world of alienation and we fail to see how all these forms of alienation are interconnected. We fail to see that one level cannot be dealt with for conversion without dealing with the other two. Because we have such an "unrealistic" approach to our world, we accomplish very little real change. The sense of true joy and peace that should characterize our lives is elusive. To people who come to us seeking a serious response to the world's alienation and a realistic Christian life in the modern world, we stand for little.

Social psychology has shown that individuals and groups are able to unite around goals and values that are bigger than their ordinary forms of adaptation and alienation. When previously divided individuals and groups are forced to work together in face of a bigger reality that is seen as a threat to all, there is an "increase in in-group solidarity and co-operativeness."[6] If we can accept the influence and pervasiveness of sin throughout our world and its infrastructures, we may begin to see our reality as bigger than all of us individually or in isolated groups. To take away the sin contained in this reality becomes more important than our appeals to the past or our adaptations to our alienations from the present. To confront the sin of the world would again be accepted by us as our common task for the future.

SPIRITUALITY IN A WORLD OF ALIENATION

If we are to become aware of the dynamics of our situation, we must look very closely at the inputs that come from its individual (intrapersonal), interpersonal (group), and infrastructural (systemic) levels. In fact, we will conclude that the only adequate way we can pray the Lord's Prayer as adults will be if we live on all three levels, with our grounding in the third level of faith.

The following paragraphs will attempt to show the threefold influence of reality in our lives and how these levels affect our spirituality in its prayer and ministry dimensions. The table on page 15 outlines these levels (with the exception of the ministry dimension, which will be added toward the end of the chapter).[7]

The maturity dimension includes the child or body level which parallels the individual level of reality itself. The adolescent or ego level corresponds to the interpersonal level, while the infrastructural level deals with the systemic network that undergirds all of life. This level can be recognized and dealt with only by an adult.

The three levels of reality have corresponding expressions in our spirituality. An individual on the first level of spirituality is controlled by systemic forces. The second tier, that which reflects an adolescent, ego-centered stance, is expressed in imitation of and transference to others of what we hope to be ourselves. The final level is that of participation or union, wherein our spirituality is expressed in an identification with God and his purpose for our world.

All these dimensions and the three levels in each dimension have significant expressions for us as we approach the Lord of our various histories and as he enters our lives to meet our needs in response to our request, "Lord, teach us to pray." Our prayer on the first level can be described as controlled by ritual, myth, and various recipes for success (certain words, formulae, etc.). The second level of prayer is that of projection. With our interpersonal, adolescent, ego-centered needs, we continually look to others as models to be imitated and with whom we want to relate as our intercessors. Like teenagers idolizing pop record and movie stars or peer leaders, we find the model of such heroes or saints beyond our possible achievement. The result is a feeling of guilt for our lack of "perfection," with concomitant feelings of alienation, insecurity,

DIMENSIONS OF HUMAN LIFE				
	REALITY	MATURITY	SPIRITUALITY	PRAYER
SURFACE	Individual	Child (body)	Systemic Control	Ritualized Myth
SURFACE	Inter-personal	Adolescent (ego)	Imitation	Projection
FAITH	Infrastruc-tural	Adult (self)	Participation	Identification

loneliness, and even anger (including often unconscious anger against our Father).

However, when our spirituality is of the third level, so is our prayer of the third level. It is the prayer of identification, of union. By faith we come to discover our identity in God's sharing of his life with us. We are given the vision to see ourselves as part of the trinitarian God through our share in the Spirit of Jesus in his community. Participating in him as members through his Spirit—who is given to each of us according to our need so that no one is wanting (cf. Rom. 12; 1 Cor. 12)—we take on the mind of Jesus. Nurtured by the Spirit both in prayer and ministry, we see ourselves as children of our Father.

If we live out our lives only on the individual and interpersonal levels, it remains on the surface—a surface we have not scratched to see the infrastructures that have such great influence on the other two levels. Similarly, a person living psychologically on only the first two levels of child (body) and adolescent (ego) is also a surface person, and thus becomes alienated from his or her self. The spirituality dimension is no different. The first two levels of spirituality, according to St. Paul, are characterized by law, by externals, by death. In contrast, one living as a true adult is free, is Spirit-guided, is alive in Christ by faith in the self and the Other. Third-level prayer, as a result, reflects this reality. It is rooted in a contemplative vision wherein we experience God to the point of identification, rather than through certain forms and models.

Persons living on the third level live past the surface of things, on faith. Such people have developed a contemplative vision that enables them to look at reality as adults, integrated human beings, able to see that enmeshed in all reality are infrastructures whose survival depends on keeping people locked into the first two levels. Such persons are able to see beyond the externals.

The assumption made in this book is that the reader, praying the Our Father as subversive activity, will have to go beyond the first two surface levels to pray and live on the adult level of self, as a participant in the Godhead, by truly living the gospel.

Perhaps we have been mesmerized by our childhood interpretation of the Our Father, which we naturally understood in light of our worldview at that time. However, if we, as adult ministers of the Word, are to accept a view of the world that in fact finds the individual and interpersonal levels influenced by and subservient to the infrastructures of our world, then we know that individual and communal prayer can never be separated from their relationship to both God and our world. If we can accept this fact, we know that we need an adult worldview in order to pray as Jesus would have us pray. When we reach this stage we find ourselves at the third level of spirituality. We are ready not just to unlearn much of what we have been taught. With the first disciples we can say to Jesus, "Teach us to pray." The result offers the possibility in the Spirit to pray as Jesus himself prayed—by word and ministry in the world of his Father.

PATHOLOGY AND THE MINISTERIAL DIMENSION OF HUMAN LIFE

An understanding of our world is essential if we are to enter it as fully as Jesus did his, with a living Word. When Jesus looked at his reality, especially on its individual and interpersonal levels, he found it greatly alienated from God. It was sinful. Thus, the first words Mark places on Jesus' lips as he enters his world, with his new brand of ministry, are a call for conversion from sin (cf. Mark 1:15). Jesus made it clear to his followers from the beginning of their ministry (cf. Luke 9:1) that their words would be a call to convert from sin.

The notion of sin and conversion brings us to the final dimension of our lives: our ministry, which involves a call for conversion on the three levels we have been discussing.

As we look at our twentieth-century world, we face a level of sin that was not so apparent in Jesus' time, namely, the influence and dominance of sin throughout the infrastructural, systemic level, which seeps into the other two levels, becoming like the soul of both. To speak the word of conversion to twentieth-century people on only their first two levels is both unrealistic and futile, for no real, lasting conversion can take place when they are highly influenced by and even controlled on the third level. As Morton Mintz and Jerry S. Cohen have shown in their *Power, Inc.*, [8] we are living in a society where the large institutions, with their corresponding ideologies, have gained control over the lives of individuals, families, and groups. Thus, where calls to conversion on the first two levels may produce surface change, no real metanoia or change of heart can take place, for the underlying causes of sin and alienation remain.

Sigmund Freud offered a helpful insight to this point in *Civilization and Its Discontents.* Freud had spent his life in therapeutic treatment of pathology in individuals. Later, psychologists showed how therapy could treat pathology in groups. Toward the end of his own life, however, Freud himself recognized the need for treating pathology in society itself, the need for research into the "pathology of civilized communities."[9] In other words, Freud recognized the need (as he looked at the individuals and groups he dealt with) to understand how the pathology, the "sin" of the world as evidenced in the structures that influence individuals and groups, could be healed. This pathology resulting from the infrastructures has been called by many different names—social sin, systemic or institutionalized violence, environmental alienation, cultural addiction, etc.

Remembering that Jesus linked individual sin to pathology ("Be healed and sin no more"), that Jesus viewed his and his disciples' ministry in terms of conversion from sin, and that Freud recognized a need of all society for therapy, we can better understand why we view our ministry in terms of freeing people, groups, and structures from the pathologies (sin) that grip them. In light of our

DIMENSIONS OF HUMAN LIFE					
	REALITY	MATURITY	SPIRITUALITY	PRAYER	MINISTRY
SURFACE	Individual	Child (body)	Systemic Control	Ritualized Myth	Personal
SURFACE	Inter-personal	Adolescent (ego)	Imitation	Projection	Social
FAITH	Infra-structural	Adult (self)	Participation	Identification	Societal

previous diagram of the three levels of reality and an understanding of the corresponding three levels of spirituality, psychology, and prayer, we can now add the ministry dimension, with its three levels. If we view our ministry in the world (Luke 24:47) as *calling for conversion* from sin (pathology), we find the three levels that must be addressed by us in this call (see the table on page 18).

When the Synod of Bishops met in 1971 to listen "to the Word of God so that we might be converted to fulfill the divine plan for the world's salvation,"[10] the bishops, like Jesus, began with an analysis of the world about them and found it wanting. The bishops had come from an environment that viewed sin as limited to the first two levels. Yet, under the influence of the Holy Spirit, they began to see how these two levels are sustained by a third level. As they noted:

> Even though it has not been our purpose to elaborate a very profound analysis of the world situation, we have nevertheless been able to perceive the serious injustices that are weaving over this earth a network of domination, oppression and abuses which stifle freedom and keep the greater part of humanity from sharing in the building up and enjoyment of a more just and more fraternal world.[11]

The bishops concluded that a purely individual (personal) or interpersonal (social) approach to preaching good news to the world was insufficient: "In the face of the present-day world situation, *marked by the grave sin of injustice*, we recognize our responsibility and our inability to overcome it by our own strength." This understanding of the influence of all three levels of sin in our present world enabled them to conclude: "Such a situation urges us to listen with a humble and open heart to the word of God, as he shows us new paths toward action on behalf of justice in the world."[12]

Prayer or ministry that does not include a true reality principle in its foundations is ineffective. Reality always includes all three levels. If God is to enter our total reality through our prayer and ministry, his Word must become incarnate in all aspects of our lives, bringing us the healing presence of his Spirit, who delivers us from all pathologies. Identifying with the Father through the

Spirit of Jesus enables us gradually to bring about conversion on all levels of society and so gradually build a new creation. Our ministry thus becomes grounded in the Spirit of Jesus, who enables us to bring healing to individuals, groups, and the world itself. Members of the First Latin American Charismatic Conference noted in 1973 that the Holy Spirit is moving in power in each of these three levels. Identified with Jesus in his Spirit, they said, we are:

> I. To transform individuals into a real personal relationship with Jesus through the baptism of the Spirit;
> II. To heal relationships and to build community—especially in the family and the neighborhood community; and
> III. To transform society by healing relationships of injustices and oppression. [13]

Our identification with and participation in the life of God through the Spirit of Jesus is at the heart of this process of bringing healing to the pathologies that are in and around us. Through this process we come to understand that we can know him "who art in heaven" only if he first recognizes himself in us—in our prayer and ministry—as we are on earth.

In the rest of this book we will study the Lord's Prayer with special emphasis on the third level of each area of consideration. The kind of prayer stressed will be contemplative prayer, or the prayer of identification, wherein we experience ourselves coming to know God and being known by God. The kind of ministry stressed will be that to the infrastructures, calling them to conversion. The spirituality that unites them both will be stressed as participative, wherein, as people with a unique contemplative vision, we are able to go beyond surface reality to preach conversion to our world. This third-level approach should help us to understand what it means to be identified with Christ—by growing participative in the life of his Spirit in communities with others as an integrated adult (self), and as one who participates in prayer and ministry to bring the joy and beauty of God's new creation (through conversion) into our sinful world.

2

Our Father Who Art in Heaven

The thesis of this book, that the Our Father was a highly subversive prayer, would be clearer if we applied to our age the meaning of its words as they were interpreted within the environment of Jesus' time. Just the fact that Jesus called God "Father" was enough for many of his contemporaries to want to kill him (cf. John 5:18)—because he was undermining the institutional expressions of their religion.

Jesus also broke religious categories by referring to God in an intimate way with the use of the Aramaic word *Abba*, or "Daddy," instead of using the more formal Hebrew word. The fact that he went beyond the ritual prayer forms of his day—which were intended to show loyalty to God within the institution—evidences Jesus' insistence that prayer be part of life. In his analysis of *The Prayers of Jesus*, Joachim Jeremias wrote:

> Jesus not only prayed in his native tongue in his private prayers, he also gave his disciples a formal prayer couched in the vernacular when he taught them the Lord's Prayer. In so doing, he removes prayer from the liturgical sphere of sacred language and places it right in the midst of everyday life. [1]

Jesus expressed himself in prayer in ways that often deviated from the regularly accepted modes of his society. Some of the words he used of God challenged his people to alter their normative understanding of God and adapt their traditional formulae about God as well. Yet, while some of these words may have challenged the traditional interpretation of reality, almost two thousand years of historical progression evidences that other words reinforced that vision of reality. Despite many new ways of referring to God and his relation to God—which threatened his co-religionists—Jesus shared a worldview and understanding of God that reflected the reality of his environment. It would be natural, then, for Jesus to be influenced by the third level of his infrastructural and cultural reality, which viewed God and spoke of God in almost exclusively male terms. The Lord's Prayer reflects this understanding.

That some words in the Our Father evidence a now outdated influence of a masculine dominance and interpretation of life (and even of God) should challenge us to go beyond these words to the deeper mystery Jesus was revealing. The Jews discovered that Jesus was offering a new understanding to complement their own (cf. Matt. 5:17). So, in our day, a deeper understanding of the nature of God gained from philosophy, as well as a realization that sexism is part of the historical "network of domination, oppression, and abuses which stifle freedom"[2] and part of the "grave sin of injustice,"[3] should challenge us to discover a deeper meaning of the reality behind the words that Jesus was trying to convey as God's revelation to us. Expanding on this notion, which might help us in dealing with certain words found in the Lord's Prayer, David R. Griffin writes in *Process Christology* that a

> basic question regarding the Christian belief in Jesus as God's decisive revelation is how Jesus can be understood by us as expressing the essential truth about reality, in view of the unacceptability of the explicit imagery he employed, based as it was upon an outdated worldview. The identification of the objective or giving side of revelation with Jesus' underlying vision of reality points to an answer to this question. It is the vision of reality expressed through his imagery that is of decisive importance. Whereas no finality can be claimed for Jesus on the level of the history of ideas, it is possible that his expression of a vision of God, man, and the world, and of inter-relatedness, might be unsurpassable.[4]

BEING-IN-PARTICIPATIVE COMMUNITY

What was the attitude Jesus tried to convey when he told us to pray "Our Father"? Primarily, it appears, he was indicating that God desires our relationship through the Spirit of Jesus. This relationship to him through the Son's Spirit is to be for us on earth what it is for the three persons in heaven—participative. St. Cyprian pointed to this communitarian reality in his commentary *The Lord's Prayer:*

> Before all things, the Teacher of peace and Master of unity did not wish prayer to be offered individually and privately as one would pray only for himself when he prays. We do not say: "My father, who are in heaven," nor "give me this day my bread," nor does each one ask that only his debt be forgiven him and that he be led not into temptation and that he be delivered from evil for himself alone. Our prayer is public and common, and when we pray, we pray not for one but for the whole people, because we, the whole people, are one.[5]

Realizing the Our Father is the prayer of every human being draws us out from our individual and even our interpersonal limitations into a global perspective.

The one who has taught us this prayer is God's revelation to us, the image of who God is and the sign of God's plan for the world. As we try to understand God through the life and work of Jesus by our sharing in Jesus' prayer, we necessarily discover the essential characteristic of God as participative community.

The trinitarian understanding of God as Father revealing his image in his Word is the foundation for our religious experience. In the giving of himself in his image, there is nothing God the Father holds back. Through the Word of God we have access to God, the ultimate resource. In the mutual giving that takes place between Father and Son, each availing the other of the totality of resources, we discover what love, or the Spirit, is. Herein we find evidenced the deepest meaning of the participative-communitarian life.

In the Trinity each person images the other precisely because each person has total access to the others' resources. This is the essence of community, as revealed by God. Through the Word enfleshed we are called to participate in this reality that we might grow in God's image by having access to the resources we need for living as fully as possible. The Word, then, is not only the image of God. As the image of God, the Word enables every person to have full access to the ultimate resource of all, the being that is God. In this light we can better understand what motivated Jesus to call out from the temple area (which formerly signified God's dwelling on earth):

> If anyone thirsts, let him come to me;
> let him drink who believes in me.
> Scripture has it:
> "From within him rivers of living water shall flow" (John 7:37–38).

John immediately explains that this access to Jesus, the one who alleviates the needs of the people, is accomplished through the Holy Spirit: "Here he was referring to the Spirit, whom those that came to believe in him were to receive. There was, of course, no Spirit as yet, since Jesus had not yet been glorified" (John 7:39). Through the Spirit of Jesus we have full access to *the* resource, who is God, in whom we live, move, and are able to be.

The essence of every human being, made in God's image, is to be-in-situation. The fundamental situation of reality involves each person living as an individual, in interpersonal relationships within the infrastructures of the environment. Thus, the person relates out of the horizons of his or her own historical individuality, interpersonal experience, and societal infrastructures. If, as a person, I relate only to control my own needs as a child does, or if I relate on the ego level of the adolescent to control others, I become alienated from my*self*, from the depth of my being. If I am alienated from myself, I become alienated from other selves and from God, the ground of my being. Failing to image the participative community of the Trinity wherein each self lives in union with the other persons, there is no effective participation with God or others in prayer or ministry.

However, if I allow myself to go beyond my child-level and adolescent-level need to control others (including God), I gradually enter more fully into the reality that constitutes the total environment of being-in-situation to participate in the unique mystery of the other. I become genuinely open to the other. I thus express an attitude and stance of *disponibilité*, which Gabriel Marcel interprets as "the essential characteristic of the person."[6]

Perhaps more than any other, the openness of the child best expresses what it means to be-in-situation. In effect, a child is "at home" with God and others. The child participates in community with them. This realization of "being at home" helps us to understand Matthew's concept of discipleship presented in terms of becoming like a child (cf. Matt. 18:3) or John's use of words to explain Jesus' offer of discipleship in his participative community: "When Jesus turned around and noticed them following him, he asked them, 'What are you looking for?' They said to him, 'Rabbi (which means Teacher), where do you stay?' 'Come and see,' he answered. So they went to see where he was lodged, and stayed with him that day" (John 1:38–39). Identifying with Jesus enabled his followers to begin viewing all of reality in a new way, like a child. Identifying with Christ through his Spirit enabled his followers to call his Father theirs as well.

Dwelling at home in God's Word gives meaning and hope to all reality. It offers the possibility for every person to participate fully as a member of a community in God's *dabar* (Word) through prayer and ministry. God's Word dwelling in us enables us to say, in this word, "I am," and to participate with God in his plan for the world. In the words of Mary Daly in *Beyond God the Father:*

> The God who is power of being acts as a moral power summoning women and men to act out of our deepest hope and to become who we can be. . . . This hope is communal rather than merely individualistic, because it is grounded in the two-edged courage to be. That is, it is hope coming from the experience of individuation and participation. It drives beyond the objectified God that is imagined as limited in benevolence, bestowing blessings upon "his" favorites. The power of being is that in which all finite beings participate, but not on a "one-to-one" basis, since this power is in all while transcending all. Communal hope involves in some manner a profound inter-relationship with other finite beings, human and non-human. Ontological communal hope, then, is cosmic. Its essential dynamic is directed to the universal community. Finally, ontological hope is revolutionary. Since the insight in which it is grounded is the double-edged intuition of non-being and of being, it extends beyond the superstitious fixations of technical reason.[7]

Probably more than anything else, the "superstitious fixations of technical reason" contribute to the fact that, in prayer and ministry, the average church person remains on the first two levels of reality. In our continual effort to define God according to needs evidenced on the levels of individual and group, we unconsciously allow the third level of our technologically controlled infrastructures to create for us patterns of prayer and ministry that reflect a god of its own making rather than the God revealed to us in the Word, in Jesus Christ.

Our environment should enable us to enter into deeply human relationships with all people and with nature as well. It should help us to view all as brothers and sisters—part of a larger participative community wherein resources are shared because all have equal access to one Father (cf. Eph. 2:18). Yet actually the infrastructures of the third level paradoxically reinforce the negativity of the first two levels of control. We try to manipulate both God and our brothers and sisters into images of our making. We reflect the "fixations" of technical society and its obsession to control all reality in the way we relate to others in our ministry. We go through our rituals in prayer, hoping thus to control God in order to meet our religious needs. We find, as Jacques Ellul alleges in *The Technological Society*, that "technique is not an isolated fact in society (as the term technology would lead us to believe) but is related to every factor in the life of modern man."[8]

With the structures of society leading us to operate almost exclusively on the first two levels, we end in alienation. Living on the body and ego levels, we become alienated from our self level. We find ourselves alienated from other selves, as well as *the* other, God. As a result, we cannot *know* God. We can neither pray effectively nor be effective ministers of his Word. The revelation of God to our*selves* has been stopped at the level of control.

Despite the technology that came into prominence during his lifetime, despite the growing influence of capital on human relations, Francis of Assisi was able to accept the uniqueness of all reality. Rather than trying to manipulate people or creation, he revered all things as revelations of God to whom he could be *disponible*. Over and over again, in prayer or in the presence of one of his followers, a citizen or an animal, or the resources of the earth, Francis viewed all creation as a gift of a God who made available to him all his resources. Such a realization created in Francis a spirit of wonder. The wonder was accompanied by a spirit of indebtedness, which resulted from an awareness that he had not created any part of this reality. With such a grasp of life, it is little wonder that Francis stood in awe at what was being revealed to him as a manifestation of God. There was no thought of controlling or manipulating reality. He could only appreciate it and celebrate it like any poor person aware of the power of another. "Within our awe there is no place for self-assertion," Abraham Heschel wrote, in an expression that can be applied to Francis and his vision of poverty: "Within our awe we only know that all we own we owe."[9]

Heschel's insight that "all we own we owe" brings us to the heart of our discussion of God's revelation to us—to our understanding of creation as God's inheritance to us as our Father, and how we can share in it through our prayer and ministry.

GOD'S CONCERNS FOR THE EARTH

God's purposes and ideal for creation are outlined in the first chapters of Genesis. In particular, the first eleven chapters (which should be viewed as a whole) pattern the way we ought to relate to God, each other, and creation itself. Here we find a description of God's power and how we share in this power in our world.

Following the kerygmatic focus of the Priestly tradition in Genesis, we discover two main concerns of God for his world. One relates to the dignity of every human being made in God's image. The other relates to the way all people are to share in the goods of the earth:

> Then God said: "Let us make man in our image, after our likeness. Let them have dominion over the fish of the sea, the birds of the air, and cattle, and all the wild animals and all the creatures that crawl on the ground."
>   God created man in his image;
>   in the divine image he created him;
>   male and female he created them.
> God blessed them, saying: "Be fertile and multiply, fill the earth and subdue it. Have dominion over the fish of the sea, the birds of the air, and all the living things that move on the earth" (Gen. 1:26–28).

From all eternity God held nothing back in expressing his Word. From the dawn of creation, the Word held nothing back in imaging forth the invisible God. God's first concern for the world is thus derived from creation through his Word: *every human being, created as God's image, is sacred* from the first moment of creative participation in the communitarian life of God. In each person, God's revelation, his image, is reflected and is to become more clear. The communitarian nature of all people, made in his image, is meant to reflect the communitarian nature of the Godhead. It becomes a fundamental principle of creation, then, that all people have the right to express themselves as the image of God and to make that image clearer by the way they live in the world. On the reverse side, an equally fundamental principle of creation is that each person has the duty (since God's image is fulfilled in participative community) to enable all other people to partake of their right to image God.

The way this right is to be exercised by each person is expressed in God's second concern for the world. Just as each person in the Trinity images the other by having full access to the life and resources of the other persons in the trinitarian community, so each human created in God's image is meant to grow in that image through an increasingly fuller access to the life and resources of the earth. Thus God's second great concern for creation as evidenced by the Priestly writer is that *equal access to the resources of life should be available to all.* All people in creation have the right of access to the resources of the earth that they need in order to live in dignity as images of God. Correspondingly, each person has the duty (since we are to live in community) to enable all other people to have access to the resources they need to lead dignified lives.

Individual persons, as involved in interpersonal relationships and in the world's infrastructures, manifest their participation in God's creative purposes only when they are able to (and when they enable others to) image God by having access to the earth's resources. Without these two concerns of God being evidenced in community, creation has no meaning. Such is the message of the Priestly writer for our generation.

According to Claus Westermann, the first chapters of Genesis were written in a specific historical context of alienation, which has many parallels to our own environment: "The Creation myths then had the function of preserving the world and of giving security to life."[10] These cosmic myths were to offer a sense of hope to the dispossessed Israelites, who viewed them in light of their political/historical infrastructures of oppression. (These passages of Genesis were written during the Exile). They seem to have equal significance for our time when the infrastructures of our world threaten the ecological balance of nature and exploit masses of people, all based on a false understanding of power itself. Power, as reflective of God, was not to oppress. It was to free.

The true meaning of power, as outlined in Genesis, implies the ability to live humanly on earth as an image of God. "When a human being has the power to actualize his own potentials," says George W. Coats in commenting on the meaning of the first chapters of Genesis, "he acts as creator. He shares God's power to project possibilities for the future. He envisions the world not only as it is but also as it might be. And then he sets about the task of bringing those possibilities to fruition. He is as a consequence fully *imago dei,* a creature created in the image of the creator himself."[11]

Humans image God by being co-creators, by their power over created reality. To be denied access to this power is to be forced to live in alienation, chaos, or sin. To be allowed access is to be blessed by God and to share in his creative power on earth as in heaven: God blessed them, saying, "Be fertile and multiply; fill the earth and subdue it. Have dominion . . . " (Gen. 1:28). Walter Brueggemann elaborates on this connection between God's creative activity and our participation in it when he says of the five verbs found in Genesis 1:28: (which constitute the "blessing"):

> The "blessing" is a bold and over-powering affirmation in which the sovereign's intent is clear. While the verbs are expressed as imperatives, they are not so much commands as authorizations by which the people are empowered to believe and to act toward the future. Thus the five verbs are a statement about the radical claim of God to establish his will for well-being and prosperity. And his will cannot be frustrated by any circumstance, even those circumstances of the traditionists' historical context of exile. His claim to sovereignty (according to the text) is over creation which he has just called into being out of *chaos.* Historically his claim refers to the *exilic situation* of

poverty, misery and despair which he now transforms into a situation of joy and shalom. These five assertions complete the creation of humankind, affirming their primacy and ordaining them as the agent of order in his world for which he now wills and asserts a fertile, productive order.[12]

Immediately Brueggemann offers us an approach that we can use to confront the chaotic conditions created by the sinful infrastructures of our world. Such confrontations help us to participate in the blessing that comes to those who enable the poor and alienated to share rightfully in the kingdom on earth as in heaven (cf. Matt. 5:3):

> Perhaps the five terms (of Genesis) are best understood if each is taken as a refutation of the opposite:
>
> be fruitful..no more barrenness
> multiply..no more lack of heirs
> fill the earth............................no more being crowded out
> subdue...no more subservience
> have dominion........................no more being dominated[13]

Two lessons of great importance are thus contained in the first chapters of Genesis: God names humans as his images; and humans, as God's images, name (control) their reality. The ensuing chapter of Genesis on Cain and Abel proclaims that if humans attempt to step beyond their bounds and try to name (control) each other, they take on the role of God. Although there can be control (non-exploitative) over creation by humans, no human is created to control other humans. To do otherwise is to assume God's role and to become an idol.

In fact, the very naming of their reality simply meant that Adam and Eve were to control creation in order to share it better, not to exploit it more effectively. Dominion over the earth *(radah)* and subduing the earth *(kabas)* are subservient to the command to be fruitful *(parah)*. Thus, the focus of our role, Coats concludes,

> falls on fruitful productivity, not destructive over-production or exploitation; on use of power for particular ends, not unlimited power; on life, not death. The psalmist captured the same point

about man's power to control the destiny of the world: "You gave him dominion over the works of your hands; you put all things under his feet, all sheep and oxen, and also the birds of the air, the fish of the sea, and whatever passes along the paths of the sea" (Ps. 8:6–8). And the consequence of such power lies, not in a glorification of man in his power, but a glorification of the source (and limitation) of the power. For the priestly theologian as well, man's power attests the glory of God from whom the power derives.[14]

The resources of the earth are for everyone. To use one's power to deny others access to those resources is to make oneself a god—for only God can use power in such a way as to deny other humans access to the earth's resources. To do otherwise is to assume divine power over other human beings. This applies equally to individuals, interpersonal groupings, and infrastructures (including nations).

God must recognize his image in us as he envisioned it in the Garden. This is the ideal we are to strive for as part of creation. We are to walk in participative community with God in the still of the evening (prayer) by walking with each other, side by side, in mutual support and cooperation (ministry). We can name creation and have power over it but we can never exploit it. Nor can we assume the role of God to name the reality of other humans. Respecting this makes us share in God's power of fathering and mothering humans and creation with life. It is the only way God can know himself—his image—in us.

God knows us when he recognizes his creative revelation, himself, in us. He recognizes us when we participate with him in sharing the earth's resources and image him to all. If we fail in the concerns of God for his creation, God can only ask, "Where are you?" (Gen. 3:9; cf. also 4:9). To the degree that we have resources (material goods, health, time, prayer, etc.) and keep them to ourselves unnecessarily and unconcerned about others who may need to share in them, to that degree God's image is hindered from fulfillment in the world. If we don't image God, we can't be known by God.

For this reason, the way we relate to the poor—be they poor in health or in material goods—will be the determining factor in God's knowledge of us. The person who cannot share in the earth's resources cannot become the image of God that he or she ought to be.

This realization helped Francis to make the link between his ministry to the needs of others and his prayers to God. After sharing his resources with the poor at St. Peter's and the lepers on the road, Francis had to see the need to be poor himself, to give up his family and inheritance, that he might be truly formed by the Word of God. Thus, his biographer, Thomas of Celano, tells us, "In the hearing of many who had come together, he said: 'From now on I can truly say Our Father who art in heaven, not father Peter Bernadone, to whom I give up not only the money, but all my clothes too. I will therefore go naked to the Lord!' O generous Spirit, to whom Christ alone is sufficient."[15]

In another passage, Celano reveals how both dimensions of Francis's sharing in God were realized in his relationship to the poor:

> The father of the poor, the poor Francis, conforming himself to the poor in all things, was grieved when he saw someone poorer than himself, not because he longed for vain glory, but from a feeling of compassion. And though he was content with a tunic that was quite poor and rough, he very frequently longed to divide it with some poor person. But that this very rich poor man, drawn on by a great feeling of affection, might be able to help the poor in some way, he would ask the rich of this world, when the weather was cold, to give him a mantle or some furs. And when, out of devotion, they willingly did what the most blessed father asked of them, he would say to them, "I will accept this from you with this understanding that you do not expect ever to have it back again." And when he met the first poor man, he would clothe him with what he had received with joy and gladness. He bore it very ill if he saw a poor person reproached or if he heard a curse hurled upon any creature by anyone.[16]

Immediately following this description of how Francis felt when he discovered someone with less resources than he himself possessed, is another description of Francis, who understood the poor to be the image of Christ:

> Once it happened that a certain brother uttered a word of invective against a certain poor man who had asked for an alms saying to him:

"See, perhaps you are a rich man and pretending to be poor." Hearing this, the father of the poor, St. Francis, was greatly saddened, and he severely rebuked the brother who had said such a thing and commanded him to strip himself before the poor man, and kissing his feet, beg pardon of him. For, he was accustomed to say, "Who curses a poor man does an injury to Christ, whose noble image he wears, the image of him who made himself poor for us in this world."[17]

SPIRITUALITY AS PARTICIPATING IN GOD'S CONCERNS

In making himself poor for us in this world, Christ revealed the Father. He also revealed to us this twofold truth: If you expect to share in the revelation of God in prayer, God can know you or reveal himself to you only if he recognizes himself sharing his earth's resources and his own image through you. Likewise, if you expect to be a minister of God's presence in a world marked by the grave sin of injustice and do not identify with God's purposes for the earth—that its resources be distributed so that all those made in his image might share in them—your ministry is lacking.

Through prayer one realizes the inability to have access to *the* resource, to God, unless God shares his resource, his revelation. And God will share his revelation only if he recognizes his image in us as people committed to his concern about sharing the earth's resources (1 Pet. 3:8–12).

This is what imaging God means. Being "perfect as your heavenly Father is perfect" (Matt. 5:48) means becoming a holy person, a just person in whom God recognizes his image, in whom God recognizes someone identified with his will (which is inseparable from his *self*) be it in prayer or in ministry. To identify with God and to participate in him through prayer is to reveal his purposes in our ministry. God "always so acted with me through his fatherly condescension," Francis of Assisi would say, "that he showed me when I prayed or meditated what was pleasing and displeasing to him (cf. 1 Pet. 1:12–22)."[18]

Perfection is made possible by God's sharing the fullness of his resources with us through the gift of his own Spirit who dwells within us, ministering through us, bringing us and all creation to the perfection that is God's. In the beautiful words of St. Paul:

All who are led by the Spirit of God are Sons of God. You did not receive a spirit of slavery leading you back into fear, but a spirit of adoption through which we cry out, "Abba!" (that is, "Father"). The Spirit himself gives witness with our spirit that we are children of God. . . . Indeed, the whole created world eagerly awaits the revelation of the sons of God. Creation was made subject to futility, not of its own accord but by him who once subjected it; yet not without hope, because the world itself will be freed from its slavery to corruption and share in the glorious freedom of the children of God. . . . The Spirit too helps us in our weakness, for we do not know how to pray as we ought; but the Spirit himself makes intercession for us with groanings which cannot be expressed in speech. He who searches hearts knows what the Spirit means, for the Spirit intercedes for the saints as God himself wills (Rom. 8:14–16; 19–22; 26–27).

If Christians can address God as "Father," by the Spirit dwelling in them, Raymond Brown writes in his commentary on the Lord's Prayer,

it is because they are anticipating their state of perfection which will come at the close of this age. They are anticipating the coming of God's eschatological kingdom, which is already incipient in the preaching of Jesus. It is no accident that in the beatitudes . . . the parallel to the promise that the peacemakers shall be called the sons of God is the promise that the poor in spirit shall inherit the kingdom of God. And so, the community that says the Our Father is not the Jewish nation but the poor, the sick, and the needy who accept Jesus' preaching of the kingdom, a kingdom prepared by the Father through Jesus (Luke 22:29–30).[19]

We would add that, in virtue of the gift of Jesus' Spirit in our hearts, those who minister to create this kingdom of the Father on earth not only anticipate "their state of perfection, which will come at the close of this age," but also presently participate in it in germinal form.

It should be clear from what we have said thus far that the "heaven" where our Father dwells is not situated somewhere beyond the Milky Way any more than "hell" is in the depths of the earth. Heaven is the state of participative community (as Francis of

Assisi realized, thus refusing to settle anywhere on "earth"). It is wherever God reigns and where his image is being realized by those who share their resources with others in need.

In our environment of sin, whose infrastructures deny millions of people access to resources and depersonalize them as God's images, to let the Word of God form us means that we are to witness, by our life-sharing, what God's participative community means. We are to stand within our institutions as basic communities reflecting in prayer and ministry the kind of life that is evidenced in the Trinity itself. Since creation is to manifest equality of resource-sharing and the fullness of God's image in all persons, our work and mission as participative communities is fundamentally linked to God's creative activity on earth as it is in heaven.

In this sense there can be no dichotomy between our prayers, wherein we cry to the Lord to be heard, and our ministry, wherein we respond to the cries of people in need. Both our prayer and our ministry are part of life wherein we discover the same three elements over and over again: (1) the recognition of a need, which gives rise to a petition; (2) a sense of dependency on the one with the needed resource to allow us access, to be present to us; which, in turn, is based on (3) a risk that we might not be heard along with a hope that what is asked will be accomplished, creating in us a sense of anticipation and wonder.

The call from a lonely acquaintance, asking for my help to sort things out, is made on the risk that I might let the person down. Until I assure the caller by my presence and action that I won't let him or her down, the petition is not answered. On a broader scale, the developing nations issue pleas to the developed nations to stop raising prices on the items they need. The request might be broader, but it too is based on risk and hope: risk of not being heard and hope that we will share our resources with them according to our ability. The fact that I sit in the quiet of my room aware that I am unable to control and manipulate my relationship with the Lord helps me to ask God to reveal himself to me that I might sense his presence and "taste and see how good the Lord is" (Ps. 34:9). This too is based on the risk of faith in his promises. All our prayers demand the ministry of presence and hope. Prayer and ministry are all based on need and an expectation that there will be someone available to respond to the need, with the resulting sense of wonder and awe. "We should praise him and pray to him day and night, saying 'Our Father who art in heaven' (Matt. 6:9)," Francis wrote all the faithful, "because we must always pray and not lose heart."[20] Francis could pray this way because he came to prayer with a ministry based on purity of heart and participation with God in the fulfillment of his revelation on earth.

God allows us to be truly free to pray and minister on all three levels of our reality. Even though we have been named by God, he does not control us. As Father, he frees us from his control. There are special moments when a father and mother look at their child and discover that, despite their efforts to control the child on its body and ego levels, they cannot fully manipulate that life that has come from them. In those moments they can only stand back in stillness and awe, in an attitude of wonder and hope. God, our Father, does the same with us. By his word and inspiration he may try to persuade us, as any parent will, but he will not control.

God gives us the freedom to act on his behalf in the world. He asks us to look at the world, marked as it is by the "grave sin of injustice" and to participate with him in redeeming it from this enslavement, to create it anew. We work for the reallocation of the earth's resources, knowing that this must be our task if God's image is to be realized in us as fully as God intends. In this sense we can say, "God needs us to accomplish his creation's original and lasting purposes."

3

May Your Name Be Holy on Earth as in Heaven

The actual wording of the Lord's Prayer does not declare God's name holy "on earth as it is in heaven." Yet a fuller sense of the Scripture's meaning helps us see this connection. "May your name be holy" is the first of three "thou" petitions in the Our Father. This indicates some connection among the three "thou" phrases. While only Matthew has all three phrases in his version, both he and Luke support such a connection. In two different places they identify *name* and *kingdom* with the *will* of God being done on earth as it is in heaven (cf. Matt. 19:29; Luke 18:28–30). Although he does not include the Our Father in his gospel, John also connects the three petitions in his theology. According to Raymond Brown:

> Besides phrasing the mission of Jesus in terms of doing God's will, Jn also reports it in terms of manifesting God's name (17:6) and of establishing the kingdom (18:37)—thus the terms of the first three petitions of the PN. And just as the preservation of the disciples is connected to doing God's will in 6:38–39, so it is connected to manifesting His name in 17:6.[1]

In his "The Lord's Prayer in the Light of Recent Research," Joachim Jeremias clearly indicates that the phrases referring to the name, the kingdom, and the will of God represent desired conditions not found in the infrastructures and environment surrounding the early Christians:

These petitions are a cry out of the depths of distress. Out of a world which is enslaved under the rule of evil and in which Christ and Antichrist are locked in conflict, Jesus' disciples, seemingly a prey of evil and death and Satan, lift their eyes to the Father and cry out for the revelation of God's glory. But at the same time these petitions are an expression of absolute certainty. He who prays thus, takes seriously God's promise, in spite of all the demonic powers, and puts himself completely in God's hands, with imperturbable trust: "Thou wilt complete Thy glorious work, *abba*, Father."[2]

The book of Genesis contains the first instance in the Scriptures where humans named any part of reality (2:19–20). As we saw in chapter 2, to name reality is to enter into a share in the creative power of God. By naming the various resources—the birds, the plants, the land—Adam and Eve had power over them. Because of this tremendous power given human beings, there is a tendency for us to try to overstep our power by also naming our God, to create a god of our own making. Thus, when God calls us by name, as with Adam and Eve, we hide our face from him because we recognize this sin and we are afraid he will not recognize his image in us (cf. Gen. 3:10). Sin is the reason why God cannot recognize us—his name in us.

The difference of perspective between God and humans, intensified by sin, is expressed quite clearly by Isaiah: "For my thoughts are not your thoughts, nor are your ways my ways, says the Lord. As high as the heavens are above the earth, so high are my ways above your ways and my thoughts above your thoughts" (Isa. 55:8–9). When we pray that God's name may be holy, we do not presume that our prayer makes it holy; rather, we pray that the holiness of his name may become evident in our lives. Yet, because our lives are not always identified with the Lord, often he cannot discover his name, his presence, or his power within us. We end up separated not only from him but from ourselves as well. We cannot even think of ourselves without feeling the results of this alienation in our very bones. Jürgen Moltmann writes:

> Our thoughts are thoughts of judgment. We are forsaken. We are forgotten. We have no future, our anxiety tells us. The thoughts of God are not like our thoughts. Our ways under the law we keep are

not his ways. We condemn ourselves, but he does not condemn us. We are resigned to our fate, but he is not. We judge ourselves and others according to the iron law of reciprocity; but his is a law of "much forgiveness." Therein God *is*—no actually—becomes different.[3]

Because we are unable to accept God as truly different from our ways, we continually try to name him even in prayer. Many of us live on the first level of manipulation and control, and we seldom experience God on the level of self. As a result we must admit that many times (despite our good intentions) our prayer is merely an exercise in meeting our emotional needs (an effort to come away with good feeling). Rarely do we truly meet God. We haven't entered into his reality, into his thoughts and, thus, can never discover ourselves as truly known and loved by God. And so we keep on searching for the Lord—and for ourselves.

LIBERATION: THE REVELATION OF THE NAME

Life is a process of seeking our name; it is the search for who I am and what I am to do. It was just this search for his identity that led a restless Moses to the mountain, unwilling to let society of his day place its name on him. In Moses' search we discover that God's revelation of himself through his name is inseparable from the process of liberation. In Moses we also discover that the revelation of God and of who we are must be found in the process of liberation, if his name is to be upon us. As we participate in this process we come to know Yahweh.

In both the Yahwistic version (cf. Exod. 3:4ff.) and the Priestly version (cf. Exod. 6:1ff.), God calls Moses by name in the form of a prayer. There is a *need* created by an intolerable situation. God identifies with this need and enters Moses' *presence*, asking him to respond. Moses stands in *awe* in face of this presence, realizing he can say Yes or No. This parallels the situation of prayer that God heard expressed through the lips of his people: "I have witnessed the affliction of my people in Egypt and have heard their cry of complaint against their slave drivers, so I know well that they are suffering" (Exod. 3:7).

The first condition for prayer is the recognition of a *need* that cannot be solved by oneself. A risk is made requesting *presence*. It was because he heard the cry of his people that God determined to enter their presence in response to their need. "Therefore I have come down to rescue them from the hands of the Egyptians and lead them out of that land . . . " (Exod. 3:8). What resulted from such a revelation can only be described in terms of *awe*, as an event of great wonder—a new relationship based on liberation.

Often we find ourselves known by God only in our cry, our loneliness, our inability to control our reality. In this condition of need and helplessness, like Moses, we discover God revealing his name to us. The revelation of his name enables us to share in the process of our own liberation: "I mean to liberate them (us)." God shows fidelity to his name in the process of liberation. After the Lord told Moses that he was called to lead the people to the freedom of the promised land, Moses queried the Lord, "If they ask me, 'What is his name?' what am I to tell them? God replied, 'I am who am' " (Exod. 3:13–14). "This is my name forever; this is my title for all generations" (Exod. 3:15). God reveals his name (his presence) in the process of liberation, which has for its goal the restoration of his original purposes for creation.

The Exodus restoration is based on the promises of Genesis, especially those often found in the Priestly tradition of Genesis. In many places the Priestly version unites three elements to outline God's message about creation's purposes (cf. Gen. 1:26; 8:17; 9:7; 17:20–25; 28:1–4; 48:3–4): (1) the mention of God's name as the *agent* of this message; (2) the promise of a blessing that will be realized when the people have access to resources, which serves as the *central element* of this message; and (3) the reference to the possession of land (along with the historical and political realities to ensure this possession), which is the *goal* of the message. Walter Brueggemann insists that, for the Priestly writer,

the name of God is linked to if not subordinated to the command/promise of fruitfulness and the promise of land. While the name of God is not unimportant for the schematic history of P, it has probably been overstressed by scholars at the expense of the blessing and anticipation of land. P is not as interested in a theory of revelation as the reality of land-promise which survives even for the exiles. It is when the name is linked together with the other two elements (verbs of formula, land) that it takes on importance and power for the tradition. Without the other elements which are typically linked to it, the name has little power for the tradition. [4]

In other words, God's name is not revealed (nor, by implication, can it be invoked) outside of the fulfillment of God's plan for the world: the realization of his image in all who are able to have access to the resources they need. Thus we find, with Brueggemann, that the Priestly theme "stretches from creation to liberation, from the blessing announced to its realization, and that is the perennial story in Israel and the stress which P wishes to make."[5]

God reveals his name (his presence and purposes) in the process of liberation. He reveals himself as the "I am" when he hears the prayers of his people who are oppressed. He reveals his identity when others are unable to name their reality in freedom. In this process of salvation and the experience of their liberation, the people discover God's presence among them: "This is the name they give him: 'The Lord our justice' " (Jer. 23:6).

Because God both witnessed his people's exploitation and heard their prayerful cry, he *therefore* (Exod. 3:8) had to enter their history with his justice, to right the wrong—to reorder creation. While we might try by prayer to determine how God should enter into our history or the history of our world, God has made it clear what *causes* him to reveal himself: that his people are in need.

Examining the Exodus passage wherein God reveals his name in the process of the people's liberation, we come to understand better the connection between seeing, caring, and calling humans to the fullness of life and our responding, caring, and seeing God. The Israelites' experience of being seen ("I have witnessed the affliction of my people" [Exod. 3:7]), of being cared for by God ("I have heard their cry of complaint, . . . so I know well that they are suffering" [Exod. 3:7]), results in a call to participate in God's freedom ("Therefore I have come . . . to rescue them" [Exod. 3:8]).

This experience of God's seeing, caring for, and calling them created the foundation for Israel's religious experience. Out of this religious experience, Israel was able to respond to God's call by identifying with his care and by seeing him as it was seen. This contemplative experience of God's seeing it, caring for it, and calling it became the foundation for Israel's contemplative ministry that enabled it to respond to God's call, identifying with him in his care for the world and by entering into the vision of God.

This religious experience of Israel becomes the basis for our religious experience as well. Our contemplation, which results from our experience of God's contemplating us, caring for us, and calling us, enables us to enter the world with a ministry wherein we respond to God's call by caring for his people to the point that we come to know God, or "see" him, just as we are seen, cared for, and called. As with the Israelites, a rhythm is thus created in our life wherein we participate in God and he in us. This rhythm of contemplation-action in our living is clearly diagrammed by Richard Byrne, O.C.S.O., in his *Living the Contemplative Dimension of Everyday Life:*[6]

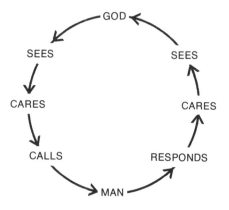

Exodus has shown clearly that God intervenes in history when his power and resources are being exploited by a few instead of shared by all and/or when his image is not being revealed in his people. When God's creative purposes, his justice, are not being fulfilled, the rhythm of creation is disturbed. A need is created for him to intervene in history. In witnessing his people's affliction and hearing their cry, God saw his creative purposes frustrated. The covenant he made with and for creation was broken. In making the people's cry part of himself, he had to reveal himself.

We discover that God reveals himself in his pathos, his identification with the oppressed that they might know him by name. In this way the covenant is restored for all of creation from its chaotic condition of alienation. The victory of justice is achieved (Isa. 42:6). People experienced God's pathos in experiencing his care for them. According to Abraham Heschel, God's pathos

> is not to be seen in its psychological denotation, as standing for a state of the soul, but in its theological connotation, signifying God as involved in history, as intimately affected by events in history, as living care. Pathos means: God is never neutral, never beyond good and evil. He is always partial to justice.[7]

God's Pathos and Our A-pathos: The pathos of God directly opposes the apathy, the a-pathos of society, especially in its systemic level that has a deaf ear to the cries of the poor and the oppressed. This is especially important for Christians to note, since often so-called religious people refuse to act—in the name of neutrality. In a "network of domination," such as that evidenced by our world, to refuse to act means that others will use our power to act. Often they will even act in our name, trying to make it appear that this name is of God. Yet it is this neutrality, this failure to use our power for justice as individuals, groups, or part of the infrastructures of society, that connotes our a-pathos, ranging us against God, who reveals himself in this pathos.

God's pathos is experienced, Heschel noted, as living care. Care, it can also be stated, is the fundamental condition needed in life for contemplative vision. If I do not care about my reality, I cannot experience God. I cannot truly contemplate, for God is not separate from this pathos, which is manifested in his care for reality, for the world. To think that I can contemplate God and not be filled with pathos means I have contemplated a god of my own making. Because, in contemplation, I have experienced God's care for me, my contemplative vision enables me to care for others. "If I am to unite with reality through contemplation, I must care for reality," Richard Byrne writes in *Living the Contemplative Dimension of Everyday Life*. Not to care is to have a-pathos, to be against God. Yet, in discovering a lack of this pathos in my life, I can ask, with Byrne:

> Is there anything I can do? Yes. I can begin looking at my own life and asking, "Do I really care? Who or what do I care about?" And when I see my lack of care—my lack of humanity—I can begin taking the first faltering steps toward a life of care. I can make my own the words of T. S. Eliot:
>
> > Blessed sisters, holy mother, spirit of the fountain, spirit of the garden,
> > Suffer us not to mock ourselves with falsehood.
> > Teach us to care and not to care.
> > Teach us to sit still. . . . [8]

By our em-pathos and sym-pathos we begin to show our care. We identify with God's creative purposes, over against a society whose ways are not those of the Lord. By intervening in the history of his people suffering injustice, the Lord showed that his caring love was creative of justice. On our part we know we cannot be identified with the Spirit of the Lord if by a lack of empathy and sympathy we refuse to show our love and care to those in need by a ministry of justice. As John writes, "I ask you, how can God's love survive in a man who has enough of this world's goods yet closes his heart to his brother when he sees him in need?" (John 3:17). In John's eyes such unresponsiveness is nothing else than a form of hate. We find this insight of John's reflected in what Rollo May writes in *Love and Will*:

> Hate is not the opposite of love; apathy is. The opposite of will is not indecision . . . but being uninvolved, detached, unrelated to significant events. . . . The interrelation of love and will inheres in the fact that both terms describe a person in the process of reaching out, moving towards the world, seeking to affect others or the inanimate world, and opening himself to be affected; molding, forming, relat-

ing to the world or requiring that it relate to him. This is why love and will are so difficult in an age of transition, when all the familiar mooring places are gone. The blocking of the ways in which we affect others and are affected by them is the essential disorder of both love and will. Apathy, or a-pathos, is a withdrawal of feeling; it may begin as playing it cool, a studied practice of being unconcerned and unaffected. But as one continues this gradual letting go of involvement . . . one finds that life itself has gone by.[9]

God's Pathos and Our Sym-pathos: Paradoxically, it can only be when we overcome our apathy that we can come to know God. For if God reveals himself in his pathos, his justice, we can only know him if we do not have a-pathos, are not against God. By our empathy and sympathy, by our ministry of justice, we identify with God in his concern to respond to the affliction of his people and their cries. In this we come to know God, for in this he knows us—he recognizes his image in us. "Woe to him who builds his house on wrong, his terraces on injustice," Jeremiah writes:

Who works his neighbor without pay
and gives him no wages.
Who says, "I will build myself a spacious house,
with airy rooms,"
Who cuts out windows for it,
panels it with cedar
and paints it with vermillion.
Must you prove your rank among kings
by competing with them in cedar?
Did not your father eat and drink?
He did what was right and just,
and it went well with him.
Because he dispensed justice to the weak and the poor,
it went well with him.
Is this not true of knowledge of me?
says the Lord (Jer. 22:13–16; emphasis added).

To know Yahweh is to do justice. To do justice is to be known by Yahweh. This is the essential message of such prophets as Isaiah, Jeremiah, and Hosea. Each of these found himself in conflict with the religious institutions of his day, which defined God's concerns for their members in light of their own ritualistic norms and traditions that supported their institutional survival. It was love that the Lord desired, not sacrifice; it was knowledge of God the Lord desired, not holocaust (cf. Hos. 6:6). Priests and people perished for want of knowledge as they tried to control God through their rituals and prayers in order to maintain "the religion."

Hear, O heavens, and listen, O earth,
for the Lord speaks:
Sons have I raised and reared, but they have disowned me.
An ox knows its owner, and an ass, its master's manger;
But Israel does not know, my people has not understood.
Ah! sinful nations, people laden with wickedness,
evil race, corrupt children!
They have forsaken the Lord,
spurned the Holy One of Israel, apostatized.
Where would you yet be struck,
you that rebel again and again?
The whole head is sick, the whole heart grown faint.
From the sole of the foot to the head there is no sound spot:
Wound and welt and gaping gash,
not drained, or bandaged, or eased with salve.
Your country is waste, your cities burnt with fire;
Your land before your eyes
strangers devour as waste, like Sodom overthrown—
And daughter Zion is left like a hut in a vineyard,
like a shed in a melon patch, like a city blockaded.

Unless the Lord of Hosts had left us a scanty remnant,
we had become as Sodom, we should be like Gomorrah.
Hear the word of the Lord, princes of Sodom!
Listen to the instruction of God, people of Gomorrah!
What care I for the number of your sacrifices? says the Lord.
I have had enough of whole-burnt rams and fat of fatlings;
In the blood of calves, lambs and goats I find no pleasure.

When you come in to visit me, who asks these things of you?
Trample my courts no more!
Bring no more worthless offerings; your incense is loathsome to me.
New moon and sabbath, calling of assemblies,
octaves with wickedness: this I cannot bear.

Your new moons and festivals I detest;
they weigh me down, I tire of the load.
When you spread out your hands, I close my eyes to you:
Though you pray the more, I will not listen.
Your hands are full of blood!
Wash yourselves clean!
Put away your misdeeds from before my eyes;
cease doing evil; learn to do good.
Make justice your aim: redress the wronged,
hear the orphan's plea,
defend the widow (Isa. 1:2–17; emphasis added).

Through prayer, Isaiah came to experience the Lord. In this experience, he came to know the concerns of the Lord and to distinguish between false and true religion (cf. also James 1:26–27). In preaching conversion from their ways to the priests and institutional leaders of his day, he, like Jeremiah, Amos, Hosea, and the other prophets, identified with God's pathos.

The prophet, then, is one whose ministry results from prayerful religious experience which takes one beyond surface forms of prayer to a life of faith to become that just person who lives by faith (cf. Rom. 4–7). Having experienced God in prayer, the pattern of the gospel takes root in one's life. The result is a life of faith expressed in justice, "for in the gospel is revealed the justice of God which begins and ends in faith" (Rom. 1:17). The empathy and sympathy of the prophet toward the plight of the poor attest to the authenticity of the prayer and religious experience wherein one comes to know the Lord.

In his classic work *The Prophets*, Abraham Heschel discusses at length how the sympathy of the prophet is a human way of identifying with and expressing God's justice. Although his explanation is lengthy, it would be wrong to summarize the fine presentation by Heschel in weaker words from ourselves. Speaking of the personality of the prophet, the great Jewish author and promoter of justice until his death in 1974, wrote:

> His sympathy is an overflow of powerful emotion which comes in response to what he sensed in divinity. For the only way to intuit a feeling is to feel it. One cannot have a merely intellectual awareness of a concrete suffering or pleasure, for intellect as such is merely the

tracing of relations, and a feeling is no mere relational pattern. . . .

The unique feature of religious sympathy is not self-conquest, but self-dedication; not the suppression of emotion, but active co-operation with God; not love which aspires to the Being of God in Himself, but harmony of the soul with the concern of God. To be a prophet means to identify one's concern with the concern of God.

Sympathy is a state in which a person is open to the presence of another person. It is a feeling which feels the feeling to which it reacts—the opposite of emotional solitariness. In prophetic sympathy, man is open to the presence and emotion of the transcendent Subject. He carries within himself the awareness of what is happening to God. . . .

Sympathy, however, is not an end in itself. Nothing is further from the prophetic mind than to inculcate or live out a life of feeling, a religion of sentimentality. Not mere feeling, but action, will mitigate the world's misery, society's injustice or the people's alienation from God. Only action will relieve the tension between God and man. Both pathos and sympathy are, from the perspective of the total situation, demands rather than fulfillments. Prophetic sympathy is no delight; unlike ecstasy, it is not a goal, but a sense of challenge, a commitment, a state of tension, consternation, and dismay.[10]

Since the Lord is just in all his ways and since God can know only himself (his image), only the person who does justice can be known by God. Only the person doing justice can be recognized as an image of God.

JESUS REVEALING GOD'S NAME

Just as God revealed his name to Moses in the process of liberation, so when God revealed himself in his Word-made-flesh, he chose a name that identifies him and his mission in terms of liberation. The name of "Jesus" means "Yahweh Saves," "Yahweh is Liberator." The child born of Mary was to be named " 'Jesus' because he will save his people . . . " (Matt. 1:21). Jesus is to save his people from their sins as individuals and as members of groups. In his person (name), he is also to take away the very sin of the world (John 1:29).

Jesus is God's presence in history. He stands in history to free people from *whatever* sin may control them. Signifying God's presence, he begins his ministry by naming others to enter into participative community with him (cf. Mark 1:15). He calls people to follow him, to identify with him through participation. Jesus shows them, more by action than by words, that he is what his name implies. Thus when he was asked if he was the one to come, who would show forth God's justice to the nations, as was promised, Jesus merely pointed to his ministry, which enabled people to be free, and declared those "blessed" who would find "no stumbling block in me" (Matt. 11:6).

Jesus' ministry enabled people to pass over from their childish and adolescent levels of relationship with God and others, by calling them, in love, to the fullness of their being. He called people to the fullness of self. Calling his disciples by name, he established community with them, and in this participative community they came to the fullness of themselves. In the words of Jacques Ellul, "Every act of love shown in scripture involves causing a person to *come out* of his status of anonymity, derived from collectivity, the crowd, etc., in order, through a purely personal relationship, to transform into a person known and distinguished by his name."[11] If we could only imagine what went through Zacchaeus' mind when Jesus called him by name and asked to stay in his house (cf. Luke 19:2ff) to begin a whole new way of life! In calling her name, Jesus not only enabled Mary Magdalen to be recognized as someone known and loved; he opened himself to be named by her, "Rabboni." God does the same with us. He calls us by name. He has empowered us that we might recognize ourselves to be known and loved by him, that we, in turn, can call on his name and reveal his name to the world for its salvation.

In a society of false gods, all competing with the true God to name reality and be the way of salvation for all, the first disciples learned in the presence of Jesus what true liberation meant. Our society equally vies for our loyalty, spending millions of dollars to discover brand names that might control our decision-making, proclaiming messianic prowess in its ads: "Datsun Saves; Datsun Sets You Free." Madison Avenue proclaims that the new trinity is woman-washer-child(ren) and that salvation (clean clothes) comes from Tide. Yet into this reality wherein it often seems that there is little difference which trinity has more influence over our decision-making, the Lord promises: "I will remove from her mouth the names" of the false gods (Hos. 2:19). In the midst of such propaganda, which sustains society's infrastructures, the Christian stands in history as evidence and testimony that "there is no other name in the world . . . by which we are to be saved" (Acts 4:12) and that "at Jesus' name every knee must bend in the heavens, on the earth and under the earth, and every tongue proclaim to the glory of God the Father, Jesus Christ is Lord" (Phil. 2:10–11). In a society that places its god in the desire to control and exploit the earth's resources for the benefit of some and the detriment of God's image in others (often in the name of freedom and democracy), the disciple of Jesus declares, "I have neither silver nor gold, but what I have I give to you" (Acts 3:6). What we give, in the name of Jesus Christ, is our effort to free people from anything that separates them from themselves, each other, their world, and their God.

Continually we are torn between salvation as it is offered by God or by the world with its resulting alienation. If the latter controls us, we continually tell ourselves we are alienated, we are not loved, we are not cared for, we are not known. Yet into this alienation the God of care comes, saying that these thoughts are not his thoughts. God enters into our histories to reveal to us that he sees us, that we are known; that he cares for us, that we are loved; that he calls us to be a liberating force with him in history because we have been baptized (called) in his name. And his name, stamped on our being, becomes the name of salvation to the gentiles, who shall "name him Wonder-Counselor, God-Hero, Father-Forever, Prince of Peace" (Isa. 9:5).

BAPTIZED IN THE NAME

The Christian is able to participate in the reality of God by being baptized in the name of the Father, the Son, and the Holy Spirit (cf. Matt. 28:19). By participation in the Christian community, the follower of Jesus is called to experience the very community of justice. This community is to enable the various gifts of its members to be fostered so that, together, they might be used for service to each member, the community, the world. Baptized in the name of Jesus, the Savior, the Christian also stands as liberator, as minister of healing and justice in the world. "You must reform and be baptized . . . in the name of Jesus Christ, that your sins may be forgiven," Peter declared to his society; "then you will receive the gift of the Holy Spirit" (Acts 2:38). Peter came to realize that having access to the Spirit and the Spirit's gifts would create a community that would give glory to the name of the Lord, rather than profane it as his society was doing. Thus, "in support of his testimony he used many other arguments, and kept urging, 'Save yourselves from this generation which has gone astray' " (Acts 2:40).

The result of baptism in the name of Jesus was to identify with Jesus as a new creation, a new covenanted community wherein all who joined would freely share their resources of prayer and goods as members of a participative community. Thus immediately after Peter called upon the people to live a life in opposition to the prevailing culture, Acts adds (2:42, 44):

> They devoted themselves to the apostles' instruction and the communal life, to the breaking of bread and the prayers. . . . Those who believed shared all things in common; they would sell their property and goods, dividing everything on the basis of each one's need.

The church becomes the liberated zone to which all people can come seeking the resources that can be provided by its members. Wherever people gather and liberation is taking place in the name of Jesus, the church is present: "Where two or three are gathered in my name, there I am in their midst" (Matt. 18:20). The church stands forth in the midst of a world marked by sin as the body of Christ, as co-liberator, as instrument of God's creative purposes, as sign of God's pathos to his people. Baptized in his name, we become co-liberators, co-creators of God's pathos in history. We become for our world, in effect, the very justice, the holiness of God (cf. 2 Cor. 5:21).

To give praise to the name of the Lord by our prayer and

ministry means that, in order to bring about God's justice, we will probably incur the "justice" of the institutions in our world. This was so true in the early church that the phrase "to sanctify the name of God" or "to make the Lord's name holy" involved the strong possibility of persecution at the hands of one's religion, one's government, and even one's family. According to the *Prayer of Jesus*, the phrase *kiddousch haschem*, or "sanctification of the name,"

> did not signify simply honor or praise rendered to God's name. It was a technical term already in use in the first century with a very precise meaning; to sanctify the name was to give witness to God at the risk of one's own life. It was to glorify God, in case of necessity, even to the shedding of blood. The sanctification of the name became almost synonymous with martyrdom.[12]

The first persecution of the church was occasioned by the preaching of the name and the resurrection of Jesus. This resulted in healing and the creation of participative communities by the followers of Jesus, which threatened that society's institutions. "To stop this from spreading further among the people," the leaders, elders, scribes, the high priest, and all who were of the high-priestly class, gave them (Peter and John) "a stern warning never to mention that man's name to anyone again. So they called them back and made it clear that under no circumstances were they to speak the name of Jesus" (Acts 4:17–18). In another place, preaching in the name of Jesus was viewed in the same context as movements of insurrection (cf. Acts 5:38–42). In response to such threats from society, Peter and John declared, "But now, O Lord, look at the threats they are leveling against us. Grant to your servants, even as they speak your words, complete assurance by stretching forth your hand in cures and signs and wonders to be worked in the name of Jesus, your holy Servant" (Acts 4:29–30).

The Jews—sick in the desert—had been liberated from personal disease by the outstretched hand of Moses that they might share in the milk and honey of a land replete with resources. The Jews of the first century were delivered by the laying on of hands by Peter and John in the name of Jesus. In our day, our invoking of the name of Jesus to enable others to have access to resources of health and material goods will bring liberation to some. Yet, it may also result in persecution from others who have become addicted to their culture and its gods of control. Such is a consequence of praying that the Lord's name may be holy on earth as it is in heaven. The early Christians gladly suffered on behalf of the name. In our present-day world, marked by the grave sin of injustice, a prayerful confession of the name of Jesus and a faithful witness to the authenticity of our prayer by our ministry may enable this phrase of the Lord's Prayer to mean again for us what it meant for the first Christians. The fourth chapter of the Acts of the Apostles (which should be expressed in our acts as apostles) continually notes the *boldness* that characterized the confession of Jesus' name and the preaching of the gospel. Applying this notion of boldness to our preaching today we agree with Cardinal Suenens, who wrote in *A New Pentecost?*: "It is time we change our vocabulary and stop calling 'prudence' what is fear, and 'wisdom' what is timidity, when faced with implementing the Gospel."[13]

Implementing the gospel message in our milieu may have consequences for us in our day like those it had for Peter and John. "I for one don't like to be a martyr," said Cardinal Jaime Sin of Manila in reference to the reaction of the Philippine government to his 1974 resistance to unjust conditions in that country. "I would like to be a confessor."[14] Today, as with the early church, to confess Jesus publicly and to work prayerfully to achieve God's purposes for his people in the face of unjust systems may result in forms of misunderstanding, persecution, and even martyrdom. Such a realization should make us all the more determined to base our lives on the way God has revealed himself in history and how we must reveal his presence in our history.

LIBERATION AS NAMING REALITY

God revealed his name, we are told, in the process of liberation when he witnessed the affliction of his people and heard the cry of the poor. In his statement on the *Evangelical Witness of Religious Life*, Pope Paul VI carried this insight one step further. "From their personal distress and collective misery, you hear 'the cry of the poor' rising up more pressing than ever. Was it not in order to respond to their appeal as God's privileged ones that Christ came, even going so far as to identify Himself with them?"[15] If, then, the cry of the poor caused God to intervene on behalf of justice, and Christ *had* to become poor so that we might become rich, the Pope concludes, "In a world experiencing a greater degree of development, this persistence of poverty-stricken multitudes and individuals constitutes a pressing call for a 'change in everybody's thinking and habits,' especially for you who follow Christ more closely in this condition of self-emptying."[16]

The question that Pope Paul raises, as a result of a basic understanding of how God uses his people to accomplish his purposes, must be faced seriously by us: "How then will the cry of the poor find an echo in your lives? That cry must first of all bar you from whatever would be a compromise with any form of social injustice. It obliges you also to awaken consciences to the drama of misery and to the demands of social justice made by the Gospel and the Church."[17]

Pope Paul offers two ways that we can identify with God's pathos and hear the cry of the poor. First, since God's pathos means that God is never neutral to injustice, it means that, as individuals, in our local and base communities as well as in our institutions themselves, we can never be neutral. We can have no "compromise with any form of social injustice." In a society wherein individuals, groups, and institutions are interrelated and interdependent, to remain silent in the face of any form of injustice means that others will use our silence loudly to name reality as just—as it meets their interpretations and their gods. To be silent means that others will use our power in our name, in the name of our God, to justify their sin.

Second, Pope Paul tells us the cry of the poor can be heard in our lives if we identify with God's creative purposes and, as disciples of Jesus, call for conversion: "It obliges you to awaken consciences to the drama of misery and to the demands of social justice made by the Gospel and the Church." Awakening consciences means to help people see that many of our individual, group, and institutional ways are not God's ways; that they stand in need of conversion; that they need God's name to be present in their prayer-forms and ministries as he revealed his name—in the process of liberation.

Our ministry, supported and reinforced by prayer, should be a true action-reflection model. It should stand in the world as a witness to God's great concerns: that the goods of the earth be distributed with equity toward all and that the image of God be manifested as fully as possible in every human being. The cry of the poor must be echoed in our lives. To believe that we can approach God in any other way, especially prayer, without having heard (responded to) the needs of the oppressed is to believe God will hear our needs when we have been deaf to those of his people. Ministry and prayer, then, are based on the common realization that all people stand in need, all people are poor; that if God is to identify with us in prayer we must identify and participate with those who are physically poor and systemically kept poor. "He who shuts his ear to the cry of the poor will himself also call and not be heard" (Prov. 21:13).

In his life, St. Francis identified with God's creative purposes as outlined in Genesis to such a degree that Celano writes, "that original goodness that will be one day all things in all already shown forth in this saint all things in all."[18] On our part, whoever does justice, St. John writes, is born of God as a new creation. The name of God is thus worshiped and ministered to in society (cf. 1 John 2:29), reestablishing the original purposes of creation. This is in direct opposition to society's effort to claim loyalty from its members, a society in which "the beast will be worshiped by all those inhabitants of earth who did not have their names written at the world's beginning in the book of the living, which belongs to the Lamb who was slain" (Rev. 13:8).

In our ministry of liberation, we identify no longer with the name of the beast but with the name of God himself. This name of God is Yahweh, "I am." The goal of our ministry, then, is to be able to say "I am" and to support all people in their effort to say "I am." Together we are to become subjects, rather than controlled objects, of our destiny. With God's name upon us, we discover ourselves known and loved; we discover that we are different. This difference, based on the unique "I am" of each individual as God's image is needed by our world in order to be truly free. Jürgen Moltmann asks, "How does freedom thus begin? It begins with prayer, with the permission to be different and with the way into the joy of God. Where does it end? It ends in the new creation of all things and relationships."[19]

This freedom begins with prayer. In prayer we experience God calling us by name. We experience God naming himself in us, saying "here *I am.*" Through the revelation of his name, we are offered the possibility of freedom, of "going out" of ourselves (ecstasy) into identification with him. Paradoxically, this "going out" of ourselves is, in effect, achieved only by entering into ourselves to the very ground of our being, by passing through the first two levels of prayer to meet God as the other, the ground of our being. Here we find we are not only named by God but can call on his name. We have no need to control God or see him as outside our experience. We can pray with our heart. Francis did this by spending entire nights simply repeating the name of Jesus and saying "My God and my all." We can discover this in the same way, or by a simple repetition of a gospel word or phrase, or by reciting the Jesus Prayer in tune with our breathing, realizing that our being is filled with Jesus' own Spirit (cf. Gen. 2:7). In this way we better understand the meaning of Thomas Merton's words about praying with purity of heart:

> To invoke the name of Christ "in one's heart" was equivalent to calling upon him with the deepest and most earnest intensity of faith, manifested by the concentration of one's entire being upon a prayer stripped of all non-essentials and reduced to nothing but the invocation of his name with a simple petition for help. Macarius said: "There is no other perfect meditation than the saving and blessed Name of Our Lord Jesus Christ dwelling without interruption in you, as it is written: 'I will cry out like the swallow and I will meditate like the turtle-dove!' This is what is done by the devout man who perseveres in invoking the saving Name of our Lord Jesus Christ."[20]

In the experience of prayer we discover God's name in our heart. It is a name of salvation, of freedom that cannot be limited only to ourselves. Thus we find ourselves participating with God in the new creation of all things and relationships. We find ourselves participating with God and with all those who need to "go out" from whatever condition is naming them that they might enter into the fullness of their total freedom as well.

Our experience of freedom in prayer cannot be separated from our ministry for freedom and justice in our world. Perhaps this is what Christ meant when he told the "parable on the necessity of praying always and not losing heart" (Luke 18:1ff). Prayer is viewed in the framework of a person in need who approaches another asking for a share in resources that are one's by right. When we minister to the call (prayer) to share our resources we become just. Living by faith we share in the justice of God: "Will not God then do justice to his chosen who call out to him day and night? Will he delay long over them, do you suppose? I tell you he will give them swift justice. But when the Son of Man comes, will he find any faith on earth?" (Luke 18:7–8).

As a result of our prayer we find ourselves united in Christ with God's purposes in history, enabling people to name themselves. We find ourselves co-creators with God in history. One of the most radical and revolutionary acts we can be part of is the effort we make to empower people to name themselves, their reality, and their God. What Mary Daly says in reference to women has to be said of every human being—that all are called by the "I am" to name their world:

> The power of *naming* [has been] stolen from us. We have not been free to use our own power to name ourselves, the world, or God. The old naming was not the product of dialogue—a fact inadvertently admitted in the Genesis story of Adam's naming the animals and the woman. Women are now realizing that the universal imposing of names by men has been false because partial. That is, inadequate words have been taken as adequate. To exist humanly is to name the self, the world, and God. The "method" of the evolving spiritual consciousness of women is nothing less than this beginning to speak humanly—a reclaiming of the right to name. The liberation of language is rooted in the liberation of ourselves.[21]

Naming one's reality in Genesis was the sign of participation in the creative purposes of God; to have that power taken from us is to frustrate the creative designs of God. Thus, whether it be women, groups or communities that have been denied jobs, mortgage loans, and fair taxes; the loneliest person in a hospital ward or counselling room; the poorest person in Appalachia or the favellas of São Paulo—God's name is to be placed within all human beings that they might again name their reality. This will enable them to be subjects of their own destiny, rather than objects meeting the destiny defined for them by others.

In the loneliness and isolation of life lived on a purely body or ego level, God steps into our history and reveals to us our true selves. In this revelation of ourselves we become free and we become empowered to offer this same freedom to our brothers and sisters. If they are not being liberated as we walk in their midst, if they do not have this kind of good news preached to them, then the Scriptures are not being fulfilled (through us) in their hearing.

We have had the name of God written on our foreheads (cf. Ezek. 9:4; Rev. 7:3) as a sign of our participation in God's pathos toward his people. Consequently we share in his creative concern for the world by our sympathy, by our prayer and ministry of justice. Prayer and ministry dedicated to achieve this goal of creation make God's name holy on earth as it is in heaven. It enables us to have passed over from death to life (1 John 3:14) to share in the new creation and vision prepared for those who are faithful:

> The heavens were opened, and as I looked on, a white horse appeared; its rider was called "the Faithful and True." Justice is his standard in passing judgment and in waging war. His eyes blazed like fire, and on his head were many diadems. Inscribed on his person was a name known to no one but himself. He wore a cloak that had been dipped in blood, and his name was the Word of God. The armies of heaven were behind him riding white horses and dressed in fine linen, pure and white. Out of his mouth came a sharp sword for striking down the nations. He will shepherd them with an iron rod; it is he who will tread out in the winepress the blazing wrath of God the Almighty. A name was written on the part of the cloak that covered his thigh: "King of kings and Lord of lords" (Rev. 19:11–16).

4

May Your Kingdom Come on Earth as in Heaven

The call for God's kingdom to come on earth as in heaven —possibly more than any other words—testifies to our thesis that, for the first Christians, the Our Father was a subversive prayer. The early community viewed themselves as residing in Babylon where the politics of emperor worship and the economics of exploitation had become united in the oppression of the poor. As followers of the one who was crucified on contrived charges of subversion of the politico-economic forces of his day (cf. John 19:12), these Christians knew that it was impossible to separate the religious realm from the politico-economic realm when they considered the infrastructures of their reality. Indeed, the politico-economic realm was able to shroud itself in religious garments (reinforced by the silence, if not the outright support, of the religious institutions of the day). The infrastructural milieu that found an ideology perpetuated by the alliance of organized religion and the politico-economic power of the state had become the god. As a result, Heinrich Schlier notes in his *Principalities and Powers in the New Testament:*

> . . . refusal to worship the image of this god is punished with death. This intelligence is capable of deciding which men are to be counted loyal and god-fearing, and, therefore, deserving to live, and which are of the godless types who will not be tolerated in that religious empire. As the power of the beast is present in the image, the refusal to worship is equivalent to the total denial of this god. The crime of *laesae Romanae religionis* is simply *laesae maiestatis.* And

how was a Christian to escape the death penalty, when his public refusal to worship Caesar and swear by his genius always raised the presumption that he had acted through *dolus*, the malice legally required for condemnation? The image, supported and inspired by the prophetic force of political power, is thus an instrument by means of which the state can distinguish friends from enemies, and punish those who are enemies. The "intelligence" of the "image" ultimately constitutes a body of living law, for the judges of this empire.[1]

No other book of the Christian Scriptures better indicates the relationship between religion and politico-economics than Revelation. Probably the most misunderstood book of the Christian Scriptures, it might well be the clearest articulation of the mindset that guided the founders of our community as they ministered God's presence in an alien world. Written in the context of the first century, its message is perennial: Whoever will not worship the beast will be placed on the enemies list (cf. Dan. 11:2; 1 Thess. 2; Rev. 13).

The book of Revelation was written for Christians whose lives were influenced by the environment of Domitian's reign (A.D. 81–96). He was the first Roman emperor who seriously believed the public's proclamation of his divinity. He institutionalized this by applying to himself the title *dominus et deus noster*, "our lord and god." According to Suetonius, an early writer, Domitian commanded that he be referred to by no other name in any writing or speech.

However, one group of people refused to abide by such a proclamation—a small group who lived by an ethic that another name was holy and to be worshiped and another kingdom was to come. Of them it was said, "To a man, they disregard the Emperor's decrees and claim instead that a certain Jesus is king" (Acts 17:7). They had given another, Jesus, the title "King of kings and Lord of lords" (Rev. 19:16) as a direct affront and challenge to the self-proclaimed legitimacy of the Roman system. Thus the group who did this would bear the brunt of Domitian's wrath.

The early Christians, while nonviolent, definitely were a community of resistance, as the Our Father attests and as the book of Revelation indicates.

Babylon the great city
shall be cast down like this, with violence,
and nevermore be found! . . .
Because your merchants were the world's nobility,
you led all nations astray by your sorcery.
In her was found the blood of prophets and saints
and of all who were slain on the earth (Rev. 18:21, 23–24).

From its beginning, when John refers to Jesus as the "ruler of the kings of earth" (1:5), and applies the common imperial acclamation "to him be glory and power forever" (1:6), all the way to its end, with the imperial advent cry, "Come, Lord" (22:20), the book of Revelation witnesses to the fact that Christians stood in the society of their day as delegitimizers of that order desired by its controlling institutions. They created, in turn, an ethic that declared that any effort by any institution to equate itself with God's kingdom would not have their allegiance.

This delegitimization and demythologizing of the powers and principalities is quite evident in the words John chose to apply to Christ. Until that time these words had been reserved exclusively for reference to the emperor. According to Robert Sabath:

> Throughout the Apocalypse John continually ascribes to God other forms of worshipful acclamation from the common store of formulas that the emperor had come to reserve for himself on the most festive state occasions: "hail," "victory," "Lord of earth," "invincible," "power," "glory," "honor," "peace," "holy," "blessed," "great," "unequalled," "Thou alone," "worthy art thou," "worthy is he to inherit the kingdom," "come," "come and do not delay."[2]

In the transference of these words and phrases to Christ, the early Christians were stating that another kingdom had already come on earth; Babylon was fallen (Rev. 18:1); idol worship was in vain. In such an environment these phrases were as much political as they were theological affirmations. Transferring to God and Christ words that formed the ideological cement that held the empire together was to register a political protest. In face of the link between the economic and political realities that conspired to create enormous wealth by the exploitation of slaves and the poor (cf. Rev. 18:1–18), the early church gave the example to future generations to live by a comparable ethic based on the need to delegitimize any power or principality that takes to itself the divine prerogatives and interprets itself consciously or unconsciously as the kingdom of God.

THE NATION AS GOD'S KINGDOM

Almost two thousand years have passed since the reign of Domitian and the writing of the book of Revelation. Yet the powers and principalities of our world still appropriate to themselves many of the same prerogatives of the Roman emperors. Sen. Mark Hatfield caught something of this when he spoke before economic and political leaders at a 1972 National Prayer Breakfast in a setting less than a mile from Washington, D.C.'s squalor and poverty: "Let us beware of the real danger of misplaced allegiance, if not outright idolatry, to the extent we fail to distinguish between the god of an American civil religion and the God who reveals Himself in the Holy Scriptures and in Jesus Christ." He concluded, "If we as leaders appeal to the god of civil religion, our faith is in a small and exclusive deity, a loyal spiritual advisor to power and prestige, a defender of only the American nation, the object of a national folk religion devoid of moral content."[3]

Since "kingdom" is a political concept (outdated, as well as quite sexist), it is important that we go beyond it as a word in considering America in a political context. The "Founding Fathers" of the United States desired to move beyond both the word and the reality of kingdom. We need to look more closely at this phenomenon to analyze how America began to see itself as God's new Israel, envisioning itself as blessed by God with the mission of interpreting reality for the world in light of its own norms and traditions.

From the sixteenth to the eighteenth centuries, especially in Britain, people began to reflect on their reality and discovered, through their leaders (new Moses types) that they were oppressed, unable to worship God as freely as they liked. These men and women began to realize that the source of their oppression was symbolized in the crown worn by people like George III, who became for them other pharaohs. In order to escape their oppressor, they crossed the Atlantic (the Red Sea) to dwell in a promised land. Like the Jews before them, who gradually displaced the Canaanites, Hittites, Amorites, Perizites, Hivites, and Jebusites (cf. Exod. 3:8), this movement gradually displaced the Mohicans, Powhatans, Narragansetts, Pequots, and Iroquois.

Both the Jews and the colonists interpreted their oppression of the less powerful as part of God's plan. Even if this could never be justified in light of God's desire to share his earth's resources with all people made in his image, once they become settled on the land they started defining it and its use to meet their own needs.

As colonists formed communities in the new land, often centered around the church, they felt the need to put down in writing the values and ideals that had brought them together. Interpreting reality only from their understanding of God's activity in *their* lives (excluding God's intervention in the lives of women, their black slaves, and displaced native Americans), these white males declared that their new nation would be founded on the principles (values and ideals) of equal access to the prime resources (rights) and the promotion of equality of all before God as his images. "We hold these truths to be self-evident," they wrote, "that all men are created equal, that they are endowed by their creator with certain unalienable rights; that among these are life, liberty and the pursuit of happiness; that to secure these rights governments are instituted among men, deriving their just powers from the consent of the governed."[4]

However, with the institution of the government, the movement gradually became mechanized, transferring the original values and ideals into laws and traditions, generally favoring the white, rich, and powerful over the nonwhite, poor, and powerless. This mechanization became so institutionalized in the movement that was created that, less than two hundred years later, citizens who professed to believe in the values and ideals of the Declaration of Independence declared they could no longer believe in them. Neither would they practice them. This was made clear recently in Rochester, New York, when twenty citizens were asked if they could subscribe to the statement, "whenever any form of government becomes destructive of these ends, it is the right of the people to alter or to abolish it, and to institute new government, laying its foundation on such principles and organizing its power in such form as to them shall seem most likely to effect their safety and happiness."[5] Only one teenager from the twenty could subscribe. The rest found such a statement subversive, "communistic," "anti-American," even though it forms the second part of the famous sentence beginning with "we hold these truths to be self-evident." What is evident from this example is that America and its declaration of democracy are often beyond the experience of a freedom-professing-but-not-practicing population.

As its civil religion evolved, America's schools and inauguration day speeches, its churches and prayer breakfasts found people waxing eloquently on America as God's new Israel. Its two great historical events would become the framework for a new kind of religion within which all could rest assured that, for America, "God's blessing rests on thee."

CELEBRATING AMERICA'S CIVIL RELIGION

EVENT .... Revolutionary War .... Civil War ....
MEANING .... Foundation of Nation........... Purification ....
HEROES ...... George Washington .... Abraham Lincoln...
SCRIPTURE... Declaration of Independence.. Gettysburg Address
LITURGIES ... Fourth of July .... Memorial Day.......

Having come to the stage of monumentalization and institutionalization, America was able to create for itself the trappings of religion. Before this civil religion eager representatives of other religious institutions stood in awe, eagerly vying to lead the faithful in obedience to its officials as those divinely led by God. This evolution of the American political institution as allied with the religious institution reached a pinnacle under Richard Nixon. According to Laurence Leamer:

Early in his career Nixon had tapped into the religious vein of America and used it for part of his political sustenance. As President, Nixon did not go to God, God came to Nixon. He became the first President to hold weekly religious services in the White House. . . . And in the end there was no one left protecting Nixon but the pathetic refuse of that religious-political tradition. There was no one left but what someone at the White House called Nixon's holy trinity: Father McLaughlin, the Jesuit; The Reverend Mr. Graham, the Protestant; and Rabbi Korff, the Jew, linking hands around the body and spirit of the President, seeking to sustain him. [6]

As America of that period continued a war taking hundreds of thousands of lives, as its courts continually reinforced the power of the wealthy over the rights of the poor, as it sought to invade the freedom of expression of its own citizens, and as its citizens (6 percent of the world's population) consumed almost 35 percent of the world's goods, the prophetic and fearless voice of a church that once sang "Amen" and "Alleluia" in anticipation of Rome's destruction was muffled by the silence of a church and religious orders concerned about maintaining respectability, credibility, and good face. In such muffled preaching, political expediency becomes justification, the language takes on salvific overtones, and political leaders become saviors. Rabbi Louis Finkelstein attested to this when he declared that "in the period of great trials and great tribulation, the finger of God pointed to Richard Milhous Nixon, giving the vision and the wisdom to save the world and civilization."[7]

Watergate and the fall of Nixon have not helped Americans remember that the Babylon described in the book of Revelation wherein "all shipowners grew rich from their profitable trade with her" (Rev. 18:19) is the archetype of all nations, including America (cf. John 17:20). Somehow Americans have forgotten that Babylon is fallen (Rev. 18:2). Just as Domitian tried to advance Pax Romana under the slogans of nationalism, so Pax Americana continues to be advanced under such banners as "Project Independence," "America Right or Wrong," "Making the World Safe for Democracy"—all summarized in songs sung in churches and communities on the court-appointed days of prayer.

As Christians we have allowed the nation to take the place of God's kingdom. We have allowed a situation to be created wherein "church people" have attitudes little or no different from those of other citizens toward materialism and consumerism (sharing the earth's resources), and race, sex, and age (the image of God in all). Yet our role, as named by God and identified with his ways, is to judge America and the reality of sin—and to do this biblically. As Christians it is not our role to judge the Bible, the church, or existing institutions from the perspective of America's participation in the network of sin.

THE CHURCH AS GOD'S KINGDOM

It has not been only the American nation that has tried, through its civil religion, to identify its norms and traditions with the kingdom of God. The church in its institutional expression has often made the effort as well.

In chapter 1 we discussed how the church, through the men and women in it, went through the stages of creating a movement that becomes mechanized into a monument; how the effort of such institutionalization is to define its reality as the institution determines it must be practiced by its members (norms and traditions) through the profession of various words (values and ideals). Just as all political movements go through the stage where the institution becomes savior (the kingdom come on earth as in heaven), so Christianity is always tempted to interpret salvation in terms of membership in its institutional expressions. To "leave" the institution, even if it be in the name of more clearly bridging the gap between what is professed and what is practiced, is often viewed in light of fidelity, loyalty, and even salvation (or usually the lack of it). On the other hand, to remain within and raise a voice calling for reform is often interpreted as "secular" or "unchristian," just as to do the same politically is "un-American."

Jesus' concept of the kingdom undermines any effort of church institutions to define their reality as eschatological fulfillment. To the religious leaders of his own Jewish religion, who were not fulfilling God's concerns, Jesus said, "Let me make it clear that tax collectors and prostitutes are entering the kingdom of God before you" (Matt. 21:31). To those who believed their religious obligation in the world could be fulfilled by observance of rituals and norms with no concern for the oppressed, he said, "None of those who cry out, 'Lord, Lord,' will enter the kingdom of God, but only the one who does the will of my Father in heaven" (Matt. 7:21). To those who find their salvation in a personalistic religion divorced from concern about conditions in their world that created and sustained the cry of the poor, to those who pride themselves on prophesying in his name and exorcising demons by his power, Jesus says, "I never knew you" (Matt. 7:23).

Jesus cannot *know* those who claim membership in his kingdom if they do not incorporate now on earth, in their prayer and ministry, the effort to realize the signs of the kingdom that Revelation says will be in heaven. To know Yahweh is to do justice, to create on earth the kind of kingdom envisioned by Jesus in the Scriptures. Belonging to any institution whose members equate its external rituals with obedience to the kingdom of God contradicts what God has envisioned: "The Kingdom of God is not a matter of eating or drinking, but of justice, peace, and the joy that is given by the Holy Spirit" (Rom. 14:17).

While the church is in the world, it is not of this world; thus the church can never be equated with the world. While the church is to be a sign of the kingdom, it is not the kingdom, for not even all its members who say, "Lord, Lord," will enter the kingdom. While the kingdom is to come on earth as it is in heaven, it is not of this earth (cf. Matt. 26:53).[8] Therefore, our role as heralds of the Great King is to try to create in the world and in the church those conditions that best signify the kingdom of God—conditions that may not always be what the world or the church interprets for itself as kingdom. "If the church appears among the rich and powerful of this world," the Synod of Bishops states, "its credibility is diminished."[9] It is our role to judge America biblically and not the Bible Americanly. It is also our role to judge the church and the world biblically, and not vice versa.

One of the biggest obstacles to this effort is the tendency of institutional religion to conform itself to the world, to be among "the rich and the powerful of this world." When the early church no longer found itself resisting Babylon, with all its idolatry, it had already adapted to its environmental condition. It took on the forms of political and economic entities in the name of religious observance and faith. Whether it was transferring the clothes of the Roman elite into its liturgical garb or Roman law into church law, the result was a never-ending tension within many of its members who found it difficult to bridge the gap between what was professed as biblical faith and what was practiced. While sociologists may say such an evolution represents an inevitable development in religion, the words of Soren Kierkegaard represent quite clearly its effect on the people: "The crisis of biblical faith concerning conformity to the world, in one form or another, occurs whenever the anomaly of an established church appears."[10]

PILGRIMS AND STRANGERS IN THIS WORLD

The crisis of biblical faith vs. conformity to the world evokes many responses in believers. For some it may be fear, for others it may be forms of rejection, while for still others it provides reason for renewed fidelity to call for conversion and work for it. For all, however, realizing that America and the church often fail to practice what they preach and profess creates a deep sense of alienation within us. Our common response often places us as pilgrims and strangers both within America as the promised land and within the church as the kingdom of God. Having nowhere else to turn in this confusion, we turn again to God as ground of our being, and we begin to pray. With James Carroll we find:

> Our contemplative vision begins with what our bones know in September and October: We are living here in this place, at this time in exile. I am not at home and neither are you. Unlike the birds I have no nest. I have no place in which to lay down my head. Once I thought with John Kennedy and Martin Luther King and Eugene McCarthy and Bobby Kennedy and before them with Tom Jefferson and Abe Lincoln that I could be at home in America, that I could lay down my head on her dreams of liberty and justice for all. That was before Dallas, Memphis, Chicago, Selma, Los Angeles, Attica. That was before Vietnam. I am in exile in my own country, and so, perhaps, are you.
> Once I thought with Pope John and Hans Küng and Teilhard de

Chardin and Daniel Berrigan and before them with Isaac Hecker and St. Francis that I could be at home in the Catholic Church, that I could lay my head down on her dreams of spirituality and service to those in need. That was before the great movement of reform begun at the Vatican Council degenerated into bickering over the lifestyles of priests and nuns. That was before several heroes and more than a few friends of mine quit the church. That was before I discovered in myself a kind of inert numbness about the faith where once there was passion that risked extremities. I am in exile in my own church, and so, perhaps, are you.[11]

To go beyond the institutional demands defined by the nation and religion to accept the call to discipleship can mean that we will have nowhere to lay our head (Matt. 8:20). It was because he also felt compelled to preach another kingdom that Jesus found himself alienated from the institutional forms of his day. Not only did he feel alienated within them, but the leaders of those institutions showed how similar they were to each other and how conformed to each other's "kingdoms" they had become when for the "good of the nation" (cf. John 11:50ff.) they conspired to kill Jesus as an insurrectionist, as one who delegitimized their reality.

It was because they could not accept the kind of kingdom Jesus preached that the leaders of his religion instilled fear for the survival of the empire as a way of keeping control over the members of the religion (John 11:48). Thus again the theological implications of Jesus' death cannot be separated from political realities. According to Robert Sabath:

> The political implications of "kings" are nowhere more evident than in the trial scenes. According to standard procedure, the basis of Jesus' indictment was posted publicly over the cross, the inscription stating a purely political crime: "KING OF THE JEWS"—which in legal jargon meant that he was condemned to death by Roman execution as a rebel against the state in one of the subject provinces ("everyone who makes himself out to be a king opposes Caesar" Jn. 19:12). The charges brought against the revolutionary resistance movement of the Zealots were similar to those brought against him: "misleading our nation and forbidding to pay taxes to Caesar and saying that he himself is Christ, a king" (Luke 23:2). The same political implications are evident in opposition assertions such as "we have no king but Caesar" (Jn. 19:15).[12]

Between the Pax Romana or Pax Americana and the real peace
resulting from the "fulfillment of all justice" in God's kingdom
stands the cross. "The peace of God is thus a critical peace," Jürgen
Moltmann writes. "Peace with God means, therefore, not gratifi-
cation of the world and contentment in the world, but throughout,
also healthy discontent and unpeace with the powers and lords of
this world."[13] The combined effort of the powers and principalities, manifested in the united effort of the various institutions
to crucify Jesus, proved to be the sign of their alienation from God.
In their very instrument of death, the sign of alienation, they
unwittingly exemplified that "the message of the cross is complete
absurdity to those who are headed for ruin, but to us who *are
experiencing salvation* it is the power of God. Scripture says, 'I will
destroy the wisdom of the wise, and thwart the cleverness of the
clever' " (1 Cor. 1:18–19).

THE CROSS: SIGN OF CONFLICT
AMONG KINGDOMS IN THIS WORLD

By sharing in God's justice, achieved through the cross, we
identify with the mission of Jesus to delegitimize any and every
attempt of the powers and principalities to make themselves kingdoms:

> In Christ the fullness of deity resides in bodily form. Yours is a
> share of this fullness, in him who is the head of every principality
> and power. . . . In baptism you were not only buried with him but
> also raised to life with him because you believed in the power of God
> who raised him from the dead. Even when you were dead in sin and
> your flesh was uncircumcised, God gave you new life in company
> with Christ. He pardoned all our sins. He cancelled the bond that
> stood against us with all its claims, snatching it up and nailing it to
> the cross. Thus did God disarm the principalities and powers. He
> made a public show of them and, leading them off captive,
> triumphed in the person of Christ (Col. 2:9–10, 12–15).

Jesus offered new life in company with himself as he ministered
God's creative purposes to his world. He made it clear to all who

would follow him that to do so in the kind of world that they lived in would end up on the cross. Such persons would have to reject the forms of salvation offered by the world, and deny themselves the feeling that would come from submission to such institutional forms:

> If a man wishes to come after me, he must deny his very self, take up his cross, and begin to follow in my footsteps. Whoever would save his life will lose it, but whoever loses his life for my sake will find it. What profit would a man show if he were to gain the whole world and destroy himself in the process? What can a man offer in exchange for his very self? The Son of Man will come with his Father's glory accompanied by his angels. When he does, he will repay each man according to his conduct. I assure you, among those standing here there are some who will not experience death before they see the Son of Man come in his kingship (Matt. 16:24–28).

People took these words literally. They believed in them and were willing to give up their lives to preach the coming "in his kingship" of Jesus. As a result eleven of the first twelve apostles died violent deaths at the hands of society. To accept the cross of Jesus as disciples means to be ready to suffer the consequences of delegitimizing the powers and principalities wherever they may be. To answer the call of discipleship concretely in a world marked by sin means to participate with Jesus in the style of life that culminates in the cross.

While it is difficult to see the real implications of "taking up the cross" when businesses are formed to produce the image of the cross on assembly lines, when Park Avenue jewelry stores display it in gold and bands march to its formation at the Astrodome, we can never forget, with John Howard Yoder, that

> the cross [was] the standard punishment for insurrection or for the refusal to confess Caesar's lordship. . . . "Take up the cross" may even have been a standard phrase of Zealot recruiting. The disciple's cross is not a metaphor for self-mortification or even generally for innocent suffering; "if you follow me, your fate will be like mine, the fate of a revolutionary. You cannot follow me without facing that fate."[14]

Because he had read so well the reality of sin in his world, Jesus made it clear to his recruits that their call for the world's conversion would incur the wrath of its existing powers. If any contemporary community is calling for conversion in today's world, it must emphasize to its recruits that if they preach a gospel of God's insistence about sharing the earth's resources and his equal insistence on the dignity of his image in every person, this can easily result in persecution and suffering. Such persecution may not be only at the hands of the powers that keep this sin abounding, but even at the hands of loved ones who have been led by the institutional norms and traditions to accept this condition of sin as salvation. This entails the willingness to be alienated from others who are closest to oneself—parents, family, and friends—and even one's own human respect (cf. Luke 14:28).

We must be realistic that today's recruits, like those of Jesus' time, will continually be bringing their own agendas into the living of the reality. We must make it very clear—as did Jesus—that the concrete following of him in history will mean the cross (Mark 8:31ff; 9:30ff; 10:32ff). The willingness to accept persecution, poverty, misunderstanding, and forms of death must be clearly accepted by any community whose members accept the need to call for change in society.

One of the greatest costs that disciples in such a community will have to accept is the temptation to return to the categories of reality-interpretation defined by the environment within which they were nurtured. They have to free themselves of the temptation the Israelites faced—to return to their days of slavery wherein they were taught how to adapt, thinking it would be better under slavery than to be free (cf. Exod. 16:3; 17:3).

The infrastructures that control ideology are able to define right and wrong through its norms and traditions; they also have the power to define "sanity" and "insanity." Yet, if we believe that these infrastructures indicate to Christians where the real pathology of world-sin lies—in societal structures, with their cultural addictions—the community of disciples and any individuals working to change the society will have to accept the inevitability of being termed radical, subversive, or even a crusader. If such terminology brings about rejection of the bearer of the message to keep the hearer from dealing with the content of the message, the pathological sickness remains undisturbed.

Because Francis accepted the role of the cross in his life, he redefined the words and attitudes of his society to indicate a deeper reality, which effectively resulted in the subversion of his society. In an environment supporting the crusades, he called himself "the Herald of the Great King," and began a crusade against militarism and hate by preaching conversion and nonviolence not only to the sultan, but within his institution, to the crusaders themselves. In both cases, society reacted to his words with various forms of rejection. As long as *he* could be defined as the crusader, the unrealistic one, this would keep people from judging reality as it was in light of the Scriptures. This would be especially the case with members of his own religion. As Celano writes, Francis said to a companion:

> "If I tell them this, I will be considered a fool; if I am silent, I will not escape my conscience. What therefore seems best to you?" His companion answered saying, "Consider it as nothing to be judged by men, for it is not only now that you will begin to be thought a fool. Keep your conscience free of blame and fear God rather than man." The holy man therefore arose and approached the Christians with salutary warnings, forbidding the war, denouncing the reason for it. But truth was turned to ridicule, and they hardened their hearts and refused to be guided. [15]

Anyone serious about preaching conversion to a society that has defined itself as the kingdom and offers to that society the possibility of looking at reality in another way will have to be prepared to suffer rejection, undermining, and ridicule at its hands. If Francis could be classified insane by his "sane" society, people could be kept from perceiving that reality might be the other way around. The distinction is subtle, but it has the effect of keeping people enslaved. This was recently exemplified in a *Wall Street Journal* column written by a member of its Board of Contributors, which was a subtle attempt to undermine effort for system-change in the United States by calling it a "crusade." Its two lead paragraphs summarized many of the historical realities we have dealt with in this chapter. The way they were interpreted, however, points out to the disciple of Jesus the need to have battle gear ready to struggle with the powers and principalities of our day (cf. Eph. 6). "There is in the United States a tradition of evangelical reform that has no exact counterpart in any other nation," the writer stated, alluding to America's civil religion:

> It emerges, one assumes, from our Protestant origins, with its conception of this new nation as being "a city upon a hill," "light unto the nations"—in short, as properly striving for and being able to achieve a degree of perfection that is beyond the reach of less blessed peoples elsewhere. All of us, for the most part without even realizing it, subscribe to this American dogma—which is why we constantly find ourselves being enlisted into movements of enthusiastic reformation.
>
> In some respects, this reform impulse is one of our glories. It gives American politics a permanent moral dimension and moral thrust that is entirely proper to a democratic republic, one of whose major functions must be to ennoble the common men and women we all most certainly are. But it has its dangers, too. It is so easy to move from the moral to the moralistic, for a concern for what is right to a passionate self-righteousness, from a desire to improve our social reality to a blind and mindless assault against the real world which so stubbornly fails to conform to our ideological preconceptions. In short, the great temptation which all American reform movements experience is to become a crusade. It is a temptation, also, that the reform impulse will frequently succumb to, with all the disagreeable results that have always attended upon crusades.[16]

As long as the infrastructures control the ideology, their interpretation of reality becomes the basis for normalcy. It becomes the shaper and interpreter of the "real world." Those who try to offer another way, in turn, are called ideological, blind, mindless, abnormal, rebels, and crusaders. As long as the public can be convinced that the latter represent ideological preconceptions, the ideology that continues through the massive monies and influence of the infrastructures remains unscathed.

At the 1976 Annual Meeting of General Electric shareholders, the difference between individual "ideology" and infrastructural "ideology" was made clear. A young man spoke at the meeting, seriously challenging the commitment of General Electric to nuclear power. In response to the young man, whose concern was not matched by his ability to speak clearly, Reginald Jones, the chairperson of General Electric, called him an "anti-nuke" and stated about opponents of nuclear power (such as that man and three General Electric scientists who quit their jobs with the company because of their concern over nuclear power): "And if you are not in an adversary mode, you can't get a headline. It is most unfortunate." The idea was clearly left with the shareholders that only "crusaders" effectively influence public opinion.

After two other speakers addressed the chair and shareholders, I began a dialogue with Mr. Jones that went as follows:

MICHAEL CROSBY: . . . I read a few weeks ago in the *Milwaukee Journal* that there was a group of industries that were involved in nuclear power, in one way or another, who have come up with a five to seven million dollar war chest to fight public interest groups [against nuclear power], with much of it related to the California Proposition 15. I am wondering if any monies of General Electric are involved in this effort?

REGINALD JONES: We have made a very modest contribution to the efforts in California to explain to the voters the nuclear power system situation.

MICHAEL CROSBY: Will you explain how much that has been?

REGINALD JONES: Oh, my God, I think it was twenty or twenty-five thousand dollars.

WALTER SCHLOTTERBECK: No more than that.

REGINALD JONES: It is less than one hundred thousand dollars, isn't it?

WALTER SCHLOTTERBECK: Oh, yes, much less.

REGINALD JONES: Well, less than that, so we are not pouring millions into this.

MICHAEL CROSBY: Great. I would think the fact that this much money has been put into that effort should be balanced with your previous comment that if you aren't in an adversary role you can't get ahead. My point is that I don't think that General Electric needs to get a headline when it has monies to get its point across in those ways.[17]

General Electric's "modest contribution" was made "to explain to the voters the nuclear power system situation." Why an effort by one person or other groups to "explain the nuclear power system situation" would be a sign of a crusade while General Electric's effort to do the same (behind the scenes) would not, staggers one's logic. Yet adversaries of the infrastructures continue to be branded as crusaders, while we forget the "crusade" of the infrastructures. The powers and the principalities remain unchecked.

5

Signs of the Kingdom Come on Earth as in Heaven

When we reflect on the early community of disciples, we discover certain sociological traits that characterize any movement purporting to change society: (1) a visible, organized gathering of people (cf. Acts 2:42ff.); (2) a clearly defined lifestyle that separates the selected community from the wider community's interpretation and support of existing reality (cf. John 11:45ff.); (3) a decision of its members, based on conversion from a normal acceptance of reality as defined by traditional institutions and forces, to accept costs resulting from such discipleship (cf. John 6:68–69).

When the early Christians looked at their milieu, they knew acceptance of discipleship involved resistance to the world's effort to dominate their thinking and lives. They agreed to "battle" with these forces as true soldiers of Jesus Christ. However, the church gradually adapted its values and ideals to conform with the norms and traditions of the politico-economic reality of which it had become a part. This conformity reached a peak when the phrase *miles Christi*, a term Paul used to associate the followers of Jesus with his passion and death at the hands of the forces of the world, was given an institutional expression to support the war effort of the church's crusade.

Jesus rejected violence as a way of dealing with the powers and principalities (cf. Matt. 25:52), but he offered an alternative action/reflection model to deal with opposition. In this spirit, Paul wrote the early Christians at Ephesus (Eph. 6:10–17):

Finally, draw your strength from the Lord and his mighty power. Put on the armor of God so that you may be able to stand firm against the tactics of the devil. Our battle is not against human forces but against the principalities and powers, the rulers of this world of darkness, the evil spirits in regions above. You must put on the armor of God if you are to resist on the evil day; do all that your duty requires, and hold your ground. Stand fast, with the truth as the belt around your waist, justice as your breastplate, and zeal to propagate the gospel of peace as your footgear. In all circumstances hold faith up before you as your shield; it will help you extinguish the fiery darts of the evil one. Take the helmet of salvation and the sword of the spirit, the word of God.

In commenting on this text, the Franciscan Giulio Basseti-Sani makes it clear that

St. Paul did not picture the "soldier of Christ" with sword in hand, intent on the slaughter of the enemies of Christ. As opposed to the soldier of the Roman army or any other, the "soldier of Christ" must not inflict suffering on others by brute force, but is himself called to suffer in union with the passion and death of Christ. To apply the words of St. Paul to a context of war and aggression, as became the custom after St. Bernard even in papal documents, is to betray the true spirit of St. Paul. But when applied to St. Francis, as it was by his first biographers, *miles Christi* takes on its own particular meaning. Any prophet comes with a message and uses the categories of his time to reverse the values contained in those categories. Thus, St. Francis, the authentic *miles Christi*, was to lead the Church back to the true meaning of St. Paul's words.[1]

What meaning underlies Paul's words? What does it mean for our milieu when he says that the "battle gear" we are putting on consists of *truth* as our belt, *justice* as our breastplate, and *zeal for peace* as our footgear?

In this chapter we will attempt to apply these values and ideals to a lifestyle of prayer and ministry as it might be lived by those fully aware of their need to stand ready to resist in a world marked by sin. These values will be considered in the light of faith, which Paul tells us must be held up continuously as our shield (cf. Eph. 6:16).

TRUTH: NONPARTICIPATION IN LIES

In a society that suffers from "credibility gaps" and needs "truth-in-lending" bills, "truth-in-advertising" campaigns, "truth squads," etc., Jesus' words represent a refreshing break with existing reality, as well as a forewarning of what dedication to truth implies for his disciples.

> I gave them your word,
> and the world has hated them for it;
> they do not belong to the world
> any more than I belong to the world.
> I do not ask you to take them out of the world,
> but to guard them from the evil one.
> They are not of the world,
> any more than I belong to the world.
> Consecrate them by means of truth—
> "Your word is truth."
> As you have sent me into the world,
> so I have sent them into the world,
> that they may be consecrated in truth (John 17:14–19).

It would seem from these words that Jesus is saying that truth is essential for personal and interpersonal survival in our world. And just as the consecration, the completion, for Jesus was culminated in the giving of his body on the cross, so our consecration in truth involves being the bodies totally given by baptismal vow and confirmational promise to the pursuit of truth: "As you have sent me into the world, so I have sent them into the world."

Truth is the foundation people need to make ethical judgments about reality. If there is no access to truth, people become confused. Today's disclosures indicate large-scale efforts in the politico-economic realm to control reality and its interpretation. Watergates, CIA coverups, failure to disclose illegal political contributions from businesses, corporate payoffs to foreign governments, and media manipulation by those who influence our politico-economic situation—all these evidence the fact that secrecy dominates a large part of our reality. If secrecy persists, we do not have the information needed from the decision-makers. Information is needed to know how to act. Ethical decisions must be founded in truth. Without access to information and truth, grounding in ethics is impossible. For want of information Christians often fail to act. Thus, the reality of sin continues as the Christian relies on information that is not forthcoming from key institutions. The grave sin of injustice is allowed to continue. Stringfellow is correct when he states: "Whatever forms or appearance it may take, demonic aggression always aims at the immobilization or surrender or destruction of the mind and at the neutralization or abandonment or demoralization of the conscience."[2]

Because our world is so interconnected, if people can be confused enough to refrain from using their power, that very same power will be used to reinforce the existing power-control. Often it will be exercised in the very name of those who admit their immobilization owing to the way truth has been manipulated.

There are several ways powers and principalities manipulate truth to maintain their control over the interpretation of reality. Some of these will be outlined in the following pages.

Half-truths and simple denials are regularly used by those institutions that wish to deny people access to information upon which to base their judgments. While we have become accustomed to the words "The story was denied" from the White House, the Pentagon, the corporation, etc., the half-truths are much more subtle, because often they are shrouded in an aura of righteousness. For example, in its effort to respond to the public's growing feeling of being manipulated by the large oil firms, Mobil took out an advertisement in major U.S. papers under the title "Big Oil, Little People," in which it said that "the middle-class, middle-income man or woman is more likely to be an owner of one of the big oil companies than millionaires." In addition it stated: "A recent survey found that nearly 14 million Americans own shares—more than two million directly and nearly 12 million indirectly—in the six largest U.S. oil companies. And nobody was counted twice." Thus, in their seeming effort to answer possible objections to their statements ("And nobody was counted twice"), Mobil concluded, "Well, the popular misconception that 'Big Oil' is run by the few for a privileged few is nonsense."[3] But is it?

What Mobil did say is true. What Mobil didn't say is another matter. Yet it spent more than any other U.S. corporation to say what it wanted the public to believe—$10 million a year on "corporate image" advertising. A large section of the American public does hold its shares, and their median family income is $16,400 a year. Yet such "truth" pales when it is revealed (not by Mobil) that 17 percent of its total shares of common stock are consolidated in just seven New York banks. Two of them, Chase Manhattan and Bankers Trust, held 11.3 percent at the time Mobil ran its ads. According to government statistics, 5 percent is enough to constitute control of a corporation;[4] yet the "popular misconception that 'Big Oil' is run by the few" Mobil declared to be nonsense. In 1976 the Midwest Capuchins filed a shareholder resolution asking Mobil to disclose, in the interest of truth, the other half of the story regarding their shareholdings. Mobil opposed the resolution and the shareholders, who tend to abdicate their powers to management, supported Mobil with over 97 percent of the vote. At the meeting, speaking against Mobil and its crusade, I was viewed as the crusader. The vote of the shareholders was evidence of the power to name who the crusader was.

Half-truths are often accompanied by another manipulation of truth: through deception and the use of symbols. Again, Mobil has proved itself a case in point. While it may be true that advertising has discovered that red, white, and blue are among the most effective colors to attract consumer attention, the fact that these same colors happen to be symbols of loyalty to America do not hurt a corporate image either, especially when the appeal for "truth" is often made in the name of concern for Americans. This was evidenced in the Mobil ad mentioned before, which stated: "While broad-brush attacks based on misinformation or political expediency may be aimed at large companies, they also damage millions of Americans who work for and share ownership in those firms."[5]

What Mobil with its red, white, and blue advertisements will not mention, however, is that, as a transnational corporation, its goal is not loyalty to America or to its workers but to growth, which comes through profits. This latter often comes at the expense of the average American. Thus, when there was the possibility in 1975 that foreign tax credits for oil companies might be cut back or rescinded, Mobil seemed to forget possible "damage" to Americans working for the company. It made clear that such action might result in the company moving from the country. A vice chairman said (although the statement was subsequently "denied"), "We would have to take every step we could to get out of U.S. jurisdiction."[6] Finally, the fact that the politico-economic institutions have the power to control the dissemination of information to create reality as they see it seems best summarized in the words of the Mobil vice president for public affairs who stated, "We want others to see Mobil as we do."[7] Such a goal is worth ten million dollars a year, if it can be accomplished.

Institutions use language to reinforce their reality and to dull people's minds—like Humpty Dumpty in *Through the Looking Glass:* "When *I* use a word it means just what I choose it to mean." Naturally, "when I make a word do a lot of work," said Humpty Dumpty, "I always pay it extra."[8] One of the ways words are manipulated is through "double-speak." Taking a life through abortion becomes "terminating a pregnancy," killing and maiming countless innocent people results from "protective reactionary strikes," the sale of countless needless consumer items from detergents to deodorants ensures "security."

This consumer-oriented, economic use of the word "security" has its counterpart in other areas besides the "need" for individual and interpersonal security. Especially through the use of the term "national security," the security concept pervades and creates an environment based upon keeping our defenses up—in the fullest meaning of the term. In the name of "national security," the Indochinese War was allowed to drag on, a bloated military budget becomes sacrosanct, resources continue to be exploited, domestic and foreign policies that interfere with human rights are tolerated—and people asking what "national security" means find their loyalty questioned. Despite this fact,

> a committee of the National Council of Teachers of English, which is investigating the use of language by public officials, has found that the Department of Defense could give no adequate definition of "national security." This is at least as important as the fact that Nixon and his advisors were willing to reach to "national security"

as a defense of their actions. The phrase was available, imported into the language of politics and used by almost all of us at some time or another in the past thirty years. One can give a meaning to "national defense"; one can give no meaning to "national security," with the result that one can give any meaning to it that one likes.[9]

In a society dedicated to "security," it is difficult for Christians to be freed from enslavement to a false security that has little, if anything, to do with God's meaning of the word. The scriptural meaning involves the necessity of conversion from false concepts of security.

Probably the best scriptural interpretation of what happens when the followers of Jesus become seduced and enslaved by false concepts of security can be found in the Letter to the Hebrews. Linking security to the notion of "rest," the author finds a parallel between the contemporary Christian and the Jew who continually was tempted (and who often gave in) to false notions of what security would mean: "Therefore, while the promise of entrance into his rest still holds," Hebrews (4:1–3, 7–11) warns,

> we ought to be fearful of disobeying lest any of you be judged to have lost his chance of entering. We have indeed heard the good news, as they did. But the word which they heard did not profit them, for they did not receive it in faith. It is we who have believed who enter into that rest, just as God said: "Thus I swore in my anger, They shall never enter into my rest. . . . Today, if you should hear his voice, harden not your hearts." Now if Joshua had led them into the place of rest, God would not have spoken afterward of another day. Therefore a sabbath rest still remains for the people of God. And he who enters into God's rest, rests from his own work as God did from his. Let us strive to enter into that rest, so that no one may fall, in imitation of the example of Israel's unbelief.

God was able to rest only when his creative purposes had been accomplished, when he had made the goods of the earth available to all he had created, and when his image was expressed in all people. For the Jews to think that false kingdoms could provide this kind of "God-rest" was a delusion. The author of Hebrews warns the Christian that one cannot "enter into God's rest," until one identifies with God's creative purposes. To identify with any other "kingdom" or its interpretation of "security" is to believe in delusion and alienation. Because centuries later Francis did identify with God's kingdom, Celano writes, "they were everywhere secure. Because they had nothing, loved nothing, they feared in no way to lose anything."[10]

"As a poet," W.H. Auden once wrote of his role, "there is only one political duty, and that is to defend one's language from corruption. And that is particularly serious now. It's being so quickly corrupted. When it's corrupted, people lose faith in what they hear, and this leads to violence."[11] Since the basis of participative community rests upon the trust its members invest in each other, to have one's language abused, manipulated, or controlled by those with power creates mistrust. This results in violence.

In response to such an effort to control reality through communications one can give in (apathy) and become enslaved, or resist and be free. "Is there really no way out?" Alexander Solzhenitsyn asked in what seems to have been his last work before leaving Russia:

> And is there only one thing left for us to do, to wait without taking action? Maybe something will happen by itself? It will never happen as long as we daily acknowledge, extol, and strengthen —and so not sever ourselves from—the most perceptible of its aspects: Lies. When violence intrudes into peaceful life, its face glows with self-confidence, as if it were carrying a banner and shouting: "I am violence. Run away, make way for me—I will crush you." But violence quickly grows old. And it has lost confidence in itself, and in order to maintain a respectable face it summons falsehood as its ally—since violence can conceal itself with nothing except lies, and the lies can be maintained only by violence. And violence lays its ponderous paw not every day and not on every shoulder; it demands from us only obedience to lies and daily participation in lies—all loyalty lies in that.[12]

Solzhenitsyn concludes with the way to maintain one's integrity and be freed from enslavement (to be consecrated in truth by means of truth; cf. John 17:17): "The simplest and most accessible key to our self-neglected liberation lies right here: personal non-participation in lies."[13] Truth is the fundamental demand that must be met by individuals and groups if they are to preach the gospel in a world marked by the grave sin of injustice.

The underlying reasons why the search for truth is so essential in our present reality relate to its connection with the influence over our lives by institutional ideology. Allowing one's reality to be defined by "the powers and principalities" is to submit to a deviation of God's creative purposes. To allow oneself to be thus led away from God's creative plan and deceived through the interpretation of reality given to those with power, means, according to St. Paul, to be led by others' injustice, which suppresses truth. It is to undermine the distribution of resources in equity and the realization of God's image in all. It is to submit to idol worship, a violation of the true God as he is to be known within the things that are made. St. Paul wrote:

> The wrath of God is being revealed from heaven against the irreligious and perverse spirit of men who in this perversity of theirs, hinder the truth. In fact, whatever can be known about God is clear to them; he himself made it so. Since the creation of the world, invisible realities, God's eternal power and divinity, have become visible, recognized through the thing he has made. Therefore these men are inexcusable. They certainly had knowledge of God, yet they did not glorify him as God or give him thanks; they stultified themselves through speculating to no purpose, and their senseless hearts were darkened. They claimed to be wise, but turned into fools instead; they exchanged the glory of the immortal God for images, . . . these men who exchanged the truth of God for a lie (Rom. 1:18–23,25).

To know Yahweh is to do justice and prayerfully to minister God's justice in the world. If one refuses to be seduced by falsehoods, half-truths, deceptions, and lies, one begins to walk in truth as God's image. This path will find one following the lonely way of crucifixion, but such truth will be the basis for making ethical decisions as the foundation for a just lifestyle. This path will find us facing the same kind of people Jesus faced and with the same results. We too will be called liars, malicious sinners, blasphemers. With truth as the belt around our waists we will be battling those whose weapons for undermining us are calumny and propaganda as well as misunderstanding. For those who have begun the pilgrimage of the cross, truth provides the reality principle to be just and to identify with God's implementation of justice in God's world.

JUSTICE: KNOWING GOD AND
BEING KNOWN BY GOD

"Unless your holiness [justice] surpasses that of the scribes and Pharisees," Jesus once stated, "you shall not enter the kingdom of God" (Matt. 5:20). The word for "holiness" used by Jesus means justice. Such a statement should make us want to investigate what the "justice" of the scribes and Pharisees was, to make sure we do not find parallels in our lives that will also frustrate the presence of the kingdom in our midst.

For our purposes we do not want to become involved in the discussion of whether the scribes and Pharisees were closed groups with no disagreements, or to what degree Jesus might be identified with either or both general schools of thought. But Matthew's discussion of Jesus' words about justice receives specification in Mark 7, where Jesus himself categorized both Pharisees and scribes when he said to them: "How accurately Isaiah prophesied about you hypocrites when he wrote, 'This people pays me lip service but their heart is far from me. Empty is the reverence they do me because they teach as dogmas mere human precepts.' You disregard God's commandment and cling to what is human tradition" (Mark 7:6–7). Having said this, Jesus immediately used the example of how the Pharisees misused the *korban* (temple offering), transferring a value and an ideal to a norm and tradition in a way that was in violation of God's concern about sharing resources with those in need. In this case those in need were one's parents. To take the resources God commanded to be shared with one's parents and transfer them to the temple and religion was to become involved in idol worship and false religion.

The scribes and Pharisees had systemically created a religion based on the practice of their own norms. Followers were chastised as "irreligious" for "disobeying" these norms (Mark 2:23ff.). Such systemization can be concluded from Jesus' allegation: "You have made a fine art of setting aside God's commandment in the interests of keeping your traditions" (Mark 7:9). As a result of their transgressions of God's commands, injustice would become sanctioned as a religious act. In no way could God identify with them, because all of his "commands are just" (Ps. 119:172).

The Hebrew Scriptures consistently identify God's commands with the implementation of justice among people. By observance of the commands, the people identified with God's creative purposes in history and came to be at one with God. In fact, it was only because God's original purposes were frustrated by sin—which resulted in the misappropriation of the earth's resources and the failure to honor God's image in others—that the commands had to be given. *Mispat* ("justice," "salvation of the oppressed," "righteousness," etc.) became the reason for the need of the law. As José Miranda writes:

> *Mispat* is the defense of the weak, the liberation of the oppressed, doing justice to the poor. The fact that laws were originally called *mispatim* (for example, in Exod. 21:1; Exod. 15:25b; cf. also Exod. 18:13–27, to cite only strata of the most widely acknowledged antiquity) is a datum of incalculable importance, for it indicates the intention and original meaning of the legislation. In the philosophy of law as well as in the theology of authority and above all in biblical exegesis, we are thereby given the criterion for discerning when later legislators were really in accord with the will of God.[14]

Isaiah used military terms ("day of the Lord," "day of punishment, of wrath") to indicate God's victory over forces of injustice and oppression:

> Lo, the day of the Lord comes cruel,
> with wrath and burning anger;
> To lay waste the land and destroy the sinners within it! . . .
> Thus I will punish the world for its evil
> and the wicked for their guilt.
> I will put an end to the pride of the arrogant,
> the insolence of tyrants I will humble (Isa. 13:9, 11).

In another place Isaiah warned:

> Woe to those who enact unjust statutes
> and who write oppressive decrees,
> depriving the needy of judgment
> and robbing my people's poor of their rights,
> making widows their plunder, and orphans their prey!
> What will you do on the day of punishment,
> when ruin comes from afar?
> To whom will you flee for help?
> Where will you leave your wealth,
> lest it sink beneath the captives
> or fall beneath the slain? (Isa. 10:1–4).

Following the spirit of Isaiah, Jesus castigated the scribes and the Pharisees with their norms and traditions because they nullified "God's word in favor of the traditions you have handed on" (Mark 7:13). In fact, such norms and traditions, Jesus points out, can be the exact opposite of the values and ideals upon which they purportedly are based. In the case of the *korban*, for example, the law (as the interpreters judged and articulated it) became the instrument of oppression and injustice—which flouted the very reason God gave the command in the first place. Thus they "disregard God's commandment and cling to what is human tradition" (Mark 7:8). By pointing to such inconsistencies—all in the name of a "religion" defined by its institutional leaders—Jesus seemed to be calling for a conversion to justice not only of individual hearts, but of the system, with its myriad underpinnings and supports.

While it is true that societal morality ultimately rests on individual morality, it is also important to realize how the various levels of morality and justice (individual, group, and environmental) interplay with and reinforce each other. A good scriptural example of how individual and interpersonal immorality are also indicative of infrastructural immorality or systemic immorality is found in God's asking Hosea to marry a prostitute as a sign of the infidelity of the nation. The nation was unfaithful to the Lord's plan to which it had at one time covenanted itself in prayer and ministry: "Everything the Lord has said, we will do" (Exod. 19:8). The adultery of Gomer, her not "knowing" Hosea in fidelity and justice, symbolized the idolatry of the nation. Israel did not "know" God, for it did not promote the fulfillment of the covenant through justice. God's complaint through Hosea's words undeniably links fidelity, compassion (mercy), justice, and "knowledge of God." "It is love that I desire, not sacrifice, and knowledge of God rather than holocausts, . . . they, in their land, violated the covenant; there they were untrue to me" (Hos. 6:6–7). God found the people's religious forms in opposition to his will. In a special way, God found himself in opposition to the priests, who had the power to articulate the real values and ideals of the covenant but instead promoted their own needs with religious reinforcements.

Hear the word of the Lord, O people of Israel,
for the Lord has a grievance against the inhabitants of the land:
There is no fidelity, no mercy,
no knowledge of God in the land.
False swearing, lying, murder, stealing and adultery!
In their lawlessness, bloodshed follows bloodshed.
Therefore the land mourns.
and everything that dwells in it languishes;
The beasts of the field,
the birds of the air and even the fish of the sea perish.
But let no one protest, let no one complain;
with you is my grievance, O priests!
You shall stumble in the day,
and the prophets shall stumble with you at night;
I will destroy your mother.
My people perish for want of knowledge!
Since you have rejected knowledge,
I will reject you from my priesthood;
Since you have ignored the law of your God,
I will also ignore your sons.
One and all they sin against me,
exchanging their glory for shame (Hos. 4:1–7).

The Lord's complaint that the Israelites—priests and people —exchanged their glory for shame (Hos. 4:7) parallels Paul's allegation that the people of his day "exchanged the truth of God for a lie" (Rom. 1:25). It also makes us aware of the way in which individuals, groups, and societal infrastructures reinforce each

other, resulting in hurt and division among people. Hosea's pointing to the priests and false prophets as especially responsible for the
unjust situation, and Jesus' pointing to the scribes and Pharisees as
particularly responsible for the situation in his day, should make us
aware that leadership in religious institutions continues (at times)
to reinforce systemic injustice in our day. Likewise, we glimpse
the difficulty of changing individual hearts and those of groups
without at the same time addressing the social system and its whole
network of oppression. It should also make all leaders in the church
aware of the often unconscious way they can be co-opted so that
they can proclaim a word that won't be contradicted by their lives.

As we try to be faithful to the prophets and Jesus by calling for
the conversion of institutions of which we are a part, we find the
need for God's *mispat*, his justice and liberation, in a special way.
"In the face of the present-day world situation, marked by the
grave sin of injustice," the Synod of Bishops stated in 1971, "we
recognize both our responsibility to confront it as well as our
inability to overcome it by our own strength."[15] As Isaiah used
military terms to indicate God's victory over systems of injustice
and oppression that manifest the powers and principalities, St.
Paul advises the same for us. As individuals and members of
groups we each have our own sins and are also part of a much
bigger reality marked by the grave sin of injustice; thus Paul's
words for us who recognize the inadequacy and the poverty of our
own resources make more sense than ever: "Finally, draw your
strength from the Lord as his mighty power" (Eph. 6:10).

The strength we have to support us is not only our understanding that our ministry of justice is identified with God's purposes in history, but that God identifies himself with us when we
are united in this effort.

The early disciples of Francis were called "true followers of
justice."[16] Today it becomes essential for all Christians to unite the
practice of gospel living with its profession through our ministry
for justice, for justice is an essential dimension of the preaching of
the gospel.[17] If justice is constitutive of gospel living and the
salvation of the world, we must begin holding each other account-
able for its implementation in our lives—just as we have done with

other constitutive elements of the gospel such as community, faith, hope, and love. If we are not concerned about justice we cannot be Christian, we cannot have gospel community, poverty, or simplicity. If our prayer and ministry are not identified with the *mispat* of Yahweh, our declaration of "living the gospel of our Lord Jesus Christ" becomes empty words and, as such, liable to the same condemnation Jesus hurled against the scribes and Pharisees of his day: "This people pays me lip service but their heart is far from me" (Mark 7:6). If our hearts identify at all in prayerful experience with the Lord of history, like him we will be compelled to be present to his people in the world. In the heart of God our hearts will hear the cry of the poor (cf. Exod. 3:7) and, sharing in God's justice for the world, we will become ministers of liberation (Exod. 3:8). We will be in harmony with the statement of the Synod of Bishops:

> Listening to the cry of those who suffer violence and are oppressed by unjust systems and structure, and hearing the appeal of a world that by its perversity contradicts the plan of its creator, we have shared our awareness of the Church's vocation to be present in the heart of the world by proclaiming the Good News to the poor, freedom to the oppressed, and joy to the afflicted. The hopes and forces which are moving the world in its very foundations are not foreign to the dynamism of the Gospel, which through the power of the Holy Spirit frees men from personal sin and from its consequences in social life.[18]

As Christians we must find the world itself to be both the springboard for our contemplation and the springboard for our ministry. The injustice in the world should force us to be more closely identified in prayer and ministry with the Lord of history. "Just Father," Jesus prayed on the night of his death (cf. John 17:25–26) "the world has not known you." The world did not *know* Yahweh because it was not just. " . . . But I have known you" by being the image of your creative justice. " . . . These men have known that you sent me [because] to them I have revealed your name" which, as on Sinai, was revealed in a ministry of liberation from sinful oppression. In prayer and ministry, we find ourselves identified in God's name, God's presence, "I will continue to reveal it so that your love for me may live in them, and I may live in them."

Prayer and ministry, then, can never be separated from the world. United to God in the Spirit of Christ, we continue to battle with the powers and principalities. Francis's struggle against sin in his world was not divorced from his contemplation or from his action. As a result, Celano writes, he helped advance the new creation:

> Hurrying to leave this world inasmuch as it is the place of exile of our pilgrimage, this blessed traveller was yet helped not a little by the things that are in the world. With respect to the *world-rulers of this darkness*, he used it as a field of battle; with respect to God, he used it as a very bright image of his goodness. . . . Who could possibly narrate everything? For that original goodness that will be one day *all things in all* already shone forth in this saint *all* things in all.[19]

PEACE: SHARING RESOURCES AND RIGHTS

The account of the admission of Brother Bernard into the early Franciscan community provides an understanding of how essential it was for the recruits to share the resources of the earth if they were to become members of what Celano calls "the delegation of peace."

> Brother Bernard, embracing the delegation of peace, ran eagerly after the holy man of God to purchase the kingdom of heaven. . . . He hastened therefore to sell all his goods and gave the money to the poor, though not to his parents; and laying hold of the title to the way of perfection, he carried out the counsel of the holy Gospel: *if thou wilt be perfect, go, sell what thou hast, and give to the poor, and thou shalt have treasure in heaven; and come, follow me.* When he had done this, he was associated with St. Francis by his life and by his habit. . . . His conversion to God was a model to others in the manner of selling one's possessions and giving them to the poor.[20]

Francis had the clear insight that peace depended on the just sharing of the earth's resources with all who were made in the image of God. If the brothers or sisters would appropriate anything to themselves, he knew that community peace would be disturbed. Since he wanted his communities to signify the peace of the participative community of the Trinity wherein all resources are shared equally, he stressed poverty as the way to reflect this in the world. In forging a common identity with all creation by his poverty, Francis was no threat to anyone or anything. Celano tells a tale about Francis's relationship to birds that serves as an object lesson of the need to share resources in order to live in peace.

> One day the blessed Francis was sitting at the table with his brothers. Two little birds, one male, the other female, came up, and, solicitous about the bringing up of their newly born little ones, they took the crumbs from the table of the saint as they pleased and as they had been doing day by day. The holy man rejoiced in creatures like these and he coaxed them, as was his custom, and offered them grain solicitously. One day the father and the mother offered their little ones to the brothers, as having been reared at their expense, and after they had given their little ones to the brothers, they did not appear in that place again. The little birds grew among the brothers and they perched on their hands, not indeed as guests, but as belonging to that house. . . . They became completely tame among the brothers and took their food together with them. But greed broke up the peace, in that the greed of the large bird persecuted the smaller ones.[21]

In Francis's time grain was often the property over which division among creatures arose, with the more powerful denying access to the weaker. Francis was not unaware that the example of the birds had all too many parallels in the way human beings and nations relate to each other. Having learned from his whole environment that disputes over property and rights stemming from ownership often resulted in war, he continually warned his communities: "If we had any possessions we should also be forced to have arms to protect them, since possessions are a cause of disputes and strife."[22]

For American Christians it is significant to recall that in the minds of those who founded the United States the relationship between disputes and possession was also quite clear. For instance, James Madison viewed all rights as ultimately related to property.

He concluded that the fundamental role of the state was to "break and control the violence of faction." Of these disputes, "the most common and durable source of factions has been the various and unequal distribution of property."[23]

Because the earth is the Lord's (cf. Ps. 24:1), no people should feel they have a right to its goods over another, especially if they already possess goods necessary for life. St. John Chrysostom wrote that what God has bestowed on us is not for individual ownership but for joint possession. This agrees with nature. He gave property to us in common so we could learn to share it in common.[24] Conflicts arise because of pure human greed or because people are denied access to the goods of the earth by those who control the resources. This happens when the distribution of rights is founded in property.[25] "Where do the conflicts and disputes among you originate?" St. James asked the early community. "Is it not your inner cravings that make war within your members? What you desire you do not obtain, and so you resort to murder. You envy and you cannot acquire, so you quarrel and fight" (James 4:1–2).

Conflicting viewpoints about real or alleged violation of property rights affect the peace and harmony in relationships among individuals, groups, and nations. Because of the unequal sharing of resources or property among the members of a community—be it within a local community or the world community—mistrust and suspicion generate alienation and division to the degree that a truly participative community cannot be established. And, as we noted earlier in this chapter, false attitudes about security flow from this mistrust. Security, or "peace," becomes synonymous with being defensive rather than participative and interdependent.

In *Nobody Wanted War*, Ralph K. White shows that all conflicts need underlying causes as well as (a) precipitating cause(s). Without underlying causes there will be no outbreak of hostility. Thus his six basic steps that seem to be involved in every conflict that leads to an outbreak of hostility among nation-states should be pertinent here. Since our thesis is that we can find the same basic interrelationships and connections among all levels of society (individual, interpersonal, and environmental), we can apply these same six elements to the breakdown of peace in any community, no matter what size. This should be true of conditions in families, religious houses, and basic communities as well as among groups and nations. Interestingly, White finds that all parties involved in conflict tend to view reality within the same categories in such a way that righteousness reinforces their position.

The first step in any conflict is to perceive the other as the *diabolical enemy-image*. Others are seen as opposed to the truth that we see as essential to the community. In the effort to maintain one's position in relation to this truth, there is a need to maintain strongly one's power of interpretation of reality. A firm stand must be taken. This occasions the rise of the second step, a *virile self-image*. Whether the weapons be words, silence, or arms, one cannot back down from the position. The need not to back down is fortressed by the third step, the *moral self-image*. All parties must see themselves as peace-loving, rational, orderly, and just. Above all, God must support their viewpoint as well, which enables the parties to submit to the fourth step of *selective inattention*. "It is involved on both sides of a black-and-white picture," White notes: "White or gray elements on the enemy side are glossed over and attention focuses only on the black, and vice versa."[26] Through selective inattention one does not put things into proper perspective, in terms of time or of space. Above all (as much as it might be tried), one is unable to put oneself into the other's shoes. This results in the fifth step, the *absence of empathy*. This inability to empathize with the position of the other side can reach such a degree that the worst possible disaster is conceived as being "unprepared for battle." What results then is the final step: overconfidence based on *irrational interpretation of reality*. When all these steps are taken by both sides, the result is readiness for war. While we know this can happen among groups and nations, it can represent the environment and style of families and basic communities as well. And, on all levels, unless alternate structures based on peace are built in, mistrust and conflict will become the norm.

The realization that there is such an unequal distribution of the world's goods has created continual tensions in the world community. With this realization has come an awareness that the unequal distribution of resources reflects a denial of God's image in people, a frustration of basic rights. However, rather than call for empathy and conversion of the systems that create this tension, most Christians remain silent as countries, one after another, become armed camps sustained by mistrust. Order is maintained by arms, not justice. Thus there can be no peace. This situation is clearly outlined in the 1971 Synodal document on Justice in the World, under the heading, "Crisis of Universal Solidarity." "The world in which the church lives and acts is held captive by a tremendous paradox," the Synod declares. It continues:

> The paradox lies in the fact that within this perspective of unity the forces of division and antagonism seem today to be increasing in strength. Ancient divisions between nations and empires, between races and classes today possess new technological instruments of destruction. The arms race is a threat to man's highest good; it makes poor peoples and individuals still more miserable, while making richer those who are already powerful; it creates a continuous danger of conflagration and in the case of nuclear arms, it threatens to destroy all life from the face of the earth. At the same time new divisions are springing up to separate man from his neighbor. Unless combatted and overcome by social and political action, the influence of the new industrial and technological order favors the concentration of wealth, power and decision-making in the hands of a small public or private controlling group. Economic injustice and lack of social participation hinder a man from attaining his basic human and civil rights. [27]

Both the affirmation of human rights and equal access to resources are necessary if there is to be an environment of peace. If the basic community of the Trinity, which is the model and life of all community, represents total access among all three members to all their resources and complete mutual sharing, then Christians trying to work for peace and participative community among individuals, groups, and the environment today must battle against whatever opposes the fulfillment of that kind of community. With this gospel of peace as our footgear, we proclaim the message of Jesus and Francis: "Peace be to this house and to all who dwell herein" (cf. Matt. 10:12; Rule, 3; Testament).

6

Thy Will Be Done on Earth as in Heaven

God's will is inseparable from his plan for the world. This conviction has enabled us to add the phrase "on earth as it is in heaven" after the reference to God's will—as well as after the phrases "may your name be holy" and "may your kingdom come." In John, nowhere is the unity of God's plan for the world and his will more clearly evidenced than in the words Jesus addressed to the Jews: "It is not to do my own will that I have come down from heaven, but to do the will of him who sent me" (6:38).

What constituted the Word's relationship to the Father in heaven was to be accomplished on earth as in heaven, not only by the Word but by all those given to the Word in the world:

> It is the will of him who sent me
> that I should lose nothing of what he has given me;
> rather, that I should raise it up on the last day.
> Indeed, this is the will of my Father,
> that everyone who looks upon the Son and believes in him
> shall have eternal life (John 6:39–40).

With these words, Jesus refers to himself as the fulfillment of God's plan for creation and identifies all those united by faith in him as those committed to continue that plan in history. For Jesus, as well as for us, this will of God is realized fully in the cross.

The sequence—that Jesus was "raised up" and that we are to "look upon" him in belief—is patterned after the liberation experience of the Jewish community. "I, . . . once I am lifted up from earth, will draw all men to myself" (John 12:32) was Jesus' way of saying he was fulfilling the prophecy that his death would be the "blessing" that would draw the nation and "all the dispersed children of God" into one (John 11:52). John uses the phraseology in light of the original promise of liberation made to Abraham: "All the communities of the earth shall find blessing in you" (Gen. 12:3). This promise was frustrated by such immorality as that of Sodom and Gomorrah, which expressed itself in a lack of social justice.[1] The cry of the poor (cf. Gen. 18:21) became the trigger for the Lord to articulate his concerns for the world:

> Shall I hide from Abraham what I am about to do, now that he is to become a great and populous nation, and all the nations of the earth are to find blessing in him? Indeed, I have singled him out that he may direct his sons and his posterity *to keep the way of the Lord by doing what is right and just, so that the Lord may carry into effect* for Abraham *the promises* he made about him (Gen. 18:17–19; italics added).

The way of the Lord is accomplished by people doing what is just and right. Only if this way of the Lord is observed will the promises be fulfilled in those who seek to be identified with God's will in history.

One of the first steps in gathering the nation together in Abraham was accomplished through the liberation experience of the desert, where the Jews were tempted to return to their enslavement. Punished by the Lord with a plague of serpents for their unbelief, they recognized their lack of faith and repented. So Yahweh said to Moses: " 'Make a serpent and mount it on a pole, and if anyone who has been bitten looks at it, he will recover.' Moses accordingly made a bronze serpent and mounted it on a pole, and whenever anyone who had been bitten by a serpent looked at the bronze serpent, he recovered" (Num. 21:8–9). John applies this theme to the injustice of the world, which, by its evil deeds, alienates itself from God. In contrast to this he finds people identifying with Christ by identifying with the great deeds of justice:

> No one has gone up to heaven
> except the One who came down from there—
> the Son of Man [who is in heaven].

Just as Moses lifted up the serpent in the desert,
so must the Son of Man be lifted up,
that all who believe may have eternal life in him.
Yes, God so loved the world that he gave his only Son
that whoever believes in him may not die
but may have eternal life.
God did not send the Son into the world
to condemn the world,
but that the world might be saved through him.
Whoever believes in him avoids condemnation,
but whoever does not believe is already condemned
for not believing in the name of God's only Son.
The judgment of condemnation is this:
the light came into the world,
but men loved darkness rather than light
because their deeds were wicked.
Everyone who practices evil hate. the light;
he does not come near it
for fear his deeds will be exposed.
But he who acts in truth comes into the light,
to make clear that his deeds are done in God
(John 3:13–21; italics added).

In his First Epistle, John spends the first three chapters on the theme of walking in the light by doing just deeds instead of walking in the darkness of the world's sin. He equates doing justice with knowing that we are identified with God, having passed over to eternal life, as the Jews passed over from death to life by their practice of justice. John writes, "We should not follow the example of Cain who belonged to the evil one and killed his brother. Why did he kill him?" He answers:

Because his own deeds were wicked while his brother's were just.
No need, then, brothers, to be surprised
if the world hates you.
That we have passed from death to life we know
because we love the brothers.
The man who does not love is among the living dead.
Anyone who hates his brother is a murderer,
and you know that eternal life
abides in no murderer's heart.

> The way we came to understand [to know] love
> was that he laid down his life for us;
> we too must lay down our lives for our brothers.
> I ask you, how can God's love survive in a man
> who has enough of this world's goods
> yet closes his heart to his brother
> when he sees him in need?
> Little children, let us love in deed and in truth
> and not merely talk about it (1 John 3:12–18; italics added).

Some scribes and Pharisees and other religious leaders were content to talk about the observance of the law and the commandments. They were unable to identify their faith with that of Jesus who made love applicable in reality as well as in theory. It was this concern of his for those without access to resources—bread in the desert, wine for a wedding, peace in one's heart, and even life itself for Lazarus—that "caused many of the Jews . . . [who] had seen what Jesus did, to put their faith in him" (John 11:45). Yet, while some people were able to have faith in him, there were others, led by tradition-bound leaders, who saw such a link between what was professed and what was practiced as threatening in light of the faith they demanded from their people. Unwittingly, they had created their own god out of deeds of darkness.

> The result was that the chief priests and the Pharisees called a meeting of the Sanhedrin. "What are we to do," they said, "with this man performing all sorts of signs? If we let him go on like this, the whole world will believe in him" (John 11:47–48).

The fact that they realized that belief in Jesus has definite economic, political, and religious consequences is evidenced in their words:

> "Then the Romans will come and sweep away our sanctuary and our nation." One of their number named Caiaphas, who was high priest that year, addressed them at this point: "You have no understanding whatever! Can you not see that it is better for you to have one man die [for the people] than to have the whole nation destroyed?" (He did not say this on his own. It was rather as high

priest for that year that he prophesied that Jesus would die for the
nation—and not for this nation only, but to gather into one all the
dispersed children of God.) From that day onward there was a plan
afoot to kill him (John 11:49-53).

It is important to make a distinction between, on the one hand,
God's will for Jesus to call for a conversion of hearts that would
result in sharing resources and preserving human integrity (and the
concomitant threat to the forces of law and order which sustained
opposite "wills") and, on the other, God's will for Jesus to be
crucified. Because Jesus entered the world to be faithful to the
former plan of God, the world responded with the latter plan of
Caiaphas. To interpret Jesus as primarily coming into the world to
die, rather than coming to do the will of God, would be to place
Jesus among the greatest of masochists with one of the most
powerful death wishes on record.

GOD'S WILL AS MISSION IN THE WORLD

Jesus entered the world, the Letter to the Hebrews relates,
saying, "Sacrifice and offering you did not desire, but a body you
have prepared for me; holocausts and sin offerings you took no
delight in. Then I said, 'As is written of me in the book, I have
come to do your will, O God' " (Heb. 10:5-7). The will of God was
that Jesus reorder among his people the injustice that was a violation of God's covenant and a manifestation of sin. In other words,
the will of God was that Jesus fulfill in himself, through his prayer
and ministry, God's plan for history. Such a fulfillment would
become the nourishing source for his contemplation as well as his
action: "Doing the will of him who sent me and bringing his work
to completion is my food" (John 4:34). "I am not seeking my own
will but the will of him who sent me" (John 5:30).

According to John, the will of God for Jesus constitutes a
mission. This mission can be understood only in viewing Jesus
from the perspective of Isaiah's Servant Songs. Isaiah declares that
"the will of the Lord shall be accomplished through him" and that
"because of his affliction he shall see the light in fulness of days;
Through his suffering, my servant shall justify many, and their

guilt he shall bear" (Isa. 53:10–11). Such affliction, however, does not come from God, but from the surrounding society to whom the servant is sent to "bring forth justice to the nations" (Isa. 42:1). The servant is to enable the poor, the brokenhearted, and the prisoners to have access to resources needed to restore their dignity (cf. Isa. 61:1). God's justice will be accomplished on earth as in heaven, restoring the original purposes of creation:

> Thus says God, the Lord,
> who created the heavens and stretched them out,
> who spreads out the earth with its crops,
> who gives breath to its people
> and spirit to those who walk on it:
> I, the Lord, have called you for the victory of justice,
> I have grasped you by the hand;
> I formed you, and set you as a covenant of the people,
> a light for the nations.
> To open the eyes of the blind,
> to bring out prisoners from confinement,
> and from the dungeon, those who live in darkness.
> I am the Lord, this is my name;
> my glory I give to no other
> nor my praise to idols (Isa. 42:5–8).

In his prayerful reflection on the Scriptures, Jesus came to identify more closely with the Isaiah Servant. Through insights gained from Mary's prayerful reflection, offered to Jesus as a youth, and from his own reflections on the society in which he lived, when it came time for him to define his ministry, Jesus applied the Isaiah text to himself (cf. Luke 4:18ff.). Later he would declare to a questioning world that upon the fulfillment of Isaiah's texts he was ready to be judged by the world (cf. Matt. 11:3ff.). Paradoxically, because he was to fulfill God's justice (cf. Matt. 3:15) Jesus would suffer in the name of "justice" as defined by his institutional reality. Jesus' style of life fulfilled the will of God, if not of the world. Since this life was a contradiction to that of the world's powers and principalities, it was against their will. To do God's will would be interpreted as resistance to their will. This would not be tolerated. "He began to teach them he would be rejected by elders, the chief priests and the scribes" (Mark 8:31). Because their deeds were evil, they would not be able to recognize God's justice in Jesus (cf. John 3:17). Because they did not do justice, they could not know Jesus or profess faith in his name as the presence of Yahweh as Liberator (cf. Matt. 1:21).

The will of God reached perfection in Jesus when he was put to death by the will of scribes, Pharisees, Pilate, and Caesar. God's will was done exactly on earth as in heaven, but it required tremendous suffering. "Not my will," he said in prayer the night he knew the representatives of the powers and principalities were on their way to put him to death for being faithful, "but yours be done" (Mark 14:36).

St. Francis tried to incarnate God's will for Jesus by preaching good news to the poor of the world. He was ready to be rejected by the world, whose will would interpret this as subversive. He was ready, as a result, to be punished by their crosses. Celano tells us that Francis, in his desire to allow God's will to come to perfection in him, was filled "with the Spirit of God, he was ready to suffer every distress of mind and to bear every bodily torment, if only his wish might be granted, that the will of the Father in heaven might be granted, that the will of the Father in heaven might be mercifully fulfilled in him"[2]—on earth as it was in heaven.

THE WILL OF THE POWERS
AND THE PRINCIPALITIES

The cross becomes the consequence as well as the possibility for anyone who will be faithful to the following of God's will in a world of sin. Jesus' parable of the talents relates how those unwilling to share the earth's resources and to recognize the image of God (the property owner) in his representatives on earth would say, "Let us kill him and then we shall have his inheritance" (Matt. 21:38). Precisely because their justice was not God's justice, Jesus would conclude, "Did you never read in the Scriptures, 'The stone which the builders rejected has become the keystone of the structure. It was the Lord who did this and we find it marvelous to behold.' For this reason, I tell you, the kingdom of God will be taken away from you and given to a nation that will yield a rich harvest" (Matt. 21:42–43).

By being raised upon the cross Jesus gathered together the lost children of Abraham and those of all the nations of the world (cf. John 11:52). By submitting in a way that gave the institutional powers and principalities of his day the impression that they had conquered him, he cut through their pretensions of "knowledge." He showed that true knowledge consists in fidelity to God's creative plan, not to theirs.

> The message of the cross is complete absurdity to those who are headed for ruin, but to us who are experiencing salvation it is the power of God. Scripture says, "I will destroy the wisdom of the wise and thwart the cleverness of the clever." . . . Since in God's wisdom the world did not come to know him through "wisdom," it pleased God to save those who believe through the absurdity of the preaching of the gospel. Yes, Jews demand "signs" and Greeks look for "wisdom," but we preach Christ crucified—a stumbling block to Jews, and an absurdity to Gentiles; but to those who are called, Jews and Greeks alike, Christ the power of God and the wisdom of God. For God's folly is wiser than men, and his weakness more powerful than men (1 Cor. 1:18–19; 21–25).

Caiaphas used "wisdom" to argue why it was proper that one person die for the good (read *survival*) of the nation (read *religion*). Yet this wisdom became salvation for those who believed and a total contradiction to wisdom as Caiaphas attempted to define it.

Jesus predicted that "everyone who looks upon the Son and believes in him shall have eternal life" (John 6:40). The centurion who looked upon the crucified Jesus proclaimed his faith in a new reality (cf. Luke 23:47). Now, whoever can proclaim Jesus' lordship and faith in the power of the resurrection need no longer be enslaved by any human power. Such a person enters into a new reality of influence (cf. Phil. 2:8ff.). The sovereignty, the power, and the wisdom of the powers and principalities of Jesus' day were totally broken by the very instrument they willed to use as their instrument of control. On the cross, Paul writes, God "disarmed the principalities and powers. He made a public show of them and, leading them off captive, triumphed in the person of Christ" (Col. 2:15).

In his important work, *Christ and the Powers,* Hendrik Berkhof clearly articulates at length the effects of the cross on the powers and principalities.

By the cross (which must always, here as elsewhere, be seen as a unity with the resurrection) Christ abolished the slavery which, as a result of sin, lay over our existence as a menace and an accusation. On the cross He "disarmed" the Powers, "made a public example of them and thereby triumphed over them." Paul uses three different verbs to express more adequately what happened to the Powers at the cross.

He "made a public example of them." It is precisely in the crucifixion that the true nature of the Powers has come to light. Previously they were accepted as the most basic and ultimate realities, as the gods of the world. Never had it been perceived, nor could it have been perceived, that this belief was founded on deception. Now that the true God appears on earth in Christ, it becomes apparent that the Powers are inimical to Him, acting not as His instruments but as His adversaries. The scribes, representatives of the Jewish law, far from receiving gratefully Him who came in the name of the God of the law, crucified Him in the name of the temple. The Pharisees, personifying piety, crucified Him in the name of piety. Pilate, representing Roman justice and law, shows what these are worth when called upon to do justice to the Truth Himself. Obviously, "none of the rulers of this age," who let themselves be worshipped as divinities, understood God's wisdom, "for had they known, they would not have crucified the Lord of Glory" (1 Cor. 2:8). Now they are unmasked as false gods by their encounter with Very God; they are made a public spectacle.

Thus Christ has "triumphed over them." The unmasking is actually already their defeat. Yet this is only visible to men when they know that God Himself has appeared on earth in Christ. Therefore we must think of the resurrection as well as of the cross. The resurrection manifests what was already accomplished at the cross: that in Christ, God has challenged the Powers, has penetrated into their territory, and has displayed that He is stronger than they. The concrete evidence of this triumph is that at the cross Christ has "disarmed" the Powers. The weapon from which they heretofore derived their strength is struck out of their hands. This weapon was the power of illusion, their ability to convince men that they were the divine regents of the world, ultimate certainty and ultimate direction, ultimate happiness and the ultimate duty for small, dependent humanity. Since Christ we know this is illusion. We are called to a higher destiny: we have higher orders to follow and we stand under a greater protector. No powers can separate us from God's love in Christ. Unmasked, revealed in their true nature, they have lost their mighty grip on men. The cross has disarmed them: wherever it is preached, the unmasking and the disarming of the Powers takes place.[3]

Despite the fact that the world was proved wrong about justice (cf. John 16:8) with the crucifixion-resurrection event, the word of life as defined by God in Christ's disciples would subsequently be met by similar efforts to undermine this justice, even to the point of persecution in the name of religion. "I have told you all this," Jesus warned, "to keep your faith from being shaken. Not only will they expel you from synagogues; a time will come when anyone who puts you to death will claim to be serving God! All this they will do [to you] because they knew neither the Father nor me" (John 16:1–3).

In view of what we face today—powers and principalities trying to make us serve their purposes—we must stress the need to be more loyal to revelation and God's will than to the powers' traditions and norms. In addition, today's powers must be continually reminded, as Jesus reminded them, "You would have no power . . . unless it were given you from above" (John 19:11).

It becomes necessary, then, continually to call people in power to conversion that their ways may be God's ways and that their use of power may truly be in harmony with God's creative purposes for manifesting his power among his people.

Today our right as human beings, images of God, to share in the earth's resources is being undermined systemically in its very foundations. In various countries, including the United States, people declare that even life itself is an arbitrary rather than a fundamental right. This is indicative of a systemic violation of rights and access to resources on other levels as well. Where

American society was formed to enable access to resources and reinforcement of rights, we now find it systemically either creating or allowing situations to be maintained that support and reinforce unequal access to resources and denial of the fulfillment of human rights. "There are a number of rights of which society itself cannot be the source because they exist prior to society," a 1974 statement from the Vatican's Congregation for the Doctrine of the Faith asserts, "but which society is obliged nonetheless to protect and render effective. The rights in question are the greater part of those which are today called 'human rights' and which our age boasts of having formulated. The first right of the human person is his life."[4]

Human societies serve to reinforce the basic rights of their citizens and to enable them equal access to resources as far as possible. Societies exist, in effect, for the good of their individual members. It cannot be the other way around, that individual members exist in relationship to the survival of the society. Furthermore, the state is to arbitrate between conflicting rights among individuals for the good of the whole. Morally speaking, it should represent those who are least able to speak for their rights—the poor, the oppressed, the voiceless and defenseless.

The basic right that must be protected, over all rights, is the access to life itself. In addition, those rights required for life's adequate expression must be assured as well. "Every man has the right to life, to bodily intergrity," Pope John wrote in *Pacem in Terris*, "and to the means which are necessary and suitable for the proper development of life."[5] The opinion of the United States Supreme Court that allowed the termination of life in unborn infants, the Administrative Committee of the National Conference of Catholic Bishops wrote, constitutes a violation of this primary right in favor of a secondary right. These bishops rejected the Court's opinion

> that the right of privacy encompasses a woman's decision to terminate a pregnancy, although the right of privacy is not an absolute right, and is not explicitly mentioned in the Constitution. In effect, the Court is saying that the right of privacy takes precedence over the right to life. This opinion of the Court fails to protect the most basic human right—the right to life.[6]

This conclusion of these United States bishops offers, for the twentieth century, the possibility for a renewal of the disciples' resistance to the political and economic and even religious systems that were based on injustice in the first and second centuries. Such a stance of resistance must be applicable to *whatever* situation is sustained by the denial of access to the resources needed for life and the right to live as an image of God. The American bishops thus concluded, "Therefore, we reject this decision of the Court because, as John XXIII says, 'if any government does not acknowledge the rights of man or violates them . . . its orders completely lack juridical force.' "[7]

The effort of various societies to liberalize abortion laws has made many realize that there is a need to resist any form of injustice in systems that are sustained by unjust norms and traditions. Such a radical deprivation of access to the basic resource—life—seems to have inaugurated the possibility of a new kind of institutional ethics of resistance on other levels as well. The Catholic church in America has begun to define its role in a society marked by the grave sin of social injustice that is reinforced through norms (laws) and traditions (opinions of courts) that systemically deny access to resources needed for life and to life itself. The role it has outlined involves resistance to this sin, accompanied by a call to conversion. This approach was reinforced by a 1974 declaration of the Sacred Congregation for the Doctrine of the Faith, confirmed by Pope Paul, which clearly placed such resistance in its historical setting:

> It must in any case be clearly understood that a Christian can never conform to a law which is in itself immoral: . . . On the contrary it is the task of law to pursue a reform of society and of conditions of life in all milieu, starting with the most deprived, so that always and everywhere it may be possible to give every child coming into this world a welcome worthy of a person.[8]

When the institutions of the first and second centuries—including the religious institution that equated obedience to it with obedience to God (cf. John 16:2)—tried to make the first Christians submit to the official interpretations of reality, the early community found it necessary to resist (cf. Acts 17:7). While in the eyes of all these institutions the early Christians were practicing civil disobedience, Peter and the apostles could only state: "Better for us to obey God than man" (Acts 5:29). To implement God's will on earth as in heaven meant, for the early Christians, the rejection of another will on earth that could not be equated with heaven's. In this sense, the Congregation's document continues:

> Following one's conscience in obedience to the law of God is not always the easy way. One must not fail to recognize the weight of the sacrifices and the burdens which it can impose. Heroism is sometimes called for in order to remain faithful to the requirements of the divine law. Therefore, we must emphasize that the path of true progress of the human person passes through this constant fidelity to a conscience maintained in justice and truth; and we must exhort all those who are able to do so to lighten the burdens still crushing so many men and women, families and children, who are placed in situations to which in human terms there is no solution.[9]

What we have said thus far in these chapters is reinforced by the document as it outlines ways to combat the *causes* of oppression. Political action, the influencing of morality, and various forms of social assistance are recommended. All aim at resisting the effort of institutions to try to define reality in their terms and to expect obedience to that reality if this means disobedience to God: "There will be no effective action on the level of morality," it is stated, "unless at the same time an effort is made on the level of ideas."[10] If at this level of ideas, people can be immobilized, prevented from acting, their apathy will support the continuation of whatever end may be desired. Yet, if they begin to resist they will no longer have *a-pathos*, be against God. Their sympathy will place them in union with God's pathos toward all who are denied their rights and an equitable share of resources. This must be the role of the Christian in the world today: "One can [not] remain indifferent to these sorrows and miseries. Every man and woman with feeling, and certainly every Christian, must be ready to do what he can to remedy them. This is the law of charity, of which the first preoccupation must always be the establishment of justice."[11]

Commenting on the abortion decree, and terming it "A Charter for Political Action," William H. Marshner outlined in *The Wanderer* a theory equally applicable to all situations that deny justice and rights to any human being, a theory that has been contradicted by too many Catholics, often in the name of a reality that uses God as reason for injustice in the world. "Catholics have been paralyzed by a specious conviction," he notes, "that the common good, toward which they must work as *citizens*, is a purely temporal, material and pragmatic thing, essentially different from the reign of Christ the King toward which they are supposed to work as *Catholics*."[12]

If the will of God is to be done on earth as it is in heaven, as it was for Christ, the fulfillment of this will on all levels must be seen as our mission in a contemporary world. Whoever identifies with the Lord of history, whoever shares in his pathos by sympathy against injustice, becomes identified with the perfection of God and identifies with his creative purposes in the world. By having "no compromise whatsoever with any form of social injustice,"[13] we hear the cry of the poor and become aware of the distress of the voiceless. By our sympathy we identify with the pathos of God and we fulfill Jesus' command, "In a word, you must be made perfect as your heavenly Father is perfect" (Matt. 5:48).

THE CROSS: RECONCILIATION AND RESISTANCE

It must always be understood that the goals and purposes of any kingdom that has authority over people on earth can tend to run counter to the values and ideals of the kingdom of God. When this is the case, such powers must be resisted. While resisting them, we can never stop trying to bring about reconciliation within them: among individual hearts, among groups, and within institutions themselves. It may be true that the cross was the symbol of one who resisted formally constituted society. Yet is must also be seen that, as a result of this same cross, ultimate reconciliation was achieved. This goal of reconciliation must be part of the gospel of anyone calling for the will of God to be done on earth as in heaven (cf. Col. 1:20) even if that will cannot be reconciled with the will of existing powers. Reconciliation with God in history means irreconciliation with history's gods. Whoever takes up the cross is following a man who was crucified by history's gods and idols. Yet the freedom that comes from this crucifixion engenders iconoclasm: resisting the effort to enslave. In not being reconciled with these idols, we discover the freedom of the resurrection.

"God is there where man has not sought him, but despised and rejected him. God is in that man from Nazareth, who, without power and nobility, died outside at the gates of society," Jürgen Moltmann has written. Clearly outlining the role of resistance and reconciliation, Moltmann continues:

> What did God do there in that man whose last word cried out: "My God, why have you forsaken me?" He gave himself in the pain of love and bore a hopeless death upon himself. What did he do there in that despised one? He took our contempt upon himself, my coldness of heart also. What did he do there in that suffering one? He took the suffering of the world on himself, and my sadness also. In the suffering and death of Jesus, he did not rest so that we could say, "Look, God is silent." God was creative in this pure suffering and pain of Jesus in the highest way. He "reconciled the world with himself," says Paul. "He did not account to them their sin," he continues, and further, "He has made him who knew no sin to be sin for us so that we become through him, the righteousness of God." All our unrighteousness is on him and all his righteousness is with us; all our impurity with him and all his creative joy with us. That is what reconciliation means.[14]

Just as God was in Christ trying to reconcile the world to his creative plan and will, so now, in Christ, the ministry of this reconciliation becomes that of all who would be indentified with Christ. The word *shaliach* (ambassador) used by Paul in the quotation below indicates one's alter-ego, one who represents in word and ministry the purposes of the one who authorizes the word to call for the situation desired. Paul defines our role as *shaliachim*, as God's alter-egos, as his images. In this case our word and ministry are to be identified with God's creative purposes in history. We are to call for the new creation, the reallocation of resources wherein all have equal access to them as God's image. Such reconciliation returns us to the original purposes of creation:

If anyone is in Christ, he is a new creation. The old order has passed away; now all is new! All this has been done by God, who has reconciled us to himself through Christ and has given us the ministry of reconciliation. I mean that God, in Christ, was reconciling the world to himself, not counting men's transgressions against them, and that he has entrusted the message of reconciliation to us. This makes us ambassadors for Christ, God as it were appealing through us. We implore you, in Christ's name: be reconciled to God! For our sakes God made him who did not know sin, to be sin, so that in him we might become the very holiness of God (2 Cor. 5:17–21).

As ambassadors of Christ, our words of reconciliation may be quite irreconcilable with the world's words. Even though Jesus sent his apostles as ambassadors to preach reconciliation and peace to every house, he warned them that just this effort would often be returned with violence in word and action. As God's ambassadors we should expect no better treatment in a world systemically maintained by irreconciliation in its political, economic, religious, and ideological infrastructures.

Often programs for peace and words of peace will be seen as a contradiction and threat to many, even within the church. In early 1975, for example, my province of Capuchin-Franciscans tried to take seriously its vocation to be part of the "delegation of peace"[15] by entering into a setting of irreconciliation between white and native Americans. The underlying violence between the groups reflected the conditions for hostility, as quoted from Ralph White in chapter 5. The actual violence itself was precipitated by some Menominee Indians who took over Alexian Brothers property at Gresham, Wisconsin. It had been unused for six years.

After the thirty-four day takeover ended, there was a serious attempt to promote reconciliation among people in the community. Upon the suggestion of the liaison from the U.S. Justice Department (whose purpose was to help restore order), we asked one of the local parish priests if he might find people in the parish who would go to the novitiate to work for reconciliation as part of a joint group consisting of an Alexian, a Capuchin-Franciscan, a federal official, and a Menominee. The priest, who had been working for reconciliation, indicated he did not think such could be accomplished, not because of fear of the Menominees, but because members of the parish who took on such a role of reconciliation would have to face the irreconciliation and bitterness coming, in part, from members of their own white Catholic community.

Preaching a gospel of peace that is based on justice—be it in Selma or Cicero or Gresham or Wounded Knee or Delano, at the Pentagon, at ITT, or even within church institutions—can bring about irreconciliation and division. This is the risk the disciple must be willing to take in trying to bring about peace as a follower of Jesus.

If within every basic community or provincial community or diocese there could be people ready at a moment's notice to enter into troubled areas, into conditions of sin and irreconciliation, offering prayerful ministry and their presence as ambassadors of peace, a sign of conversion would be given to an unbelieving society (cf. Matt. 12:41). What the *Vocation of the Order Today* (quoted below) envisions of the Friars Minor can be envisioned for all who are concerned about applying Paul's words to our contemporary realities: "We implore you, in Christ's name: be reconciled to God" (2 Cor. 5:20).

> Taking into account our vocation as men of peace, we will be able to take part truly in the problems and social and political struggles of our day. This requires serious and correct information so that we can avoid sentimental enthusiasm, a summary of unjust judgments, irresponsible declarations, and will be capable of an objective analysis of situations. In addition, if we seriously try to live in justice and in mutual sharing, if we take part, according to our possibilities and gifts, in the fate and in the work of the poor and the abandoned of our times, we will then have the right and the duty of joining our voices with those of the oppressed. But we will do so out of love for the person we discover in every man, regardless of the social group to which he may belong. Thus, working as true peacemakers, we will hasten the coming of the kingdom of God in which there must no longer be walls between men, nor dominion of men over men: "no longer slave nor freeman . . . but sons of God."[16]

Within church institutions, great irreconciliation occurs in clerical congregations of men. Here one group of members is systemically denied access to resources that are available to others, denying God's image in them. Nonclerical brothers are denied access to official leadership within the community. St. Francis once said, "With God there is no respect of persons, and the minister general of the order, the Holy Spirit, rests equally upon the poor and simple." He wanted this thought inserted into his rule, Celano adds, "but since it was already approved by papal rule this could not be done."[17] Thus Franciscans, through Francis, obediently responded to the call from Rome. This obedience now brings them into irreconciliation with another declaration of the Roman church. Today's inequality and elitism bring Franciscans into irreconciliation with Rome's order that religious can have no compromise whatsoever with any form of social injustice.[18] Another of Rome's decrees offers civil disobedience as a way of reinforcing human rights: "If any government does not acknowledge the rights of men or violates them, . . . its orders completely lack juridical force."[19] Given such contradictions, Franciscans and other male religious can either be "a-pathetic," or they can attempt to create within their own communities equal access to the resource of power as it expresses itself in official leadership.

Such words might sound divisive to some. Jesus' words did the same to others who unquestioningly obeyed God's will as interpreted for them by the religious institutions of their day. The religious leaders taught "as dogmas mere human precepts" (Mark 7:7); they were able to exact obedience because they had the power to define God's will and thus maintain the order desired by the institution. Today, as Jesus did in his day, we must remember our call to the gospel. Our role in our institutional environment will thus be "a leaven of evangelical challenge and non-complacency in her midst. This is a task not to be taken lightly; the seeds of evil and failure are always within us; to content ourselves with a purely verbal protest would be sheer hypocrisy."[20]

When Francis formed his communities of brothers and sisters, it was in the time of the Fourth Lateran Council, which had been called to renew the church. Francis adopted its sign of tau, or the cross, for his signature, for his communities, and for their habits. They were to stand as signs of the cross bringing salvation and freedom to a world irreconciled by sin, as tau marked the foreheads of the faithful people who had identified with God's plan at the time of Ezekiel (9:4ff.).

Francis wanted his followers to express their acceptance of this cross by forming their habit in its shape so that they would be a sign of salvation and liberation to each other and that they might never have anything of theirs coveted by anyone in the world. Celano tells us that Francis "designed a very poor and mean tunic, one that would not excite the covetousness of the world."[21] Because he wanted his community to share all its resources, it could never stand in history as a contradiction to the cross that was its trademark. This cross gave all, especially the poorest sinner, equal access to liberation. It had to be the mission of his community to preach this sign of the cross to the world (cf. Matt. 28:19).

Praying and working for the accomplishment of this mission help to create the fulfillment of God's will on earth as it is in heaven. This is our mission, as it was Christ's. To do otherwise is to become idolators, marked by obedience to the will of a reality that cannot be equated with God's vision for our world. If we are faithful to this gospel, we who have been signed by the cross will have allowed the resurrection from the cross to become real in our lives. What we have tried to do on earth will be recognized as identified with the way the will of God will be in heaven:

Then the Lamb appeared in my vision. He was standing on Mount Zion, and with him were the hundred and forty-four thousand who had his name and the name of his Father written on their foreheads. I heard a sound from heaven which resembled the roaring of the deep, or loud peals of thunder; the sound I heard was like the melody of harpists playing on their harps. They were singing a new hymn before the throne, in the presence of the four living creatures and the elders. This hymn no one could learn except the hundred and forty-four thousand who had been ransomed from the world. These are men who have never been defiled by immorality with women. They are pure and follow the Lamb wherever he goes. They have been ransomed as the first fruits of mankind for God and the Lamb. On their lips no deceit has been found, they are indeed without flaw.

Then I saw another angel flying in mid-heaven, herald of everlasting good news to the whole world, to every nation and race, language and people. He said in a loud voice, "Honor God and give him glory, for his time has come to sit in judgment. Worship the Creator of heaven and earth, the Creator of the sea and the springs."

A second angel followed and cried out:

"Fallen, fallen is Babylon the great
which made all the nations drink
the poisoned wine of her lewdness."

A third angel followed the others and said in a loud voice, "If anyone worships the beast or its image, or accepts its mark on his forehead or hand, he too will drink the wine of God's wrath, poured full strength into the cup of his anger. He will be tormented in burning sulphur before the holy angels and before the Lamb, and the smoke of their torment shall rise forever and ever. There shall be no relief day or night for those who worship the beast or its image or accept the mark of its name. This is what sustains the holy ones, who keep the commandments of God and their faith in Jesus" (Rev. 14:1–12).

7

Give Us This Day Our Daily Bread

The unity of the members of the body sharing in one eucharistic meal represents the way in which Jesus wanted all those identified with him to have equal access to the resource of life (cf. John 6:35, 51). In the Eucharist, as Jesus envisioned it and as Paul theologized on it, the messianic hopes of the people were to be accomplished "until he comes." In the eating of the bread and drinking of the cup, the members of the community witnessed to the belief that they would be participating in messianic fulfillment "until he comes."

The messianic overtones of the Eucharist can best be understood from Jesus' parables and teachings, and their relation to the writings of prophets like Isaiah, Jeremiah, and Amos. Thus, while the Pharisees used their categories of law and tradition to criticize Jesus for enabling people to have access to him, Jesus warned that the ideal to be striven for was to share a meal, not with those who could return the favor, but with those ordinarily denied access to the meal. Jesus explained this ministry with messianic overtones:

> Whenever you give a lunch or dinner, do not invite your friends or brothers or relatives or wealthy neighbors. They might invite you in return and thus repay you. No, when you have a reception, invite beggars and the crippled, the lame and the blind. You should be pleased that they cannot repay you, for you will be repaid in the resurrection of the just (Luke 14:12–14).

Jesus ate with publicans and sinners, the beggars, the cripples, and all those denied access to the benefits of the Judaic religion as defined by its leaders. This clearly was meant to signify the goal of the messianic feast: full access of the table-members to participation in the community of God. Such a teaching seemed scandalous to the leaders of Judaism, who had come to define access to God in terms of ritual observance, not human rights. These leaders could no longer hear God calling them to conversion in the presence of Jesus:

> Now it happened that while Jesus was at table in Matthew's home, many tax collectors and those known as sinners came to join Jesus and his disciples at dinner. The Pharisees saw this and complained to his disciples, "What reason can the Teacher have for eating with tax collectors and those who disregard the law?" Overhearing the remark, he said: "People who are in good health do not need a doctor; sick people do. Go and learn the meaning of the words, 'It is mercy I desire and not sacrifice.' I come to call, not the self-righteous, but sinners" (Matt. 9:10–13).

Because they were deaf to the cries of the poor, the alienated, and the outcasts, those thinking they were assured access to the kingdom would find their places being taken from them (cf. Matt. 21:43) by the very ones they systemically ostracized from access to the resources: "Let me make it clear that tax collectors and prostitutes are entering the kingdom of God before you" (Matt. 21:31).

WORSHIP: THE SIGN OF HAVING DONE JUSTICE

Jesus tried to explain that the definitive kingdom of God is not limited to some future heaven. Rather, it has broken into history on earth as a new way of living. The dynamics of the meal become the sign of the dynamics of the kingdom itself. In his preaching Jesus declared that those who defined the kingdom for themselves would be denied access to it because they had systemically denied access to it by others: "Mark what I say. Many will come from the east and the west and will find a place at the banquet in the kingdom of God with Abraham, Isaac, and Jacob, while the natural heirs of the kingdom will be driven out into the dark" (Matt. 8:11–12). By this statement, Jesus remains faithful to the prophetic declarations that linked the meal or cultic sacrifice with the prior need to offer justice and compassion as sacrificial gifts before partaking of the meal. For instance, Jesus quoted Hosea, who declared that the Jews "violated the covenant" by their injustice. This made their sacrifices barren: "For it is love that I desire, not sacrifice, and knowledge of God rather than holocausts" (Hos. 6:7, 6).

This constituted a violation of the covenant, because the covenant represents a commitment to create the conditions of the kingdom of God on earth as in heaven. When any people are denied participation in the fruit of the covenant (which is justice and peace in a community of equality), selfishness (that is, sin) results. When the selfishness of the Egyptians created a situation wherein the Hebrews were denied access to the resources of material goods, power, and freedom, God viewed this as a violation of the covenant and intervened in history to deliver the Hebrews: "I have witnessed the affliction of my people in Egypt and have heard their cry of complaint against their slave drivers, so I know well what they are suffering. Therefore I have come down to rescue them from the hands of the Egyptians" (Exod. 3:7–8). God's fidelity to his promise that justice would be accomplished—by enabling the Jews to have access to resources (land)—would be signified when they could celebrate a ritual meal: "I will be with you; and this shall be your proof; . . . when you bring my people out of Egypt, you will worship God on this very mountain" (Exod. 3:12).

In the Jewish Scriptures, the passover meal, the ritual sacrifice, could take place only if there was a passing over from oppression to freedom. The covenant symbolized in the memorial of the meal was valid only if the covenant of God's will for the world was observed by the people in the ministry of their daily living. The *proof* that the covenant was fulfilled on earth as in the eternal banquet of heaven would be that the meal that was celebrated would meet the covenantal conditions. This meant a passing from whatever would deny people access to resources and the image of God in them. As descendants of the community who had experienced equal access to food and water (cf. Exod. 17:1–7; 1 Cor. 10:3), they were now to create the covenantal conditions (cf. Matt. 8:7–10). To have a ritual without the reality would be idol worship and a prostitution of God's will. According to God's will, their memorials had to unite the ritual observance of God's justice with the actual practice of justice. John T. Pawlikowski, of Chicago's Catholic Theological Union, has written:

> Basic to this interpretation of the covenant was the sense that the Sinai Event had brought about an historic transformation in man's notion of the term "religion." Previous to Sinai, "religion" could generally be equated with cult or ritual. Worship was considered to be the highest religious expression of which man was capable. But the terms of the Exodus Covenant had outdated this simple interpretation of religion. The necessity of worship was never at issue. The dialogue between Moses and Yahweh includes elaborate details for offering sacrifice. But if one examines carefully the relevant passages in the book of Exodus it will become evident that the ritual prescriptions are not included in the covenant proper. Instead the vast bulk of the covenantal legislation has to do with the area of justice and mercy rather than cult. What had occurred at Sinai was the expansion of the term "religion" to include social responsibility as an integral, inseparable part of its definition. Set within the context of the history of man's developing religious consciousness, this expanded Exodus notion of religion represented a crucial breakthrough. Any future attempt to separate concern for justice and mercy from worship would be tantamount to idolatry. This was the most unique and the most crucial realization that resulted from the biblical theology of the covenant.[1]

After the Exodus event, when the liberation movement became mechanized and ritualized in norms and traditions, the prophets made it clear that Israel, despite its belief in its chosen status, did not even "know" Yahweh, because its deeds proved contrary to Yahweh's plan. Further, if Israel did not "know" Yahweh as the true God by not meeting the conditions for true worship, its worship was idolatrous. "For it is love that I desire, not sacrifice, and knowledge of God rather than holocausts" (Hos. 6:6).

Isaiah declared that, though "justice used to lodge within her" (1:21), Israel no longer knew the Lord (1:2), because it broke the covenant and believed its sacrifices could be accepted by the Lord without their having first identified with God's concerns for the world. The covenant of the nation involved the personal sacrifices of each member of the community to bring about the sharing of resources. Since the people were unfaithful, they were asked:

> What care I for the number of your sacrifices?
> says the Lord.
> I have had enough of whole-burnt rams and fat of fatlings;
> in the blood of calves, lambs, and goats I find no pleasure.
> When you come in to visit me,
> who asks these things of you?
> Trample my courts no more!
> Bring no more worthless offerings;
> your incense is loathsome to me.
> New moon and sabbath, calling of assemblies,
> octaves with wickedness: these I cannot bear.
> Your new moons and festivals I detest:
> they weigh me down, I tire of the load.
> When you spread out your hands
> I close my eyes to you
> Though you pray the more,
> I will not listen.
> Your hands are full of blood!
> Wash yourselves clean!
> Put away your misdeeds from before my eyes;
> cease doing evil; learn to do good.
> Make justice your aim: redress the wronged,
> hear the orphan's plea, defend the widow (Isa. 1:11–17).

Ritual is meant to commemorate an event. If the ritual is to be valid, the event that is signified should not be isolated from the lived experience of those who participate in the ritual. In the case of religious ritual, not to be part of the passover process in the "today" of one's historical experience is to be separated from partnership in the real meaning of the ritual. With us, as with the people of the prophet's time, sacrifices and holocaust must be secondary to compassion and true knowledge of God: "He did what was right and just and it went well with him. Because he dispensed justice to the weak and the poor, it went well with him. Is this not true knowledge of me, says the Lord?" (Jer. 22:15–16).

The only conclusion one can reach from such passages is that it is impossible to enter into full union with God in worship without having the works of justice in our hands. The covenant cannot be ritualized in our liturgies without having first been actualized in our histories. Those who enter the kingdom of God in heaven will be those who have done justice on earth. One can neither know God nor be known by God (covenant) if God does not recognize deeds that represent his image, his word. Since God can only know himself (his image), our deeds of justice determine the degree of "knowing" (or union with him) that we will have.

It is significant, then, that by linking "knowing" with the doing of justice Jesus indicated whether his followers would be considered faithful to their covenant or would be denied access to the kingdom. For instance, in Matthew's Last Judgment scene, God *recognizes* ("knows") only those who by their ministry of justice enabled the hungry, the naked, the shelterless, and all the oppressed to have access to resources they needed. The link is made between doing justice and remaining in God's sight, between fulfilling the covenant and entering the kingdom of God, between enabling others to have access to the resources of life and being given access to the banquet. As Matthew earlier compared the reign of God to a king who gave a wedding banquet, inviting all to enter (cf. 22:2ff.), so at the Last Judgment Jesus declares no less than four times that the justice of human beings on earth will determine their participation (knowing, communion) with God in heaven:

> When the Son of Man comes in his glory, escorted by all the angels of heaven, he will sit upon his royal throne, and all the nations will be assembled before him. Then he will separate them into two groups, as a shepherd separates sheep from goats. The sheep he will place on his right hand, the goats on his left.
>
> The king will say to those on his right: "Come, you have my Father's blessing. Inherit the kingdom prepared for you from the creation of the world. For I was hungry and you gave me food, I was thirsty and you gave me drink. I was a stranger and you welcomed me, naked and you clothed me. I was ill and you comforted me, in prison and you came to visit me."
>
> Then the just will ask him: "Lord, when did we see you hungry and feed you or see you thirsty and give you drink? When did we

welcome you away from home and clothe you in your nakedness? When did we visit you when you were ill or in prison?"

The king will answer them: "I assure you, as often as you did it for one of the least of my brothers, you did it for me." Then he will say to those on his left: "Out of my sight, you condemned . . . " (Matt. 25:31–41).

In many ways this story of what we need to do on earth to be with God in heaven summarizes the whole meaning of creation. Just as the blessing came to those who would be able to have access to the goods of the earth in Genesis, so Jesus is saying that those who enable others to have access to the goods of the earth receive the blessing prepared for them from the beginning of creation.

In many ways, too, this story summarizes the whole meaning of the Our Father, where we pray that God's purposes might be fulfilled on earth (in creation) as they are in heaven. Matthew offers us a Jesus who says that to be known by God is to be a just person. To know God, in turn, is to do justice. To be known by God and to know God, in prayer and ministry, becomes justification. To enable others to have access to our resources enables us to have access to God: "Come, you have my Father's blessing! Inherit the kingdom prepared for you from the creation of the world" (Matt. 25:34). Observe the many connections to the Our Father in this verse of Matthew, Raymond Brown urges in his classic, "The Pater Noster as an Eschatological Prayer": "the title (Father); Petition 2 (the kingdom); Petition 3 (the divine will: prepared from the foundation of the world); and the present petition (a favorable judgment based on dealings with our brothers)."[2]

In this light, we can better understand how Francis indicated to his brothers that asking others for a share in their resources would enable their benefactors to be blessed by the Lord and would help them toward salvation. As Celano writes: "At times exhorting his brothers to go begging for alms, he would use these words: 'Go,' he said, 'for at this last hour the Friars Minor have been lent to the world, that the elect might fulfill in them what will be commanded by the Judge: *Because as long as you did it for one of these, the least of my brethren, you did it for me.*' "[3]

Interestingly, at the Last Judgment the king ignores protestations of prophecy, exorcisms, and miracles as signs the people offer for their entry fee into the kindgom (Matt. 7:22). Neither does the king refer to ritual observance, nor is he open to protestations about observance of liturgical norms and traditions. The actions themselves determine if his followers have been faithful to the covenant. Fidelity to the covenant signifies participation in the liberating presence of God in history. With us, as with Jesus, there should be no need for the world to ask if we are the ones who are to come. With Jesus, we fulfill the covenant by bridging the gap between what is professed and what is practiced. The world will know God by our prayerful and active fidelity to the covenant through involvement in justice:

> The days are coming, says the Lord, when I will make a new covenant with the house of Israel and the house of Judah. It will not be like the covenant I made with their fathers . . . from the land of Egypt; for they broke my covenant, and I had to show myself their master, says the Lord. But this is the covenant which I will make with the house of Israel after those days, says the Lord. I will place my law within them, and write it upon their hearts; I will be their God, and they shall be my people. No longer will they have need to teach their friends and kinsmen how to know the Lord. All, from least to greatest, shall know me, says the Lord, for I will forgive their evildoing and remember their sin no more (Jer. 31:31–34).

EATING THE BREAD AND RECOGNIZING THE BODY

In an environment where people live the covenant as well as profess it, there is no great need for society to come to know God through teaching, documents, decrees, or catechisms. Society comes to know God and experience him as alive when people recognize God in the presence of those who are committed to show forth his justice and holiness. This is accomplished by sharing in God's justice and holiness through the gift of God's own Spirit. The Spirit of God in our hearts gives us the power to fulfill the covenant in our histories:

> Thus the nations shall know that I am the Lord, says the Lord God, when in their sight I prove my holiness through you. For I will take

you away from among the nations, gather you from all the foreign lands, and bring you back to your own land. I will sprinkle clean water upon you to cleanse you from all your impurities, and from all your idols I will cleanse you. I will give you a new heart and place a new spirit within you, taking from your bodies your stony hearts and giving you natural hearts. I will put my spirit within you and make you live by my statutes, careful to observe my decrees. You shall live in the land I gave your fathers; you shall be my people, and I will be your God (Ezek. 36:23–28).

Thus we come to a deeper meaning of the words in the Our Father which ask for the gift of bread each day.

Luke places a parable on prayer immediately after the Our Father. After praying to the Father to "Give us each day our daily bread" (11:3), he quotes Jesus as saying, "What father among you will give his son a snake if he asks for a fish, or hand him a scorpion if he asks for an egg? If you, with all your sins, know how to give your children good things, how much more will the heavenly Father give the Holy Spirit to those who ask him?" (Luke 11:11–13). Matthew links the request for bread with the granting of the Spirit (cf. 7:9). The Holy Spirit, then, is the gift of God that becomes the bread of our life. The Holy Spirit being poured forth in our hearts at baptism gives us access to the Father (cf. Rom. 5:5), and deepens our relationship with him through the eucharistic banquet.

As the Word was made flesh through the power of the Spirit (cf. Matt. 1:20), by the same Spirit the Word is made flesh in us through the Eucharist: "If you do not eat the flesh of the Son of Man and drink his blood, you have no life in you; . . . it is the spirit that gives life" (John 6:53, 63). To eat the body and drink the blood of Christ means to participate in his life through his Spirit and thus to grow in the life of Christ begun in us at baptism: "The body is one and has many members, but all the members, many though they are, are one body; and so it is with Christ. It was in one Spirit that all of us, whether Jew or Greek, slave or free, were baptized into one body. All of us have been given to drink of the one Spirit" (1 Cor. 12:12–13).

The blood of Christ enabled the new covenant to be established, reconciling Jew and gentile, Greek and Roman, free and slave.

Through his passover, Christ enabled all people to have access to him without exception. Through the power of his Spirit, all barriers were broken down. "You were strangers to the covenant and its promise," Paul reminded the Ephesian gentiles, who once had no access to this resource of life:

> You were without hope and without God in the world. But now in Christ Jesus you who once were far off have been brought near through the blood of Christ. It is he who is our peace, and who made the two of us one by breaking down the barrier of hostility that kept us apart. In his own flesh he abolished the law with its commands and precepts, to create in himself one new man from us who had been two and to make peace, reconciling both of us to God in one body through his cross, which put that enmity to death. He came and "announced the good news of peace to you who were far off, and to those who were near"; through him we both have access in one Spirit to the Father (Eph. 2:12–18).

If it is true that in his blood and in one Spirit we have access to the Father as reconciled members of his body, then it is equally true that to participate in his Spirit demands the same ministry of reconciliation on our part. No longer can we live by laws or traditions that perpetuate alienation among the members of the body; no longer can we live by an environment that signifies division among peoples. The one Spirit of Jesus demands of us prayer and ministry that identify with his effort to create the new covenant, to participate with groans (cf. Rom. 8) in the new creation. If Christ died for all, Paul reasoned in his Second Letter to the Corinthians, external appearances must pass away to enable all to come to know him truly by justice and to share in the new creation.

> Because of this we no longer look on anyone in terms of mere human judgment. If at one time we so regarded Christ, we no longer know him by this standard. This means that if anyone is in Christ, he is a new creation. The old order has passed away; now all is new! All this has been done by God, who has reconciled us to himself through Christ and has given us the ministry of reconciliation. I mean that God, in Christ, was reconciling the world to himself, not

counting men's transgressions against them, and that he was entrusted the message of reconcilation to us. We implore you, in Christ's name, be reconciled to God! For our sakes God made him who did not know sin, to be sin, so that in him we might become the very holiness [justice] of God (2 Cor. 5:16–21).

The Eucharist is the body of Jesus. The church is the body of Jesus. The Eucharist is the church. If the church is divided and not reconciled it cannot be the full measure of the body. It demands reparation and healing. If the covenanted are not working to bring healing to brokenness in the body so that people in any part of the world can have access to the resources of life and thus image God, then they are not bringing the proper sacrifice of *their* bodies to the celebration of the Eucharist.

There cannot be a dichotomy between allowing injustice among the members of the church in a building and allowing injustice among the members of the body in the world. To believe so and to live so is to fail to know Jesus Christ, as Paul pointed out to the early Christians. He chastized them for creating situations within their eucharistic assemblies where the poor were not given access to the goods of others in the form of food and drink. To believe one can refuse access to such basic resources and still have access to the body and blood as true food and drink is to "show contempt for the church of God" (1 Cor. 11:22). In order to celebrate ritually the body and blood as the sign of unity, one must first be a prayerful minister of reconciliation. "Your meetings are not profitable but harmful," Paul clearly told the Corinthians.

First of all, I hear that when you gather for a meeting there are divisions among you, and I am inclined to believe it. There may even have to be factions among you for the tried and true to stand out clearly. When you assemble it is not to eat the Lord's Supper, for everyone is in haste to eat his own supper. One person goes hungry while another gets drunk. . . . Would you show contempt for the Church of God, and embarrass those who have nothing? (1 Cor. 11:17–22).

A divided community where people are not able to have access to resources is a scandal to the body and a contradiction to the plan of God. To eat the passover meal in its eucharistic form without having ministered to the passover of people from denial of resources to participation in them is to deny the very body of Christ. Alienation and tension within the body (cf. 1 Cor: 11:18) are a countersign to the messianic banquet of the kingdom of God that it represents. If one does not recognize the image of God in those who are denied resources and does not minister to their need, as Matthew relates in the story of the Last Judgment, God will not recognize that person. In the Eucharist, those who fail to work for healing and justice among the members of the body in the world bring judgment upon themselves. The Eucharist is the memorial of Christ's passover from death to life; there all are drawn together and all brokenness is healed:

> Every time, then, you eat this bread and drink this cup, you proclaim the death of the Lord until he comes! This means that whoever eats the bread or drinks the cup of the Lord unworthily sins against the body and blood of the Lord. A man should examine himself first; only then should he eat of the bread and drink of the cup. He who eats and drinks without recognizing the body eats and drinks a judgment on himself (1 Cor. 11:26–29).

Because the early community was not recognizing the needs of the members of the body, alienation in the form of physical and personal suffering, as well as irreconciliation with God, was the consequence, in Paul's view. Francis MacNutt notes this (while also showing that access to the resource of health is the ordinary will of God) when he writes:

> Far from being a sign of God's blessing, much physical sickness is a direct sign that we are not right with God or our neighbor: a person who eats and drinks without recognizing the Body is eating and drinking his own condemnation. In fact, that is why many of you are weak and ill and some of you have died. If only we recollected ourselves, we shouldn't be punished like that. But when the Lord does punish us like that, it is to correct us and stop us from being condemned with the world (1 Cor. 11:29–32).[4]

Just as the Hebrews took judgment upon themselves when they

offered their memorials, rituals, prayers, and sacrifices without having compassion and true knowledge of God (communion), so the covenant is unfulfilled when one does not actively work for the unity of Christ's body that is sealed by Christ's blood: "This cup is the new covenant in my blood" (1 Cor. 11:24). To drink the cup worthily means for us, as it did for Jesus, to become the covenant (cf. Matt. 20:22–23), standing before God in prayer and before the people in ministry as ambassadors of God's reconciling presence. In us, as in Jesus, the words of Isaiah about the Servant of God must be fulfilled: "I, the Lord, have called you for the victory of justice. . . . I formed you, and set you as a covenant of the people" (42:6), so that whoever identifies with Christ in this servanthood becomes a sign of God's covenant of reconciliation (cf. 2 Cor. 5:21).

In the context of extending healing and bread to his followers, Christ himself has given us the model for our compassion and empathy, which results in reconciliation. According to Matthew (15:13–21), the sharing of bread with the people was occasioned by Jesus' healing. As the sacrament of God's reconciling presence, Jesus enabled the people to have access to the gifts of healing and bread. As a result, they were reconciled within themselves, their communities, and their God. Although sharing resources of healing and bread with those in need was viewed by Jesus as part of his ministry, it was viewed, among the combined religious and politico-economic forces, as subversive activity that created irreconciliation. If thousands would come for healing and be given bread, soon the world would become reconciled to God by following him (cf. John 11:48).

Such reconciliation, brought about through healing and through sharing bread (a symbol of all resources necessary for life), would be met with irreconciliation in the form of suffering and poverty. Having access to resources of healing and the goods of earth as in heaven is to be out of harmony with what society considers reconciliation (read *order*).

In a society sustained by unequal access to resources of health and goods, participation in the Eucharist stands as a true sacrament. It stands as both a sign of and a source for another reality: a new covenant, which finds us identified with the Servant of God in a ministry of healing and sharing of goods that is also extended to our world. Yet precisely this ministry and witness occasion ir-reconciliation with the world. Thus, suffering and poverty should be considered as a consequence coming from society to those committed to healing and sharing of resources rather than as a consequence of God's ordinary will. Working for a reality in which there will be no more suffering is a sign that the covenant is being realized in us.

Such a covenant can be established only in a body willing to be broken so that other broken bodies can be healed, and in blood willing to be shed on behalf of the many so that they can have access to life. To participate in the eucharistic meal and not be identified in concern and solidarity with the oppressed of the world who are denied access to resources needed for life is a contradiction of the covenant. It is to refuse to do our share in promoting the unity of the body of Christ. For us to eat the bread that is Jesus without being actively concerned about members of the body who are denied access to resources because they are poor, nonwhite, or live in other nations is to fail to recognize the body. To fail to accept these conditions is to show how far we have come from the original meaning of the Eucharist as the sacrament of justice, peace, and unity. Thomas Barrosse writes:

> For the ancient Semitic world a meal, especially a communal meal, had a significance which modern man often fails to appreciate. Table fellowship, for example, implied commitment to tablemates, and this rendered eating and drinking together an apt way of sealing a covenant (Gen. 31:54; Ex. 24:3; Tob. 7:11–15) and made betrayal by a tablemate a particularly perfidious act (Ps. 41 [40]:10).[5]

One cannot eat the bread that is broken without accepting responsibility to do something about all the brokenness that is still part of the body. One cannot be recognized or known by God if one does not recognize Christ in his broken members (cf. Luke 24:35).

This realization struck me forcefully during a liturgy in which I participated while taking a Spanish course. It was at a time when attempts to learn the language had become particularly difficult and burdensome for the class. We met for the breaking of the bread.

A sister in our group not only was having a hard time being reconciled to a new language but also was suffering from much irreconciliation in the community from which she came. During the shared homily, she revealed her brokenness and weakness to the extent that she left the room in tears.

When I was handed the bread consecrated as the body of Jesus, the realization came to me that this broken bread in my hand contained her brokenness. This immediately brought me into solidarity with her as well as other broken people about whom I had particular concern—the Wisconsin farmer I talked to each day who needed rain for his crops, the millions of starving in the Sahel who lacked food itself. I understood there that by saying "Amen" to consecrated bread, I would become responsible for the healing of all these people, not just her.

We take brokenness into ourselves and it becomes part of us. And as Jesus had offered himself as covenant so that all could have access to him, somehow our lives as covenant have to be lived so that, as a result of it, as many people as possible can be brought into a deeper sharing in the earth's resources, that they may become more fully the image of God that they are called to be. Our Amens have to be a commitment to bind up wounds, to heal the broken, to enable all to have access to life—or else they become empty words.

To participate in the Eucharist without being concerned about the community of all those in the world who can neither eat nor drink what they need for life is to be identified with those who went through rituals rejected by God (Isa. 1:1ff.).

We must become the sacramental reality if it is to be real in our lives. In the case of the Eucharist, we are to become the covenant, the body broken that others may be healed, the blood poured out that others may have access to life.

RITUAL WITHOUT REALITY

One should not easily be able to eat the eucharistic bread without being concerned about the reality that 75 percent of America's bread and prepared flour is controlled by only four firms, which have continually been charged with price fixing and monopolistic control, that is, denying others access to the market. One should not easily be able to drink from the fruit of the vine without remembering the struggle of farm workers to have access to the power of bargaining with growers, without remembering how huge growers and a mighty union once created an adulterous relationship that denied farm workers access to a union of their choice.

To eat the bread and drink the wine without being concerned about justice among the members is a scandal to the cross of Christ. Yet once one becomes concerned about identifying with broken bodies and those denied access to life resources, the Eucharist can become a contradiction to the world itself. Faith in the Eucharist is a scandal to the unbeliever, for it represents a commitment in faith to a certain passing over—to the liberation of the oppressed. As a sign of the messianic community in which all are to have equal access to the banquet, those who participate in the Eucharist must be committed to make this a reality on earth as it is in heaven. The "amen" to the body and blood in its eucharistic presence is to commit oneself to a repudiation of anything that hinders Christ's presence in any of its other forms as well. The Eucharist is to become an "Amen," an acceptance of our responsibility to work against any political, economic, religious, or ideological injustice that is incompatible with the mystery of faith we proclaim when we eat the bread. The need to be faithful to this responsibility became quite clear to me on Food Day, 1976.

I was on my way to Notre Dame to teach a class about corporate responsibility. On the plane I read the *Wall Street Journal* and the *Milwaukee Sentinel*. Under an editorial entitled "The Right to Food," the *Wall Street Journal* wrote: "Famine and food shortages have plagued mankind since the beginning of time, yet finally mankind has the means to overcome hunger—provided that governments do not interfere."[6]

Such is the gospel according to the *Wall Street Journal*: free enterprise, the free market, freedom from government. Interestingly, on the same Food Day in the *Milwaukee Sentinel* a story was carried about the Federal Trade Commission's lawsuit against four cereal makers for running a "shared monopoly." While purporting to exist to supply the people's basic right to food, they were confusing consumers and allegedly inflating prices:

Their massive advertising campaign—the FTC says the four spent 13 percent of their total sales on radio, television and print ads in 1970—has made it impossible for new manufacturers to enter the market, the agency says. "Unless the barrier to entry created by intensive advertising is lowered, the American consumer will continue to pay excessive prices for ready to eat cereals and the respondents will continue to earn profits far above a competitive level," one FTC document says.[7]

To say "Amen" to the bread means to make sure no infrastructures or their ideologies perpetuate situations that make it difficult for people to have access to their daily bread on earth. In our effort to resist any such effort, we should be clear about our motivation. Our purpose in not identifying with any form of oppression is to be faithful, as individuals and as groups, to the Spirit of freedom, who enlivens us as members of one body. In this Spirit we find our ultimate liberation, which results from our fidelity to the Word and our effort to create in our world a reality that reflects that Word. As we gather together to hear the Word and break bread, we should be aware of the continual temptation to repeat, with the two disciples on the way to Emmaus, "We were hoping that he was the one who would set Israel free" (Luke 24:21). As they would learn, people can never operate from a perspective that equates freedom with or limits them to any system of an economic, political, or even religious nature that views itself in terms of messianic fulfillment. Knowing Jesus in the breaking of bread and enabling all to have access to that bread—on all levels—is what will make our own participation in the Eucharist a sacrament of true freedom.

The sign that they had been faithful to the covenant, which would result in their liberation, would be evidenced for the Jews in their worship (cf. Exod. 3:12). The sign that he had been faithful to the covenant, which resulted in his passover, was commemorated by Jesus in the meal (cf. Luke 22:19). The ritual of worship and the meal had to follow reality, not precede it. Both ritual meals—of the Jews and of Jesus—flowed from the very human experience of passing over from enslavement to freedom, from a condition of injustice to one of justice. It follows, then, that in the Eucharist, if we are to be faithful to this sign (to the reality that it represents by work and action), this ritual must also flow from our ongoing involvement in passovers from forms of death to fuller sharings in life. Unfortunately, this does not evidence itself in the lives and style of living of many American Catholics who go through the ritual every week.

Our ritual must be at the center of our daily living. It cannot be at life's periphery. We must make sure that our rituals have a decisive effect in our lives and in the life of our world. Otherwise they can easily become purely spectator rites full of empty words and meaningless actions. Furthermore, not only is our ritual to originate from our effort to create conditions of passover in our world; it should be the inspiration that enables us to remain faithful to what we celebrate. In the words of the Synod of Bishops of 1971:

> The liturgy—which is the heart of the Church's life and over which we preside—can be of great service to education for justice. For it is a thanksgiving to the Father in Christ, which vividly expresses, through its communitarian form, the bonds of our brotherhood, and reminds us incessantly of the Church's mission. The Liturgy of the Word, catechesis and the celebration of the sacraments have the power to help us rediscover the teaching of the prophets, the Lord and the Apostles on the subject of justice. . . . The Eucharist forms the community and places it at the service of man.[8]

Jesus placed himself at the service of the world by becoming the Suffering Servant. Committed to binding up the wounds and enabling all to have access to needed resources, Jesus became the passover lamb led to slaughter by the powers of this world. He became the Lamb of God who would take away the sin and alienation of the world. Through his Spirit, we are to identify in his passover as the sheep of his pasture (cf. Ps. 78:13).

Jesus reminded his followers that what happened to him could be expected by them (cf. John 15:18ff.). Whoever participates fully in the Eucharist must become identified with the Lamb of God, committed to take away the grave sin of injustice that marks our world. Having brought our sacrifice to the altar, which celebrates our effort to participate in the world's passover from sin to grace, and having celebrated ourselves in the passover of the Body of

Christ, we leave filled with the Spirit of the Lamb of God. Only now can we leave as sheep entering into the midst of wolves (Luke 10:3).

We leave, knowing we do so as a covenant and as a sign of God's plan for the world that we have celebrated in mystery. "Here again the Christian is a 'sign' of the reality of God's action," Jacques Ellul writes:

> It is the Lamb of God, Jesus Christ, who takes away the sins of the world. But every Christian is treated like his Master, and every Christian receives from Jesus Christ a share in his work. He is a "sheep" not because his action or his sacrifice has a purifying effect on the world, but because he is the living and real "sign" constantly renewed in the midst of the world, of the sacrifice of the Lamb of God.[9]

In other words, only by carrying into the liturgy our deeds of justice and from the liturgy our commitment to be its ministers in the world will our prayer be heard, our prayer in which we ask that our sacrifice be acceptable to God our almighty Father.

8

Forgive Us Our Debts as We Forgive Those Indebted to Us

What did Jesus mean when he included in the Our Father "Forgive us our debts as we forgive those indebted to us"? To understand this phrase it seems important to view it in the context of Jesus' attitude not only about prayer but about his world. We should recall the setting, recorded earlier by Luke, in which, after spending forty days in prayer, Jesus declared what his world-stance and ministry would be:

> He came to Nazareth where he had been reared, and entering the synagogue on the sabbath as he was in the habit of doing, he stood up to do the reading. When the book of the prophet Isaiah was handed him, he unrolled the scroll and found the passage where it was written:
> The spirit of the Lord is upon me;
> therefore he has anointed me.
> He has sent me to bring glad tidings to the poor,
> to proclaim liberty to captives,
> recovery of sight to the blind
> and release to prisoners,
> to announce a year of favor from the Lord (Luke 4:16–19).

This last phrase, "To announce a year of favor from the Lord," has definite overtones of *kairos,* or a sacred time of God's action in history. This becomes particularly true when Jesus immediately links this concept of *time*—the acceptable year—with the concept of *place:* "Rolling up the scroll he gave it back to the assistant and sat down. All in the synagogue had their eyes fixed upon him. Then he began by saying to them, '*Today* this Scripture passage is fulfilled *in your hearing* '" (Luke 4:20–21).

At that time and in that place Jesus announced his platform and style of ministry. Because he would begin this ministry with a call to conversion (cf. Mark 1:15), his declaration in the synagogue cannot be separated from an understanding of the "year of favor," which called for conversion on the the part of Jewish institutional religion. This year of favor was the Jubilee Year.

According to the book of Leviticus (chap. 25), the Jubilee Year was meant to remind the Hebrews that they were to serve the purposes of the Lord throughout their histories: "For to me the Israelites belong as servants; they are servants of mine, because I brought them out of the land of Egypt, I, the Lord, your God" (Lev. 25:55). Because Israel would forget its call to be servant and would try to become lord, Yahweh prescribed the Jubilee Year every fifty years so that there could be a *systemic* conversion, which would convert an unwilling people back to its original purposes as outlined in Genesis. The Jubilee Year, then, was to ensure that the goods of the earth and its resources would be available to all. It was to ensure that (by sharing in the goods of the earth) all people would be free to image God in their lives, without domination by others. This had as its goal the fulfillment of the covenant and the reordering of creation and community.

In this light we can better understand how Jesus (who declared the Jubilee would be inaugurated by his ministry) would include in the prayer that was to summarize his view of prayer and ministry the sentence "Forgive us our debts as we forgive those indebted to us." Forgiveness of debts was one of the four constitutive elements of the Jubilee Year, along with abstention from normal work, returning the land to its original control, and freeing slaves (Lev. 24:1ff.). If Jesus was trying to create a community that reflected the Jubilee, or the original purposes God intended for his people and creation, then these elements had to be included in the community's lifestyle and prayer. Jesus did not consider the Hebrew community's (non)observance of the Jubilee. The Jubilee represented a style of living he wanted fulfilled in his community of good news.

CANCELLATION OF DEBTS

The year-long celebration of the Jubilee was to begin on the Day of Atonement, which signified salvation through the forgiveness of sins. However, Jesus used words in the Our Father that did not limit forgiveness to sins only. He extended the meaning to include the cancellation of debts as well.[1] Linking the two concepts created a significant Jubilee element. According to John Howard Yoder:

> The Lord's prayer, which summarizes the thought of Jesus concerning prayer, includes the following request: "remit us our debts as we forgive those who have offended us." Accurately, the word *opheilema* of the Greek text signifies precisely a monetary debt, in the most material sense of the term. In the "Our Father," then, Jesus is not simply recommending vaguely that we might pardon those who have bothered us or made us trouble, but tells us purely and simply to erase the debts of those who owe us money; which is to say, practice the jubilee.[2]

Yoder's contention makes all the more sense when we realize that *aphesis*, the noun form of the verb *aphiemi*, is the term used by the Septuagint for the Jubilee Year.

We tend to limit the meaning of forgiveness of debts to a purely religious sense, which makes this phrase of the Our Father quite harmless, free of any reference toward our world marked by the grave sin of injustice. The Septuagint, on the other hand, contains hardly any religious notion, but stresses the legal meaning of *forgiveness* as cancellation and *debts* as that which is owed (cf. Deut. 15:1–11). The words *aphes* (forgive) and *opheilema* (debt) cannot be isolated from their material context (cf. Luke 6:34–36). Ernst Lohmeyer makes this quite clear in his classic work, *Our Father*. He links these words to Jubilee notions contained in the Sabbath Year, which was to be held every seventh year (while the Jubilee was to be held every fiftieth year):

> The association of this word "debt" with the verb *aphienai* ("remit, loose") is a common feature of Greek linguistic usage. The verb is often used in a juristic context, where it means to free from various legal ties and obligations. There is evidence of this sense not only in

Greek literature and the language of comedy and the papyri, but also in the Septuagint, where it is almost a stereotyped term for the Old Testament Sabbath year for which the regulation runs (Deut. 15:2): "Every creditor shall release what his neighbor owes *(opheilei)* to him." In Greek, then, the legal sense of the word is predominant, and a religious sense has not developed anywhere; the Septuagint usage varies between two different meanings.[3]

In Matthew's Gospel, Jesus' conclusion to the parable of the merciless official seems to paraphrase the forgiveness petition in the Our Father: "Then in anger the master handed him over to the torturers until he paid back all that he owed. My heavenly Father will treat you in exactly the same way unless each of you forgives his brother from his heart" (18:34–35).

The situation that Jesus described can be compared to the post-slavery era in the United States when indentured servants were forced to borrow from their masters to such a degree that they could never become free. In Jesus' account, the master declares a Jubilee, a pardon for the debtor (cf. Matt. 18:27). Because of his pathos, the master was moved to pity. Yet, because the debtor was in a condition of *a-pathos* by not showing *sym-pathos* and *em-pathos* with his neighbor who was indebted to him for a much less amount, he incurred the wrath of the king. There can be no heavenly Jubilee if we fail to work for it on earth. If we have the resources necessary for our life and reject other people or keep them from having access to what we have in overabundance, we sin. "I do not want to be a thief," Francis said, "for it would be considered a theft in us if we did not give to someone who is in greater need than we."[4] There cannot be forgiveness, there cannot be Jubilee, until we have become reconciled.

This realization helps us better to understand "Forgive us our debts as we forgive those indebted to us" as well as the other "us" sentence of the Our Father: "Give us this day our daily bread." Recalling our previous discussion, we find a deeper understanding for the thesis that we cannot properly worship without having first offered the gifts of justice. If we are indebted to others or they are to us (to the point of alienation), there can be union neither with each other nor God: "If you bring your gift to the altar and there recall that your brother has anything against you, leave your gift at the altar, go first to be reconciled with your brother, and then come and offer your gift" (Matt. 5:23–24). It does not matter, for our purposes, who is indebted to whom; Jesus was speaking to all Christians—those who were in debt and those who held the debt. The simple meaning is that there cannot be union with God (which implies forgiveness of sins) if we are not in union with others and they with us.

Conversion from sin in its individual, interpersonal, and social levels is needed if we are to be part of a Jubilee community. Isaiah made this clear when, after rejecting the prayers and sacrifices of the Israelites because of their injustices, he called for their conversion:

> Wash yourselves clean!
> Put away your misdeeds from before my eyes;
> cease doing evil; learn to do good.
> Make justice your aim; redress the wronged;
> hear the orphan's plea, defend the widow.
> Come now, let us set things right,
> says the Lord:
> Though your sins be like scarlet,
> they may become white as snow;
> Though they be crimson red,
> they may become white as wool.
> If you are willing and obey [he concludes with a jubilee notion]
> you shall eat the good things of the land (Isa. 1:16–19).

As a community draws further away from its original and radical origins, it tends to spiritualize its founding values and ideals, which once were expressed in concrete lifestyle. In the evolution of the Christian community, the original spirit of Jesus was mesmerized by the adaptation of the church's teaching to accept usury and interest and a system in which people become debtors for a good part of their lives. This acceptance ignored the original values that Jesus tried to create among his followers, who were to owe each other nothing but love (cf. Rom. 13:8). The Our Father should reflect the lived experience of calling for conversion of a system built on false needs that keep people indebted to those who have the power to create needs. Instead we have made the forgiveness of debts a purely religious concept having little or nothing to do with the reality of our daily lives.

There are also other religious concepts that have replaced the material, or physical, element involved in the cancellation of debts and forgiveness of sins. One of them relates to our present limitation of some signs of the jubilee such as recovery of sight to the blind (Luke 4:18) to purely spiritual or sacramental areas. This applies to other illnesses as well. Yet Jesus offered both healing and good news for the poor (cf. Luke 7:22–23) as signs of the Jubilee fulfilled through his Spirit working in him.

The gift of the Spirit within us calls us to exercise our healing power, through prayer and ministry, in various ways as a sign of the Jubilee's fulfillment in us. This can be in the sacramental dimension, or in the "healing of memories" through prayer and the counseling ministry, or even, if the gift be given us, in the sharing of the Spirit's power in us to liberate people from physical disease and the influence of the powers and principalities on any of the three levels of our reality. To have been healed by Christ's stripes and brought into Jubilee and access to God and to fail to enable others to have access to our various gifts of healing is to refuse to let the real purposes of the Jubilee take place in our lives. As Francis MacNutt has written:

> It's as if God's saving, healing, forgiving love cannot flow into us unless we are ready to let it flow out to others. If we deny forgiveness and healing to others, God's love cannot flow into us. It's all part of the great commandment in which loving our neighbor is part of the same commandment as loving God: "I love God only as much as I love my worst enemy." There is a direct relationship between our willingness to love others and the healing ministry.[5]

Another religious concept that has replaced the physical or material element in the cancellation of debts and the healing and forgiveness of sins is the indulgence, a practice particularly in evidence during the Holy Year. The paradox here is that the Holy Year's foundations are based in the Jubilee Year, as Pope Paul VI noted in his decree calling for a Holy Year in 1975.[6]

During 1974, in at least one diocese, extensive plans were made to have local "Holy Year Churches" at which full indulgences (remission of sins) could be gained. At the same meeting at which these plans were made, I offered a suggestion which would have helped to reintroduce a material element to the traditional religious concept of forgiveness of sins. It was suggested that "debt-reduction" boxes, which would be used to help the poor, be placed in the back of these "Holy Year Churches." The idea was never accepted or even seriously discussed. Instead of stressing the need to make a pilgrimage from the enslavements that keep people professing a gospel that has little evidence in their lives, plans were made for a pilgrimage to Rome by jet, which cost $1,242. Such a form of debt-reduction (arranged by Faith Tours) was accepted; the effort to return to the biblical foundation and to do something about the poor was passed over.

There can be no indulgence, there can be no forgiveness of sins if we close our ears to the cry of the poor. Real penance involves a conversion of hearts toward the poor. If we purport to accept our own poverty before the Lord and do not find ourselves in solidarity with the poor of the world, the Lord cannot know us. Our sins cannot be forgiven:

> Is this the manner of fasting I wish,
> of keeping a day of penance;
> That a man bow his head like a reed,
> and lie in sackcloth and ashes?
> Do you call this a fast,
> a day acceptable to the Lord?
> This, rather, is the fasting that I wish:
> releasing those bound unjustly,
> untying the thongs of the yoke;
> Setting free the oppressed,
> breaking every yoke;
> Sharing your bread with the hungry,
> sheltering the oppressed and the homeless;
> Clothing the naked when you see them,
> and not turning your back on your own.
> Then your light shall break forth like the dawn
> and your wound shall quickly be healed;
> Your vindication shall go before you
> and the glory of the Lord shall be your rear guard.
> Then you shall call, and the Lord will answer,

you shall cry for help, and he will say:
Here I am! (Isa. 58:5–9).

In prayer we call upon the Lord, requesting access to him as our resource. If we bring to this prayer an ear deaf to the cry of the poor, he will not hear us. However, if we allow the poor to have access to our resources, Isaiah tells us, when we call to the Lord in prayer, he will say, "Here I am."

As we look about us, how can we find ways to become involved concretely in living this petition of the Lord's Prayer in a manner to take us beyond a purely spiritual or religious notion of forgiveness of debts? In our local communities and gatherings, we subtly try to keep people indebted to us in many ways—by our office and authority, by manipulating others to feel inferior before us, by such a simple thing as expecting thanks. Even in our own communities, much less our world, how many feel alienated, marginal, left out? And what are we doing to cancel this debt?

As members of a system that holds people indebted to it for breaking its laws, we can fail to apply this petition of the Our Father to those in prison who "owe their debt to society." We know our system is established so that usually it is the nonwhite and poor who are imprisoned because they lack access to proper resources.

Besides working for conversion of our judicial and penal institutions, another area where we can work to forgive debts and set people free is by urging full and complete pardons to those who are indebted to society because they refused, for whatever reason, to participate in a war that has proved to be unjust and a waste of human lives.

We need to alleviate the results of injustice by continuing to work with the hungry, the ill-clothed, the uneducated, the widow and orphan, the poor and the alienated. We also need to work with others in a concerted effort to overcome the causes of these injustices, which are linked to oppressive structures and unjust systems. These too need conversion. There can be no indulgence, no remission of our debts, unless our fasting and penance are linked to our efforts to join with the Jubilee King in the liberation of the oppressed, the freeing of those imprisoned (cf. Luke 4:16ff.), and the forgiveness of each other's debts.

FREEING THE ENSLAVED

One of the prescriptions of the Jubilee Year as outlined by Leviticus was that the Israelite slaves were to be set free (25:50). On first glance it may appear that this has no application to the forgiveness of debts. A distinction about slaves made by Aristotle might help us, however, see our country as historically built on chattel slavery and perpetuating itself on de facto slavery. As a result, as American Christians trying to witness Jesus' Jubilee platform to the world, we will preach conversion from both.

Chattel slavery, according to Aristotle, consists of a system in which some human beings are the absolute property of other human beings and are deprived of all property, even that resulting from their own labor. This is the kind of slavery the book of Leviticus speaks of. A clear example of this is the slavery in the American south before the Emancipation Proclamation. As in Roman law, the slave codes in the southern colonies in the eighteenth century conceived of the slave as a *res*, a thing; the people as well as their work were owned by the master.

Although great effort was made to break the body as well as the spirit of the slave by separation from any visible form of property, the slave owners failed to note that this alienated people could sublimate their need for land. Differing from their owners in race and culture, feeling powerless and seeing little meaning or norm to life, slaves could, by the use of language and signs, transfer their need for property or land to an active hope for it. As the Jews who were enslaved in Babylon looked back to their promised land (cf. Ps. 137:1), so the black slaves, domesticated by Christianity and told to be obedient to their masters (cf. Eph. 6:5), used the religious words taught by the masters. From them they created songs of liberation to give hope. Just as forgiveness of sins was not purely a religious or spiritual notion but had definite implications of law and materiality, so the hope for a restoration of property or land rested not simply in the "promised land" of heaven, but on this earth as it would be in heaven as well. James H. Cone writes:

> In this context "Swing Low, Sweet Chariot" referred to the "idea of escape by 'chariot,' that is, by means which a company could

employ to proceed northward." When black slaves sang, "I looked over Jordan and what did I see, Coming for to carry me home," they were looking over the Ohio River. "The band of angels" was Harriet or another conductor coming for him; and "home" was a haven in the free states or Canada. "Steal away" meant to sneak into the woods for a secret slave meeting, and "Follow the Drinking Gourd" meant following the Great Dipper to the Ohio River and freedom.[7]

While religion served the needs of the slaves as a response to their alienation as well as their hopes, it was used by the powerful in society to keep the slaves in their place without property or the hope for it. This use of religion as a further instrument of oppression and injustice was sanctioned as evidenced by the silence of the official church as well as by official support. In a letter to southern slaveholders (1727) the bishop of London allayed fears that they, as Christians, might have to face if their slaves were to become Christians:

> Christianity and the embracing of the gospel does not make the least alteration in civil property or in any of the duties which belong to civil relations; but in all of these respects it continues Persons just in the same State as it found them. The Freedom which Christianity gives is freedom from the Bondage of Sin and Satan and from the Dominion of Men's Lusts and Passions and inordinate Desires; but as to their outward condition, whatever that was before, whether bond or free, their being baptized and becoming Christians, makes no matter of change in them.[8]

The fact that, by the seventeenth and eighteenth centuries, slavery in the West had been almost limited to black Africans contradicts the belief that in Christ there should be no distinctions. The very color of one's skin was further reason for alienation. This realization was not lessened with passing years in the United States, as the thirteenth and fourteenth amendments to the Constitution show and as is evident in the case of the red race, the native American, who was not allowed to be a "citizen" of the land until 1924.

If one considers the economic, military, and technological powers evident in the contemporary world, one faces the striking fact that, with the exception of Japan, the unequal distribution of wealth and power that has occurred (with its base in the "bundle of property rights"[9]) tilts dramatically in favor of white nations over nonwhite nations. Alienation exists within America among the races. Alienation exists between America and others based, in fact if not in theory, on color and race.

This realization brings us to the second kind of slavery or servitude that Aristotle outlined: de facto servitude wherein a human is no longer the property of another human, but has no property beyond toiling ability and is thus forced to live a dependent, servile life. Ironically, the division between the people and states who have the economic, military, and technological power and those who do not occurs at roughly 30 degrees latitude. With the exception of Japan, this generally divides the world between predominantly white and nonwhite peoples. This division is expressed in the constitution of such groups formed to influence public policy as the Trilateral Commission, which is composed of leaders from Western Europe, Japan, and the United States, who carry on 70 percent of the world's trade among each other, even though they constitute but 15 percent of the world's people. Through the pervasive influence of travel and communications, the nonwhite peoples of the world are increasingly aware of the predominantly white structures, which they perceive as keeping them alienated. Facing such power—which seems to evade public scrutiny as it promotes its own interests—the poor nations sense that this power will be the true determiner of what any New International Economic Order will be. They feel that it will be shaped primarily with the interests of these powerful nations and their transnational corporations in mind.

The former political colonialism and chattel slavery may have died. What remains is a form of economic colonialism maintained in the structures of the North that create an economic dependency in the South. Despite good intentions toward the countries of the South by individuals and even groups such as the Trilateral Commission, the will to change the underlying level of control is missing. With no new lands and frontiers to conquer, and with resources being drained, there is little chance for the peoples of the Asian, African, and Latin American countries (and the racial minorities or women in the United States) to benefit economically, culturally, or socially. Add to this the fact that they face complex issues entirely different from the development models of past centuries and we can see why Cardinal Roy, head of the Pontifical Peace and Justice Commission, declared, "Today, every circumstance in the now developing nations—internal and external —works in the opposite sense. . . . There are no external safety valves; . . . the world's free land is occupied, the frontier closed. Political decolonization has not yet altered the overwhelming balance of wealth and power in favor of the already rich."[10]

In face of the statistics revealing the huge disparity in wealth and power between rich and poor nations—which was not altered by the much heralded efforts of the First and Second United Nations Development Decades—we find the accepted notions of "development" operable among people in the United States no longer applicable to the situation. According to Denis Goulet, author of *The Myth of Aid* (a book which has done much to dispel the notion of viewing aid as a purely selfless and altruistic gesture on the part of the rich nations toward the poor nations), there are three basic approaches to the idea of development. The *first* views development in terms of the Gross National Product. A country is developed when it can independently experience a growth rate from 5 percent to 7 percent on a per capita income ranging from $500 to $1,000. The *second* takes economic growth as its number one factor, and adds social change, assuming that modernization is desirable and possible and that it will be facilitated by the developed nations. The *third* notion of development stresses ethical values such as justice and the promotion of qualitative improvements in all societies and all groups and individuals within those societies.

With the possible exception of the third type of development, the foregoing descriptions presume a model based on a form of capitalism that is the framework of such sponsors of development as the World Bank, the International Monetary Fund, United Nations agencies, and the Organization for Economic Cooperation and Development, as well as regional banks. As Denis Goulet points out, all these continue a form of de facto enslavement, no longer limited to individuals but encompassing nations and classes of peoples:

As these institutions officially see things their mission is to solve problems of poverty and technological backwardness, not to abolish structures of dependency. To do so would in fact be suicidal. Yet it is clear that the operating assumptions and working procedures of this network of institutions buttress the interests of "donors" allegedly working in "partnership" with aid "recipients." Such pervasive institutional bias renders a realistic definition of issues impossible. . . . Aid agencies, as well as development planning institutions within many Third World countries themselves, are structurally unable to accept a development model which requires basic changes in the prevailing distribution of power and decision-making in the world at large and within societies themselves.[11]

As we reflect on these words in light of God's purposes in history, as we consider that the Jubilee Year was a way of systemically converting a society to its original purpose of sharing resources as equally as possible and ensuring the image of God in all, we cannot help believing that Aristotle's definition of de facto enslavement still exists. It predominates in what the Synod of Bishops called "a network of domination, oppression and abuses which stifle freedom and which keep the greater part of humanity from sharing in the building up and enjoyment of a more just and fraternal world."[12]

Sharing the resources of the land and ensuring human rights are not only God's plan for the world; they almost seem to be the two natural goals of human society. Yet we are part of a nation whose political economy frustrates their achievement on a global basis. As Dr. Hernan Santa Cruz, former head of the United Nations commission which dealt with human rights and private property in the drafting of the International Covenant on Human Rights, stated:

The political will to tackle the development problem with a determination commensurate with its importance, gravity and urgency has not been forthcoming from the western industrialized countries—in particular the United States, the United Kingdom, the Federal Republic of Germany, and Japan, which together hold in their hands almost two-thirds of the world's financial and technological resources.[13]

He continues by declaring that it is not only a matter of the nations involved being converted. The peoples within those nations, as part of the whole system, need to be freed from false notions that reinforce those systems.

> Neither does there exist in those countries—and this is one of the causes of the above fact—a true political will to change a type of international economic relations between their world and the poor and needy that is almost exclusively favorable to them. The industrialized countries do not intend to put an end to a situation of dependency and exploitation, which constitutes a subtle, sinister form of neocolonialism.[14]

That such a system will not easily change became quite evident to me during the summer of 1976. I was part of various groups who met throughout the United States to discuss the New International Economic Order. One meeting I attended took place at Aspen, Colorado. Most participants were vice presidents of major United States transnational corporations, members of the U. S. State Department, and foreign-affairs officials from other countries. Good will, sincerity, and verbal support of more equitable economic policies marked the participants. Nevertheless, it was clear that any basic changes or conversion of the international economic system itself (recognized by all as contributing to the inequities in varying degrees), were considered radical as well as unrealistic.

This was evidenced in the generally negative reaction to a major paper delivered to the group by a former Andean Pact economist, Constantine V. Vaitsos, on "Employment Problems and Transnational Enterprises in Developing Nations: Distortions and Inequality." While he showed the good that can be fostered by the presence of transnational corporations in areas such as Latin America, his overall conclusions pointed to the perpetuation of a situation of economic dependency that reinforces the concentration of power in hands of those already rich to the detriment of the poor:

> The operations of transnational enterprises in developing countries (as it is generally also true for activities of such firms in other parts of

the world) are characterized by: a) a significantly large absolute and relative size, b) a high growth rate and industry concentration in their respective markets, c) an actively pursued process of denationalization of the local economies, d) an oligopolistic interdependence in their concentrated markets and barriers to entry confronting would be competitors and e) a command over captive markets of goods, services and factors of production through significantly large and increasing interaffiliate trade.[15]

A basic principle of distributive justice is that the few should not have at the expense of others. This principle, which enabled people to see the sin of the chattel form of slavery, must be applied for the liberation and jubilee of those now controlled by the second—economic—form of slavery. Unjust enrichment at the expense of the resources and human rights of others continues slavery, albeit in another form. Radomiro Tomic, former Chilean ambassador to the United States, declared:

> There are obvious ethical reasons to oppose unjust enrichment. Roman jurists established this centuries before our era, thus confirming what Aristotle has already expressed. All medieval law rejected what Saint Bonaventure defined as "hoarding the property of others under the veil of a contract." And Anglo-Saxon countries . . .—most relevantly the United States—have confirmed the principle of equity through common law, thereby condemning unfair accumulation of wealth. Well, then, if becoming rich at the expense of another is condemned when the victim is a private person and the harm relatively minor, why should it be accepted when it is done on a colossal scale and when the victims are whole countries?[16]

RETURNING THE LAND

People tend to appropriate property and wealth to themselves. The more cunning are able to accumulate more, often at other's expense. Thus another Jubilee prescription called for the return of the land to its original condition. In that condition it reflected the fact that the earth is primarily the Lord's (cf. Ps. 24:1): "The land shall not be sold in perpetuity; for the land is mine, and you are but aliens who have become my tenants. Therefore, in every part of the country that you occupy, you must permit the land to be redeemed" (Lev. 25:23–24).

With the rise of capitalism as an economic form, Francis of Assisi intuitively recognized problems related to property and prayerful ministry. In rejecting ownership Francis was trying to say that he did not want divisions and distinctions based on property or the "bundle of property rights" arising in his community. Celano tells us that, in terms of ownership of land itself, Francis "always wanted the law for strangers to be observed by his sons." This law for strangers, which was part of the Jubilee, meant for his followers "to be gathered under a roof that belongs to another, to go about peaceably, to thirst after their fatherland."[17] Such an expression, we shall see later, indicates how Francis also was trying to create a Jubilee community in imitation of Christ.

The form of capitalism we face today is quite different from that which caused a person like Francis to reject money and wealth as a style for his community. Because of its complexity and "mix," the economic reality we face cannot simply be defined or totally understood. Yet we can see a certain ideology resulting from the way it operates. Pope Paul VI outlined some of its implications in his encyclical on the progress of peoples:

> Out of these new conditions opinions have somehow crept into human society according to which profit was considered the chief incentive to foster economic development, competition the supreme law of economics, private ownership of the means of production an absolute right which recognizes neither limits nor concomitant social duty. This type of unbridled *liberalism* paved the way for a type of tyranny rightly condemned by our predecessor Pius XI as the source of *internationalism of finance* or *international imperialism*. Such economic abuses will never be rejected as completely as they ought to be because the economy must only serve man, a point about which it is fitting once more to give a serious admonition. But if it must be admitted that so many hardships, so many injustices and fratricidal conflicts whose effects we feel even now, trace their origin to a form of *capitalism*, one would falsely attribute those evils to industrial growth which more correctly are to be blamed on the pernicious opinions about economics which accompany that growth.[18]

Pope Paul indicated some of the opinions that underlie our present form of capitalism, which, it should be remembered, is never as bad as its theories, just as socialism is never as good as its theories. What are some of these?

One of the first principles is that profit and growth are considered the main incentives to foster economic development. Frequently this is at the expense of human beings. Regularly newspapers and television report about corporations discharging into the air, water, and land pollutants that are linked to diseases and even death in human beings. Many of these corporations resist monitoring and even threaten to close down if they are forced to abide by environmental or consumer standards. Other corporations will abide by laws created in one country for the common good of citizens there, but will still use ingredients in their product that have been judged harmful. Still other corporations exploit the natural resources and the labor of human beings until either the resources are depleted or human beings organize to share more fully in the profits—and then the corporations move from the area. This migration has occurred in the United States from the northern states to the southern states. Then, as the laborers in the southern states became more organized, the migration across the Mexican border increased—from 120 plants in 1970 to about 450 in 1974—aided by duty-free imports from the United States and cheaper Mexican labor. [19]

This transnationalism of the large economic enterprises continually expands at the expense of small and middle business, which in 1960 accounted for 60 percent of the industrial economy, but only 30 percent in 1970. Today small and medium-sized farms, businesses, banks, and communications media will face the same problems, as larger industries create a concentration in the areas of food, energy and technology, banking, and communications information. The larger industries are able to determine prices and product distribution and, consequently, who will be able to purchase their products. Since larger corporations have better credit with large banks, much of their investment results in either underbidding or buying out existing small or medium-sized businesses at home and abroad. This has given rise to an entirely new form of capitalism never envisioned by Adam Smith.

Abroad, in countries where labor is unorganized and cheaper, with technology in their control, and with less-stable governments on the one hand or militaristic governments who are reinforced by their presence on the other, transnational corporations have been able to create an entirely new reality that must be recognized and challenged on principles of justice. The assumption that still sustains belief that key American institutions, such as those in the economic sector, are based on justice achieved through the market place (equal access to resources) is no longer operable, despite millions of dollars being spent by corporations to keep people controlled by this ideological myth. The transnational corporations have become the new missionaries professing this creed of free enterprise. Because there has evolved a systemic deterioration of checks and balances to their power, they are sustained by their gospel. Their religion is the promotion of a value system as the kingdom that most people think they can attain, and to which, more and more, the people become indentured servants to promote the system's goals. "And through covetousness shall they with feigned words make merchandise of you" (2 Pet. 2:3) is how the King James version describes such an enslaving situation. As Pope Paul VI said in 1971:

> Under the driving force of new systems of production, national frontiers are breaking down, and we can see new economic powers emerging, the multinational enterprises, which by the concentration and flexibility of their means can conduct autonomous strategies which are largely independent of the national political powers and therefore not subject to control from the point of view of the common good. [20]

Pope Paul refers to the concentration of companies in industries as well as the concentration of wealth among individuals. How does this apply to the United States?

In up to two hundred of the nation's major manufacturing industries, the top four companies in each industry control half of the market. This is called oligopoly. An internal Federal Trade Commission report notes that "if highly concentrated industries were deconcentrated to the point where the four largest firms control 40 percent or less of an industry's sales, prices would fall by 25 percent or more."[21] Without historic monopoly, it has been estimated that current maldistribution of wealth would decrease by 50 percent.[22] The five hundred largest industrial corporations in the 1977 *Fortune* listing accounted for over 65 percent of the sales of all U.S. industrial companies, 80 percent of their total profit, and 75 percent of their employees.   These five hundred constitute but .0003 percent of the 1,700,000 U.S. corporations, but average seventy-five percent of their profits, sales, and employees.[23] In 1953 such corporations were paying about 37 percent of their profits in taxes to the government. By 1977 the average business paid 23 percent.

This difference was not made up by wealthy individuals, for this period also found concentration of wealth taking place among the rich, accomplished in good part by tax loopholes, which again forced the "middle class" to bear the burden. Fiscal year 1975 found the average American family paying $1,350 for these loopholes, two-thirds of which were not necessary. Such loopholes enabled the wealthiest 1 percent of all American families to reduce their payment of taxes on income from 33 percent in 1952 to 26 percent in 1967, with regular attempts to lower it even further.

Income is the money a person takes in during a given period. Wealth is the value of a person's possessions, such as real estate, homes, cars, stocks, etc. With the reduction of taxes on income for the rich, an increase of wealth takes place. The recent concentration of wealth among the rich in America has little parallel in any other nation. In 1949, 1 percent of the American people controlled 21 percent of the nation's personal wealth. In 1959 it controlled 30 percent and in 1969 it controlled 40 percent of the total personal wealth.[24] The top five-tenths of this 1 percent had 22 percent of the nations's personal wealth. This 1 percent has eight times the wealth of the lowest 50 percent of the population.

While there are different measurements for wealth in America, as the statistics above evidence, even conservative estimates and figures show the richest 20 percent of the population controlling over three-fourths of the wealth, while the lowest 25 percent has no significant control over any wealth. With the growing burden of taxation falling upon the "middle class" (where can one find a "middle" when 99 percent share 60 percent of the wealth?), the evidence points to an enrichment of a few having access to power as well as to law-formulation being made at the expense of the many.

"Any society in which a few control most of the wealth and the masses are left in want is a sinful society," the bishops of the West Indies declared. "We believe that those who own superfluous possessions are obliged in justice to share them with those who are in want."[25] The bishops' statement applies to the United States as a nation and as a member of the world community, in which it has a disproportionate share of the wealth and maintains it at the expense of the world's masses through its influence over commodity pricing, control of patents and technology, and ability to get better credit and financing to perpetuate its power and wealth.

Clearly, in the United States, just as there has evolved a systematized enrichment of some at the expense of others—a sign of sin—there must be a systematized reallocation of the wealth and resources for the betterment of all. There must be a Jubilee proclaimed to the people in this last quarter of the twentieth century, as Jesus announced the Jubilee to the people of the first century.

Jesus did not merely proclaim "the acceptable year of favor," or the Jubilee. He provided, as part of his platform, a systemic way for its accomplishment. In the spirit of John, who declared that the concrete conditions needed for Jesus' coming rested in sharing with those in need (Luke 2:11), Jesus demanded that those who would be identified with him and his purposes in history would have to sell what they had and give to those who did not have access to such resources—the poor. This was the condition demanded before they would be fit to be united in participative community with him. This community was to be a sign of the kingdom come on earth as it would be in heaven, where there would be no poverty. It became a sign of blessedness. They would be blessed who participated in the effort to make this kingdom on earth as in heaven (cf. Matt. 5:1ff.).

This shows poverty in a different light. If poverty can be defined as the inability to have access to resources, then the kingdom of God is in the process of being established when the poor have access to resources. Since poverty in itself is condemned in the Scriptures as against the plan of God for his people, to work actively for those conditions in society that realize God's plan demands that we systematically work for the reallocation of this world's resources to give the poor their proper access to them.

The early Christian community was composed of members striving to witness to this demand. As a result they sold their property, sharing *on the basis of each one's need* (cf. Acts 2:45). The aim was not to give up the right to material goods; rather, it was to enable others denied access to them a chance to receive their benefits, for the goal of equity.

In giving "some advice on the matter of rich and poor," Paul made it clear that distributive justice was the aim of the Jubilee community. Yet this was to be realistic:

> The willingness to give should accord with one's means, not go beyond them. The relief of others ought not to impoverish you; there should be a certain equality. Your plenty at the present time should supply their need so that their surplus may one day supply your need, with equality as the result. It is written, "He who gathered much had no excess and he who gathered little had no lack" (2 Cor. 8:12–15; cf. Exod. 16:18).

A Jubilee community would witness to the participative community of the Trinity. It would be a witness to Jesus, who became incarnate to witness to the manner by which this would be accomplished. Community sharing has to be based on the example of Jesus. As Paul wrote, "You are well acquainted with the favor shown you by our Lord Jesus Christ: how for your sake he made himself poor though he was rich, so that you might become rich by his poverty" (2 Cor. 8:9).

Emulating Jesus and the early community, Francis insisted on sharing with the poor as a sign of readiness to be part of his community. Assuming that relatives were generally of the same economic background as those who joined his community, Francis insisted that relatives of initiates not receive what was left behind, since they already had access to resources. If a candidate's family was to witness to the world of the kingdom and be good news and Jubilee for the poor, the poor had to be given access or the candidate would be unfit to enter the community. Celano writes:

> It happened in the Marches of Ancona that after Francis had preached there a certain man came humbly asking to be admitted

into the order. The saint said to him: "If you wish to be joined with the poor, first distribute your possessions to the poor of the world." When he heard this, the man left, and impelled by a carnal love, he distributed his goods to his relatives and gave nothing to the poor. It happened that when he came back and told the saint of his generous liberality, the father laughed at him and said: "Go on your way, brother fly, for you have not yet left your home and relatives. You gave your goods to your relatives and you have defrauded the poor; you are not worthy to be numbered among the holy poor. You have begun with the flesh and you have laid an unsound foundation on which to build a spiritual structure."[26]

This practice of the early community of not giving one's money to family but to the poor is reinforced in the example of Brother Bernard, whose "conversion to God was a model to others in the manner of selling one's possessions and giving them to the poor" and not to parents.[27] If one would give to those who already had access to resources it would hardly be a sign of a commitment to create the kind of community on earth that would image the kingdom in heaven where all would have equal access. Instead of good news being preached to the poor about this kingdom, the status quo would be further strengthened.

If we are to see that those are blessed who enable the poor to participate in resources, we need to distance ourselves from whatever today may contribute to poverty. This means relinquishing titles (certain rights) and false power. It means trying to free oneself of property as far as possible or refusing to act as the rich of the world with what property one has by not refusing access to it by the poor.

We live in a society which has convinced itself that happiness (blessedness) does not have much reference to the kind of kingdom proclaimed by Jesus, which finds the poor sharing in its blessings with the rich. Its practice and pursuit of happiness is not to be found in sharing resources but in amassing them in affluence (cf. Luke 12:19ff.). In fact, a study detailed in *Psychology Today* shows that the overwhelming number of participants in the research found people happy in direct positive correlation with their degree of affluence.[28] Thus while we Catholic and Protestant Americans preach and profess a gospel that states "the less the better," the gospel that advertises the opposite is the one that is pursued. How far we Americans have come from St. Thomas, who found ultimate happiness resting in the contemplation of truth!

How can Christians preach another gospel when this idol-mammon controls the system that is our culture and heritage and creates the mind-sets of the people in the pews, desks, and chairs around us? Do we dare ask them to join us on a pilgrimage out of such a system, which demands we leave some of these things behind despite the pleasure they give us? Dare we begin a critical investigation of the world about us? Dare we call for conversion on all three levels of society to truly make way for the Lord?

ABSTENTION FROM WORK

The fourth element of the Jubilee Year called upon the Hebrews to take time from their regular farming to renew themselves before the Lord and re-establish priorities. In our context, we would apply this to our need to "stop business as usual," to slow down for prayerful and critical reflection. Just as the land needed time to renew itself and be renourished, so we need time to reflect on the religion we profess and the world in which we live. We need to reflect critically on our living, our prayer, and our ministry within the institutions of our day in light of the demands of the gospel.

This fourth element of the Jubilee Year has its roots in the notion of Sabbath, or rest. Taking time off from business as usual affords us the opportunity to participate in the Sabbath of contemplation, of prayerful rest in the Lord. Entering into this rest frees us to look at the false notions of security that have become our idols (cf. Heb. 3–4). In prayerful rest the Spirit of the new creation we work for prays within us (cf. Rom. 8). Here we approach the Lord of history as poor people, totally unable to have access to him, totally dependent on his decision to share his resource of grace and presence with us. In face of this reality, there can be no manipulation, no exploitation, no control—if there is to be true participative community in a contemplative stance. One needs silence, space, and time in which to come to the realization that humans are totally unable to determine the destiny of prayer, or even its content. If we fail to "stop business as usual," if we fail to take time off and distance ourselves from our ordinary environment for prayer and recollection, it will become increasingly difficult to distance ourselves from its influence in our lives. We need to withdraw to our lonely places if we, in turn, are to be drawn to God.

Because no one can come to the Father unless the Father draws the person to himself, one needs an equal amount of humility, faith, and hope in which to present oneself before the Lord. And if, from his wealth, the Lord of history cares to share his resources, his presence with us, we can only make our own the words that Francis made his own. Celano writes:

> When a servant of God is praying and is visited by a new consolation from the Lord, he should, before he comes away from his prayer, raise his eyes to heaven and with hands joined say to the Lord: "This consolation and sweetness you have sent from heaven, Lord, to me, an unworthy sinner, and I return it to you so you may keep it for me, for I am a robber of your treasure." And again "Lord, take your good things away from me in this world and keep them for me in the life to come." Thus, he said, "he ought to speak. And when he comes away from prayer he should show himself to others as poor and as a sinner, as though he had attained no new grace." For he would say: "It happens that a person loses something precious for the sake of some trifling reward and easily provokes him, who gives, not to give again."[29]

In taking time for contemplative prayer, we should be able to find, with Francis, the link between the way we live our poverty and desire to concretize it in our lives, and our ability to say, "My God and my All." If we have been formed by the Word of God, we cannot let that Word be suffocated by a society that tries to enslave us through production and consumption patterns. Only Jesus is Lord. If one experiences the lordship of Jesus in prayer and does not see the necessity of making that a reality on earth as it is in heaven, the reality of that prayer should be seriously questioned. If one believes he or she is given access to the resource of God's grace and peace in prayer and is not thereby forced to live and work for a society where the poor on all other levels can image God by having access to what resources they need, a question should be raised about exactly who was met in prayer.

One of the best examples of someone who reflected deeply and who had a critical interpretation of reality gained from that prayer was Mary. She stored all things in her heart (cf. Luke 2:51)—the reality that was her environment and how this was to be interpreted in light of the Word of God. As her own canticle testifies, Mary did not limit her understanding of God's action in her life to herself or even her own community. Her personal prayer, reflecting on God's action in her life, was not separated from her sense of identification with God's liberating mission in the world. Her realization of her own personal liberation became a testimony and praise of the peoples' communal liberation:

> He has shown might with his arm;
> he has confused the proud in their inmost thoughts.
> He has deposed the mighty from their thrones
> and raised the lowly to high places.
> The hungry he has given every good thing
> while the rich he has sent empty away (Luke 1:51–53).

It may even be said that Mary's religious experience was valid because it resulted in her commitment to God's plan for history. As John would explain, one's personal experience of God's action in one's personal life has to be witnessed in a concomitant commitment to God's concern about sharing with those in need; this is an absolute test to the genuineness of religious experience (cf. 1 John 3:17). As the words attributed to Mary show, not all who think they have had the experience of the Lord, even if it seems to be highly real and personal, will enter the kingdom of God. It will be given only to those who live that prayerful experience by following his will for their concrete reality.

Given our world, it would be advantageous to examine our ministries to determine if they are facilitating or hindering God's will that relates to the sharing of the earth's resources and the promotion of his image in all. Perhaps the most important area U.S. Catholics could investigate is the area of parochial ministry, or the examination of the church in its parochial expression. In his reflection on the need for basic Christian communities to arise within existing parish structures, José Marins seems to be pointing to a direction that is essential for the conversion needed within church institutions:

> The parish has remained bonded to a type of society that has already disappeared in urban centers and is fast disappearing in rural areas. This has resulted in a progressive marginalization of the parish, which is incapable of being a leaven in a society of rapid transformation or unable to promote deeper forms of human relationships. In the large cities, the traditional parish is inadequate to unite the faithful around the word of God, the altar and into an actual lived-experience of charity. There is a need for the ecclesial community to make a profound about-face, to divest itself of those programs which reflect a society that has already died, and to form groups which will think deeply about their evangelical roots in order to find new forms of expression in our era.[30]

Only a person of prayer can begin to face the reality outlined by Marins, for to begin dealing with this reality implies a need for conversion from existing patterns, a need to "leave" the existing ways as "salvation" and forge a new road to freedom. And since these existing patterns have resulted from years of formation and acceptance on the part of a generally domesticated people, only much time and reflection will be able to begin the process of a liberation from these forms. This reality came upon me after serving five years in a central-city, predominantly black neighborhood, where the congregation remained primarily white and elderly. Reflecting on my own experience I was led to ask if others might be living and spending time as I was, being a person very tied up in administrative, program, and group development but rarely facilitating the concrete preaching of the gospel, calling for conversion on the streets, reinforcing my faith prayerfully with the people, and sharing gospel values among the people—which is essential to the very kind of communities we purport to be building.

While there may be exceptions in the U.S. parish ministry today, I no longer believe that average Catholics of any race or ethnic background have a working ecclesiology that creates a church of the third level. In such a church the members see themselves as spirited members of one body called to preach good news to their communities, their neighborhoods, their schools, offices, corporations, unions, and the wide world. Instead, too many seem to view their church membership as affording them certain rights and privileges—for the house "chaplain" to "lead us in prayer," to have squatters' rights to certain rooms and areas on church grounds, to boycott collections when the word that is preached differs from theirs, to, in effect, become a ghetto-ized club little different from any campus fraternity or sorority, a racist Eagles' Club or elitist card club.

The need to bring critical reflection to both our existing institutional expressions and the needs of the poor of the world was reinforced by Pope Paul, who declared the need for a renewal of heart and personal conversion resulting from "a complete examination of our mentality regarding two principal realities: the religion we profess and the world in which we live."[31] Taking time off, symbolically "leaving" the land of our prayers for prayer, and the land of our institutions for church, is needed on an ongoing basis if we are to create a Jubilee community of good news in a world that, as Jesus promised, will receive such an outline for a new creation as bad news.

We need the reinforcement of co-believers, of a basic support community, who will prayerfully and ministerially begin this journey with us. With such reinforcement, we can truly become pilgrims and strangers in this world as we are assured of becoming fuller participants in the kingdom of heaven.

9

Lead Us Not into Temptation . . .

"Lead us not into temptation, but deliver us from evil" is the final petition of the Lord's Prayer. For our purposes we shall discuss the two parts of the petition separately. In the next chapter we shall discuss how they interrelate.

The fact that "Jesus was led into the desert by the Spirit to be tempted by the devil" (Matt. 4:1) seems best understood in Matthew's attempt to portray Jesus as the founder of a new community based on the Exodus experience. Just as Israel experienced forty years of testing in the desert, so Jesus went "into the desert for forty days, where he was tempted by the devil" (Luke 4:1–2). An analysis of the temptations of Jesus should help us as we try to understand how we can pray to the Spirit to lead us not into temptation in our modern world.

The early chapters of this book showed that the founder of every movement, after reflection on reality, decided to follow a way differing from reality as currently interpreted and lived through various institutional expressions. The temptation in the desert, when Jesus had to determine the specific way in which he would live out his ministry, must be understood in this light.

The first way offered Jesus by the existing powers and principalities personified in the devil was to exercise a ministry that would be primarily economic in its expression. As Jesus experienced hunger from his long fast he was approached with the words, "If you are the Son of God, command this stone to turn into bread" (Luke 4:3). Even though all four gospel writers would tell the dramatic story of Jesus' enabling thousands of people to have full access to the resource of bread to satisfy their hunger and even though he fulfilled his promise to provide bread for life everlasting (cf. John 6:51), Jesus was not to address his milieu in purely economic terms: "Doing the will of him who sent me and bringing his work to completion is my food" (John 4:34). Furthermore, neither would the ministry of his followers be identified in such economic terms. Jesus would later tell his disciples that they should work "for food that remains unto life eternal," identifying with the will of God by hungering for his justice (cf. Matt. 5:6). Thus Jesus resisted the effort of the powers and principalities to offer a purely economic base for the kingdom of God.

The second way offered Jesus by the devil was to exercise a ministry that would be primarily political in its character: "Then the devil took him up higher and showed him all the kingdoms of the world in a single instant. He said to him, 'I will give you all this power and glory of these kingdoms; the power has been given to me and I give it to whomever I wish. Prostrate yourself in homage before me, and it shall all be yours' " (Luke 4:5–7). Jesus would later directly contradict a similar declaration by another voice representing the powers and principalities with the words, "You would have no power over me whatever unless it were given you from above" (John 19:11); moreover he would reject both a popular declaration of himself as a political leader (cf. John 6:15; 12:15) and any effort to make himself one by the use of force (cf. Matt. 26:53). Nonetheless Jesus rejected all efforts to relate to his environment in purely political ways. Even though all power was given to him on heaven and on earth (cf. Matt. 28:18) and he shared this power with his followers (cf. Mark 3:15), he made it clear that the exercise of his followers' power would be quite different from that of the powers and principalities. It would be based on a reorientation of power so that the least would be the greatest and the last would be first. Thus, when his own followers tried to identify his use of power in terms used by their contemporaries, Jesus said:

> You know how those who exercise authority among the Gentiles lord it over them; their great ones make their importance felt. It cannot be like that with you. Anyone among you who aspires to greatness must serve the rest, and whoever wants to rank first among you must serve the needs of all. Such is the case with the Son

of Man who has come, not to be served by others, but to serve, to
give his own life as a ransom for the many (Matt. 20:25–28).

This lesson was reiterated continually throughout his ministry;
Jesus never stopped resisting the effort, begun in the desert, for a
purely political solution for the creation of the kingdom.

The final alternative offered Jesus was to exercise a ministry that
reinforced a mythical interpretation of religion that had little or
nothing to do with the concrete exigencies of daily life:

> Then the devil led him to Jerusalem, set him on the parapet of the
> temple, and said to him, "If you are the Son of God, throw yourself
> down from here, for Scripture has it, 'He will bid his angels watch
> over you'; and again, 'With their hands they will support you, that
> you may never stumble on a stone' " (Luke 4:9–11).

The religious message he offered would prove to be a stumbling
block for those locked into a mythical and ritualistic interpretation
of their religion (1 Cor. 1:23). He would also declare no further
need of the temple building as the center of reality, presenting
himself in its stead (John 2:19). Instead, his Spirit-filled members
were to become the temple wherein praise would be offered God.

Jesus continually resisted the temptation to deal with life by an
appeal to religious observance separated from the observance of
God's concern for the world. He asked those who lived this way,
"Why do you for your part act contrary to the commandment of
God for the sake of your tradition?" (Matt. 15:3), and said "for the
sake of your tradition you have nullified God's word" (Matt. 15:6).
Furthermore, Jesus warned his followers against imitating such a
form of ministry: "Be on the lookout against the yeast of the
Pharisees and Sadducees" (Matt. 16:6). Thus Jesus continually
resisted the effort of the powers and principalities to offer simplis-
tic, mythical, legalistic, or ritualistic ways of expressing religion.

As a result of prayer, Jesus left the desert successful in his
resistance to sin as it was offered him by the powers and principalities of his day. What he began in the desert he finished on the
cross, continually resisting efforts to seduce him. He remained
constant in this resistance even when the effort reached its supreme

attempt to control him through the cross. Just as in the desert Christ proclaimed, "Away with you, Satan!" (Matt. 4:10), so on the cross did "God disarm the principalities and powers. He made a public show of them and, leading them off captive, triumphed in the person of Christ" (Col. 2:15).

In prayerfully reflecting upon our world we discover the manifestations of the powers and principalities as much at work today as Jesus found in his desert experience. The 1971 Synod of Bishops stated that the situation of our world is one marked by the grave sin of injustice.[1] Resistance must be the way we deal with any grave sin, including the very evident grave sin of injustice as it expresses itself in "a network of domination, oppression and abuses."[2] With Jesus' Spirit leading us, we become enabled to resist as he did. "Draw your strength from the Lord and his mighty power," Paul reminds us. "Put on the armor of God so that you may be able to stand firm against the tactics of the devil. Our battle is not against human forces but against the principalities and powers, the rulers of this world of darkness, the evil spirits in regions above" (Eph. 6:10–12).

In our present world, marked by the grave sin of injustice that is systemic and institutionalized, what form do the powers and principalities take? Equally important, how do they come to approach us with temptation which we know we must resist?

Today the powers and principalities in our world of sin seem to be expressed primarily in the unity created among and within *institutions, isms,* and *ideology,* as the chart on p. 167 outlines. The pages to follow will attempt to explain how they operate.

We have shown earlier how movements evolve to the monument stage we call institutions. These institutions express themselves through many kinds of isms and are reinforced with an ideology that legitimizes both the institutions and the isms. The result of this we have called the infrastructure. It is also called social sin, or the grave sin of injustice that is manifested in a network of domination that denies the freedom of people to image God and the equality of people to share in the earth's resources. As Gregory Baum describes it, the infrastructure contains the institutions, "social processes" (isms), and ideologies that represent the sin of the world contradicting God's plan:

Sin resides not only in the free choices of individuals; it also and especially resides in people's corporate life. We are born into sin. Sin inheres in corporate life, i.e., in institutionalized life, in institutions that inflict injustices and oppression on people, in the social processes that build and protect these institutitions and in collective ideas and religious symbols that legitimate these institutions.[3]

Having considered the three levels of reality as individual, interpersonal, and systemic, we can now better understand how we must expand our notion of sin.

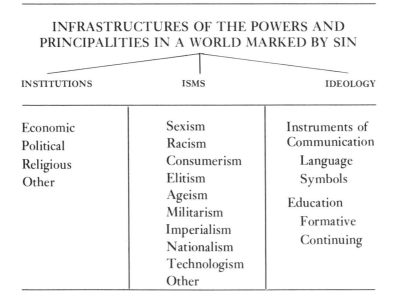

INFRASTRUCTURES OF THE POWERS AND PRINCIPALITIES IN A WORLD MARKED BY SIN

INSTITUTIONS	ISMS	IDEOLOGY
Economic Political Religious Other	Sexism Racism Consumerism Elitism Ageism Militarism Imperialism Nationalism Technologism Other	Instruments of Communication Language Symbols Education Formative Continuing

INSTITUTIONS AND SOCIAL SIN

Today we are evolving from a notion of sin related primarily to individual and group levels to include—as the pervasive reality infecting both (and reality as a whole)—the notion of social or environmental sin. Baum notes:

Social sin operates in institutions, even if the people involved in it have good intentions. In many activities of basic daily existence, we participate, whether we like it or not, in the social institutions of our society and hence derive some profit from the exploitation of other people. Personal sins compounded have created social sins, and conversely, social sins create an environment that promotes personal sins.[4]

Jesus was tempted by the economic, political, and religious infrastructures of his day. He resisted them and their efforts. The contemporary follower of Jesus must recognize the approach of the powers and principalities through the institutional expressions of reality as defined by the economic, political, and religious spheres of the present day, and try to resist them as well. Jesus was culturally conditioned to be part of a system that was based on division, and even though he broke through many of these, the social divisions of his society also influenced his outlook (cf. Luke 7:27). In our lives as well, many times we will find these infrastructures having subtle influence over us and our worldview, often without our realization. While we (and Jesus) may be individually without actual sin in such situations, this does not free us from the responsibility to unmask this sin of the world for what it is.

These three spheres of sin can frequently reinforce each other to such a degree that, in their expressions, there is little dissimilarity. The economic institutions are supported by the political and religious, the political by the economic and religious, and the religious by the economic and political. The religious institution is supported especially in the forms of contributions and tax exemptions. As a result the church in its institutional expression often does not speak against various forms of sin perpetuated by these other institutions. It becomes unable to practice in fact what it preaches in theory. It becomes compromised. In the words of Michele Cardinal Pellegrino of Turin:

> Often it is a link with economic and political power that prevents the church from speaking in complete frankness. . . . Silence, or diplomatic language in the pejorative sense of the word (which is perhaps worse than silence), is the price paid when the church does not know how to choose freedom, a choice which would obviously involve renunciation of the supports and privileges that later require a compensation.[5]

Jesus warned his followers that whoever followed him would be hated by the world because their message often could not be compromised with the vision of reality defined by the institutions of the world. Yet, as the movement of this message became a monument, we often find the ministry of his followers limited to institutional maintenance.

At times one goes so far as to see one's prime ministry in terms of the actual buildings, to the detriment of the far greater plan of God for the world. Such a possibility makes us painfully aware of the need for conversion on the part of the institution of the church. We need to evangelize the church that it might be free of the cultural addiction that has compromised its message and mission. As Stephen Cardinal Kim of Seoul declared at the 1974 Synod on Evangelization:

> When our church schools are taxed almost to extinction or taken over, when our churches are occupied or access to them denied or churchmen harassed or imprisoned, instant and loud protests of priests, bishops, and the laity make world news. But when men and women are oppressed, exploited and imprisoned simply because they struggle to exercise or defend fundamental human rights, when they are even denied just trial or defense, we church people are loath to get entangled in their cause. It would seem at times that we value more highly the temples of stone and wood than the temples of God which are living people.[6]

Support of policies and practices of economic and political institutions that reinforce an unequal distribution of resources and the denial of human rights has had its consequences. As a result, even well-meaning Christians are often unable to identify a call for a conversion from policies and practices that perpetuate such alienation and sin as relating to the gospel. If they have been taught another word which has never critiqued sin in its institutional expression, they are quite unable to believe such a Word can be of God when it is addressed to them. Thus, because they have accustomed themselves to living with the isms of the institutions, many Christians are literally unable to see how such social sins as racism, sexism, and militarism have anything to do with the church. Because Christians are unwilling to accept such realities as part of themselves, the calls for conversion made in pews and classrooms have often met with resistance. Thus, especially in the civil rights movement of the 1960s (because it proved bankrupt in its efforts to convince its own members to change), the institutional church experienced the necessity of calling for conversion as one institution to others. Church leaders were forced to go the civil rights route to Selma, Montgomery, Cicero, and Milwaukee because the people stationed in the pews would not move. When it was time to practice what was preached, the gap between the two, which had been allowed to exist in the name of peace, progress, and prosperity, proved to be so ingrained that the people *couldn't* move.

As the cause of civil rights was the issue of the 1960s, the issue of the right to life may be the cause of the 1970s and beyond. If the average Christian fails to become involved in ensuring the right to life for all people at all stages of human life, church leaders again will be forced to travel the economic and/or political route to insist on the rights of persons who might otherwise be denied access to the very resource of life. Since such resistance will be counter to existing interpretations of the law, the effort to ensure the right to life may begin the time of persecution of the religious institution by the economic and political institutions of our day. Already the response of the political structure—such as investigation of bulk mail permits of groups trying actively to work to resist the Supreme Court ruling—may be a first indication of what can be expected from the world if Jesus' community will remain faithful to his teaching about the sharing of resources and the promotion of human rights.

ISMS IN INSTITUTIONS AND IDEOLOGIES

Since in our society major institutions support each other and reinforce each other's goals, varying degrees of all isms of society can be found in all its institutions. Given the influence of the infrastructures on ideology, there is a resulting tendency to rationalize these sins as tolerable, if not actual graces. There are five isms in particular that Americans ought to be attempting to eradicate from their institutions and the ideology that reinforces them if they are to be faithful to the spirit of Jesus' unique vision in their own histories. The five to be discussed briefly here are sexism, elitism, racism, militarism, and consumerism.

Sexism. The same institutionalized violence that has systemically kept women in low-paying jobs and out of leadership in political and economic institutions can be found in other institutions, including those called religious. This includes the very Roman congregation that deals with religious life and secular institutions; its members are primarily men, although the majority of institutions with which it deals are composed of women. Of the Vatican's 3,000 employees, 250 are estimated to be women, up in 1977 from fewer than a dozen in 1967. While almost half of these are in the Curia, the ban on women priests of 1977 also bars women from any executive or decision-making post.

Throughout history, in almost every culture, women have had their reality (images and resources) defined for them by men. Such institutional sins of sexism are reinforced by an ideology that borders on idolatry. The English language is not as sexist in its words as a language like Chinese, whose ideograms include three women together to mean "noisiness" and "badness" and one woman under a roof to mean "peace." Yet our language is such that women must continually go beyond male-dominated words to discover their identity in books, sermons, the news, and the media.

Sexism is the ism that affects more people in the world than any other. It extends so far as to evidence a historical pattern of cultures, even naming God in terms that reflect the control of infrastructures by males. Some claim that culturally conditioned arguments appeal to God as "Father." We forget that Jesus, too, was influenced by the infrastructures of his day, which influenced his choosing of men as apostles. Yet God, who is beyond infrastructural influence, chose a woman to make Christ present in the world—which, we are often told, is the purpose of the priest.

Elitism. In the economic and political institutions of our day, elitism takes expression as positions of leadership are often passed on to family members generation after generation. A "ruling class" is created that systemically denies access to power to any except those born into the class or with enough financial backing to become accepted by the class.

Until the 1960s elitism expressed itself in the U.S. Catholic church through leadership exercised by bishops of a predominantly Irish background. In the majority of male congregations with priests, leadership has been allowed only to the priests (with some exceptions for the newer congregations). Yet, in a world divided by class, the Franciscans ("Little Brothers") were founded to witness to a "community of equality" and be free of any thoughts or actions that divide the community according to class.[7] With all people needing some form of equality in order to image God and have access to needed resources, Francis insisted to Cardinal Ugolino that his followers should not be in situtations that would make them *majores*, or elites:

> "Lord, my brothers are called *minors* so that they will not presume to become greater. Their vocation teaches them to remain in a lowly station and to follow the footsteps of the humble Christ, so that in the end they may be exalted above the rest in the sight of the saints. If," he said, "you want them to bear fruit for the church of God, hold them and preserve them in the station to which they have been called, and bring them back to a lowly station, even if they are unwilling. I pray you, therefore, Father, that you by no means permit them to rise to any prelacy, lest they become prouder rather than poorer and grow arrogant like the rest."[8]

A similar form of elitism, though lessening due to declining vocations to the priesthood, is the interpretation of church ministries in terms of clerical models. Somehow ministry is seen as limited to clerics, with laypeople being able to share in ministry through the clerics vicariously. Instead of basing the profession and practice of ministry on baptism and its call to all to mission, it is still linked to the priesthood and to the person; laypeople share in ministry through the "priesthood of the faithful."

While there may be grounds for linking ministry to priesthood if the ministry is cultic-related, the deputation to preach the gospel, to enhance the image of God in all, and to call for a just sharing of the earth's resources is the duty of all Christians by baptism and confirmation and their exercise of the Spirit's charisms. Yet, as long as financial considerations determine (in practice if not profession) priorities in parishes, schools, campuses, and chanceries, and as long as such monies are controlled by one class, ministry will tend to be determined according to principles that unconsciously reinforce the exercise of ministry by that class. Such a misuse of authority should be resisted as a violation of the vocation all have as members of the body of Christ (cf. 1 Cor. 12).

Racism. It has often been said that racism is the most pervasive sin in American society. It is a condition that pervades every institution within the nation and from which religious institutions are not exempt. While professing equality of opportunity among the races (and sexes) by legislation, the infrastructures of our society deny equality of results by systemic discrimination. While professing human rights for all in State Department speeches, America has systemically supported the racist regime of South Africa, even vetoing in the United Nations efforts of most of the world community to bring it to conversion through condemnations and sanctions. While professing to "better" the peoples of the developing nations, U.S. economic institutions enter these mostly nonwhite nations to advance the goals of the corporation without equal consideration being given to enable people systemically denied power over their resources to become controllers of them.

Today nonwhites might be seen as replacing the lepers of Francis's day—a group systemically denied access to full participation in the community, rejected on the basis of their skin. Though people of Hispanic background are a quarter of the U.S. Catholic church, there are less than a dozen Spanish-speaking bishops in the country. With the church acting as a historical domesticator of nonwhites in America and across the continent, Americans live with the reality of racism showing even in language such as that of the Northern Cheyenne, whose word for "*priest*" means "white man who stands between us and God."

Racism is manifest on individual levels through such forms of rejection as name-calling and on infrastructural levels through discrimination. When even these open forms are not always evident, we must be on the alert to resist racism's latent, subtle forms. These hide within prejudices that create "we" and "they" and on infrastructural levels meld into alienation or a sense of feeling out of the mainstream.

Whether it is sexism, elitism, racism, ageism, or some other ism, we need to realize how even conscientious Christians are influenced by the isms of the infrastructures to perpetuate prejudices and inequality of opportunity and of results. If it is true that the Lord's Prayer reflects a desire to build on earth the heavenly city, then no humans can be denied their right to image God by having access to whatever resources they need to bring their lives and personalities to fulfillment. Having discussed the above isms as violations of God's image in all, we now can deal with two isms—militarism and consumerism—which affect the way the world's resources will be shared.

Militarism. A militaristic society tends to solve problems in a military manner as a result of a concentration on arms, with its concomitant heightened fear and suspicion. Military personnel have a disproportionate influence in decision-making (which can lead to war), and budgetary considerations give first priority to the military. This is reflected in the United States where roughly half of every federal budget dollar is spent on military-related programs. It is evidenced by United States foreign policy, which finds 60 percent of every foreign aid dollar going for military-related expenditures, even under such programs as "Food for Peace." With entire communities throughout the nation relying on the arms race for their economic health, cities like St. Louis, Seattle, and Fort Worth become dependent on industries that maintain peoples' mutual suspicions and alienation around the world. This militarism manifests the effectiveness of the powers and principalities in our nation, which, Pope Paul VI declared, may rationalize such sin in the ideology of religion, to the detriment of peace (cf. Eph. 6:14). Linking both the political and the economic institutions into this grave sin of injustice, he stated (in language stronger than any I've used in this book!):

> Violence returns to fashion and even vests itself in the breastplate of justice. It becomes a way of life abetted by treacherous evil-doing in all its components and by all the wiles of cowardice, extortion and complicity; it stands out like an apocalyptic spectre armed with incredible tools of murderous destruction.
>
> Collective selfishness comes to life again in the family, society, tribe, nation and race. Crime no longer horrifies. Cruelty becomes inevitable, like the cutting edge of a hatred which has been declared

legitimate. Genocide is proposed as a monstrous possibility for a radical solution. And behind these horrible visions looms the gigantic armaments economy with its cold-blooded, unerring calculations and its greedy markets. Thus politics resumes its irrevocable power programs.

And peace?[9]

As a way of resisting the militarism in the society surrounding the early church, no member of the community was allowed to bear arms. Creative ways can be explored to effect institutional conversion from a military economy to a peace economy, conversion from a form of prior institutionalized violence that keeps people alienated and mistrustful and often causes acts of physical violence on individual and group levels.

Consumerism. Possibly the most serious ism influencing almost all people in the United States is consumerism. This was noted in an editorial column in a 1975 issue of the *Wall Street Journal* entitled "Getting off the Treadmill." Reflecting on thoughts that Amitai W. Etzioni had shared with political and economic leaders at a Columbia University seminar the *Journal's* columnist stated:

> What is at stake is the central project of our society, which seems to be that our society operates on a principle of the production of resources during working-hours and the consumption and destruction of them in leisure times. Americans work hard to play hard, earn more to spend more, drive themselves to drive their cars, producing and consuming in an ever-intensifying cycle that keeps gobbling up a growing portion of the earth's limited resources.
>
> It wasn't always thus, the professor reminds us. Other societies had other central projects. Ancient Sparta made war its central project. Some medieval societies ordered their activities around the cultivation of the arts and learning. In the golden age of Greece, politics was the central project.
>
> What's different now is that the central project involves the masses, whereas in the past perhaps 2 percent of the society was directly involved in the central pursuit while the masses subsisted as serfs. Now, we are all out there producing and consuming hard every day, executives and steelworkers alike, doing the proper American thing of filling our production quotas and sales goals so that we can fill our gas tanks, vacation homes and two-car garages.[10]

Probably unwittingly, the *Wall Street Journal* writer was indicating how consumerism exemplifies social sin and institutionalized departure from God's plan. He concluded his column with a question all must ask: "Is it sillier to think that six percent of the world's people can indefinitely go on consuming a third of its energy and other resources, than to think that millions upon millions of Americans will find ways to jump off the accelerating production-consumption treadmill?"[11]

Because it seems that America's huge corporations think it is easier to believe both than to make decisions that will systemically enable the disfranchised to participate in power, the top one hundred corporations spend over $4 billion a year to influence public opinion to preserve the acceleration of the treadmill.

If consumerism has become the central project of our society, it has become *the* idol—for whatever is most important in our lives will be our god. "The unbelievers of this world are always running after these things," Jesus warned in Luke (12:30). In this passage from Luke we also find today's obsession with consumerism linked to covetousness (12:13–21) and anxiety (12:22–31). Realizing the temptation continually seducing his followers to create a lifestyle controlled by this "god of the more," Jesus offered a new way to insure true security: "Do not live in fear, little flock. It has pleased your Father to give you the kingdom. Sell what you have and give alms. Get purses for yourselves that do not wear out, a never-failing treasure with the Lord which no thief comes near nor any moth destroys. Wherever your treasure lies, there your heart will be" (Luke 12:32–34). Few people, if any, who pray contemplatively (or with the prayer of the heart) are consumerists. Their security is in another part of reality. Their lifestyle reflects the quality of their authentic religious experience.

IDEOLOGY AS REINFORCING
INSTITUTIONS AND ISMS

Consumerism is reinforced by an ideology which has many people equating its various forms with God's blessing (cf. Luke 12:19). This fact reveals it as an ideology, or belief-system, that undergirds all isms and institutions. This ideology is forwarded through the communications media and education promoted by the institutions to facilitate their self-serving interpretation of reality. The institutional realities are economic, political, and religious. The ideological realities are the instruments of communication and education. How they interrelate has been clearly outlined by Donald Gaudion, a past head of the National Association of Manufacturers. Gaudion draws five boxes arranged in a circle, naming them technology-economic, media, government, religion, and education. In our environment, all relate to and depend upon each other. "One falls," Gaudion notes, "and another is damaged."[12]

At their monument level, institutions in American society differ little from each other in their way of operating. They try to perpetuate themselves and allegiance to their vision of reality by means of their own ideologies through the instruments of communication (publications, press, radio-television, etc.) and education. The education they provide serves as both integration to the uninitiated and ongoing formation for reinforcement. With education and the communications media serving as the two main arms of ideology, their interconnectedness often evidences social sin and the manifestation of the powers and principalities. It reflects the attempt to try to tempt humans into submission to worldviews countering God's plan for history. As the Synod of Bishops stated in their document on justice, "The school and the communications media, often obstructed by the established order, allow the formation only of the man desired by that order, that is to say, man in its image—not a new man, but a copy of man as he is."[13] When this happens, Paul wrote centuries ago to the Romans, the truth of God is hindered by such injustice because the image of God and God's truth has been exchanged for mere human images. It is a lie (cf. Rom. 1:19–25).

A political institution like the Soviet Union uses ideology to define reality in such a way that anyone offering another image based on a different sharing of resources or promoting another kind of image of human beings is often termed insane.[14] A politico-economic institution such as that in South Africa is able to view racism in terms of psychological normalcy. This was evidenced in a 1974 news release that stated, "An 11-year-old South African black child, who was roasted by three white railway workers, is to receive psychiatric treatment to try to cure him of his fear of whites."[15] Yet sanity and insanity have ideological connotations in our society as well, especially when some try to call the institutions and people controlled by their worldview to conversion.

An economic institution that spends $400 million annually on television advertising aimed at children is able to create consumption patterns that easily affect lifestyle patterns of entire families. The average American adult sees 40,000 commercials a year on television. Creating advertising to influence the viewer has but one goal in mind: a modern-day form of enslavement that should make us cry with the Israelites for deliverance. In the words of the Administrative Board of the United States Catholic Conference, "What American commercial television is all about is not primarily either information or entertainment, neither news nor culture. Its primary objective is to create a meeting place for consumers and advertisers. American television is essentially concerned with *the sale of consumers to advertisers.*"[16]

The communications media, especially television, whether controlled by political, economic, or even religious institutions, is recognized as a primary influence on the formation of public mores and behavior. The influence of the media in forming mindsets and even consciences is so great that in 1974 ITT, after revelations of its involvement in an effort to keep Salvador Allende from power in Chile and to influence antitrust legislation against it in the United States, spent $6.4 million in a media campaign to enhance itself in the public's estimation. Within a year its effort paid off with an increase from 20 percent to 43 percent of the numbers of people polled who viewed ITT as a company that cared about people.[17] Yet, never once during this period did ITT admit the truth of its involvement in Chile. The people could be seduced to believe in (trust) ITT through the media. The people, ITT realized, could be bought as well as sold.

With American institutions concentrated in power, the links between institutions, isms, and ideologies must be seen in light of distributive justice. This is particularly evident in the case of the economic and political institutions, as well as the ideological institutions of learning and the media which reinforce this control over power and wealth. According to Richard Barnet and Ronald Müller:

> There is also an intimate and necessary connection between growth and concentration. In a world dominated by oligopolistic competition, the quest for the one leads inevitably to the other. The result is that managerial control of the technology, the finance capital, and the instruments for developing and disseminating ideology rest in a few hundred individuals. The principal decision makers in the 200 top industrial corporations and the 20 largest banks, which control such a huge proportion of the nation's wealth and its capacity to produce wealth, number fewer than a thousand persons. These individuals are the planners of our society.[18]

An example of how institutions, isms, and ideologies reinforce each other and must, therefore, be resisted as manifestations of the powers and principalities can be found in the efforts of members of the Interfaith Center on Corporate Responsibility. The Capuchin-Franciscans were among this ecumenical group that began exploring some of the domestic and foreign practices of IBM during the mid-1970s, the isms related to those practices, and the ideology involved in the instruments of communication. How, it might be asked, did they interrelate?

As of 1975, ten of IBM's twenty-four board members also sat on the boards of six top New York banks. These six New York banks held 13.3 percent of IBM's outstanding shares in their trust departments. This constitutes effective control of the corporation, according to U.S. government statistics.[19] At the same time, these six New York banks (finance capital) that had over 13 percent control of IBM (technology) also held (as of 1973) 5.5 percent of NBC, 27 percent of CBS, and 29 percent of ABC (instruments for developing and disseminating ideology). Thus institutions and ideology were united in problems dealing with isms in IBM: domestic issues of hiring practices for women and minorities (sexism and racism) as well as cumulative voting (elitism), and foreign issues related to hiring practices (sexism and racism) as well as sales to the South African government (racism and militarism).[20]

Events that took place in late 1976 and early 1977, with the ascendancy of Jimmy Carter to the United States' presidency, indicated a further connection between the banks, corporations, education, the media, and government. Both Carter and Walter F. Mondale belonged to the Trilateral Commission. This group includes representatives from the United States, Japan, and Western Europe who generally agree that these three actors must work together to promote their common concerns in face of the Eastern European, Third World, and OPEC nations.

According to former *New York Times* diplomatic correspondent, Leslie H. Gelb, the members of the Trilateral Commission are part of the "Community" whose elite "comprise some 300 professors, lawyers, businessmen, congressional aides, foundation executives, thinktank experts and even some journalists."[21]

A significant number of people from it and the Council on Foreign Relations (both founded by David Rockefeller) were picked by Carter and Mondale for top policy-making government positions, including Paul Warnke, Zbigniew Brzezinski, and W. Michael Blumenthal. According to Gelb, they represent

> part of a small floating group that comes close to monopolizing the top foreign and national security posts in the administration. Known as the foreign policy community, it does not operate as a club of the like-minded or a conspiracy or a governing board. It acts more like an aristocracy of professionals. Its members sometimes actually make the decisions, usually define what is to be debated and invariably manage the resulting policies.[22]

Gelb should know. When he wrote these words he did so as a *New York Times* diplomatic correspondent. He also was a member of the Council on Foreign Relations. Within two months of this article, however, he was appointed by Carter to the State Department to direct its Bureau of Foreign and Military Operations. Other members of the Trilateral Commission were also selected for Carter administration posts.

As for IBM and its "Trilateral Connection," Carter chose nearly one-fourth of IBM's outside directors for his cabinet: Cyrus Vance of the State Department, Harold Brown of Defense, and Patricia Roberts Harris of HUD—all members of the Council on Foreign Relations.

Vance and Brown (who also belonged to the Trilateral Commission) were not to be the only IBMers to advise Carter. In addition, Griffin Bell's Atlanta law firm represented the company in Georgia—and the Justice Department which he was named to head began an antitrust suit against IBM in 1969 because of its alleged monopolistic practices. While Bell excused himself from the case, his Atlanta law firm partner, Charles Kirbo, was picked as a Carter advisor. Another law firm, representing IBM interests in the West, found one of its partners, Warren Christopher, in the Carter administration as Undersecretary of State. Dr. Louis Branscomb, Science Advisor to Carter, was an IBM vice-president and chief of its technology.

Such was the influence of people from IBM—whose basic values and goals reflected those underlying the Carter government—that *Forbes Magazine* would headline a pre-inauguration article: "Jimmy Carter's Computer Connection," and state, "No question about it; the new Administration will have a strong IBM tone. Two other individuals linked to the company were near misses: du Pont Chairman Irving Shapiro, an IBM director, took himself out of the running for Secretary of Treasury; and IBM Vice President Jane Cahill Pfeiffer turned down an offer to be Secretary of Commerce."[23]

The revolving doors through which top IBM personnel entered government under Carter returned to the company former IBM officials who had left the company to direct government posts under Gerald Ford. After the inauguration, T. Vincent Learson and William W. Scranton were reseated on IBM's Board of Directors after serving as high administrative officials. They were joined on the Board by William T. Coleman, Jr., former Secretary of Transportation, and Carla Anderson Hills, the Secretary of Housing and Urban Development in Ford's Cabinet.

Despite the connections of many people in top government positions to companies like IBM and groups such as the Trilateral Commission, the Council on Foreign Relations, and the U.S. Council of the Americas, there is no real evidence of conspiracy, as

Gelb, Müller and Barnet note. Yet, the "network of domination" that we have seen as synonymous with the infrastructure does become clearer. The policymakers in government—who often are the directors of our large banks and who also sit on the boards of the largest transnational corporations, of the principal schools, and of print and electronic disseminators of ideology—are not consciously conspiring to harm human beings. Yet the fact that they tend to remain secret about and often control information regarding their policies and practices does not help in their efforts to achieve credibility and understanding from the average American. Neither does the fact that they are often unwilling to provide others access to information about their operations. As a result, even with very good intentions on the part of individuals, the basic ordering and relationships of power and wealth remain unchanged. The infrastructure continues intact.

In face of such a manifestation of the powers and principalities, we are called to a life of resistance which should enable us to "accept the insecurity of institutions and of ideas."[24] It should also create the kind of pedagogy that is needed for the future in our world. Since education is another way of translating ideologies, our pedagogy should be reinforced with the teachings of Christ rather than that of the institutions about us.

Through education, the power of institutions has been able to create general adherence and support of the principles and policies that keep them in operation through the effort of loyal members. Yet, when institutions portray attitudes that are not in keeping with the values and ideals upon which they were founded, their education does not tend to call for a conversion back to the original values and ideals. Rather, it reinforces the present norms and traditions, which have become institutionalized, and promotes conformity to them. Thus, "the method of education very frequently still in use today encourages narrow individualism," the Synod of Bishops stated in 1971. Instead it should be helping people "to be no longer the object of manipulation by communications media or political forces."[25]

Today, our pedagogy can do one of two things: either facilitate an integration into the present way in which reality is defined and lived in our world—marked by the grave sin of social injustice—or offer resistance to this sin by promoting an alternative definition of reality. This alternative education would be based on the scriptural demand for a just distribution of resources and the promotion of inalienable rights of human beings created in God's image. Such an education would enable people to be "led out" *(educare)* from the temptation of sin, as the words quoted below indicate. These words (which might well be placed above the entrance of every learning center, in the textbooks and materials of every study/reflection group, and in the heart of every communicator of God's word) form the basis upon which a truly alternative educational system and approach can be based. According to the 1971 Synod of Bishops:

> Education demands a renewal of heart, a renewal based on the recognition of sin in its individual and social manifestations. It will also inculcate a truly and entirely human way of life in justice, love and simplicity. It will likewise awaken the critical sense that will lead us to reflect on the society in which we live and on its values; it will make men ready to renounce these values when they cease to promote justice for all.[26]

Until now, the manner of education promoted by most of us within our own formation programs as well as our own schools has tended to respond to the first two levels of human life—the individual and the interpersonal. The result has been a successful educational approach, which, in turn, has received support and reinforcement from the surrounding society. However, as the bishops indicate, an education or formation that does not deal with the third level and its infrastructures has little to offer our world as a truly gospel-based methodology. "Accordingly," they conclude, "educational method must be such as to teach men to live life in its entire reality and in accord with the evangelical principles of personal and social morality which are expressed in a vital Christian witness."[27] Any effort to limit our education and formation to a purely individual- or community-oriented style must be resisted as inadequate to deal with the reality of our world.

Jesus resisted the effort of the powers and principalities of his day to control his ministry by shaping it according to then-current economic, political, and religious interpretations of reality. In good part, Luke shows, Jesus resisted this temptation as a result of his prayer. Similarly, as a result of our prayer, wherein we meet the Lord of history revealing himself, his concerns, and his will for our world, we are confirmed in our effort to resist the powers and principalities of our day as they approach us through the sins of our institutions, isms, and ideologies. The effectiveness of the powers and principalities cannot be underestimated. Even though they have already been conquered, the war is not yet over.

Their influence will make it difficult to understand and implement God's will in our lives (cf. Wisd. 9:13). God's will can never be found totally articulated on any level of reality. It can only be discovered by those who pray for it (Wisd. 9:17) in the midst of temptation, as did Jesus in the Garden. Through this prayer we come to believe that God's creative plan, which is identified as his will, and the thoughts of his heart, which remain forever (cf. Ps. 33:11), are not only quite different from those of the powers and principalities (cf. Prov. 19:21); they are within our heart where we discover the chance to be identified with God's will in history. This is why Francis wanted his followers always to pray with pure hearts.

To pray with pure hearts results from having God's covenant, rather than society's apathy and alienation, written on our hearts of flesh (cf. Jer. 31). Purity of heart, gained in prayerful participation in the community that is God, helps us to be strengthened by God's Spirit in our ministry. It will help us heal the hardness of heart in individuals and groups that are made so, often without realizing it, by the social sin that envelops them and keeps them from conversion. Francis called this condition "the Babylonian stuff" that "will generate an abiding rust in the heart."[28] William Stringfellow aptly describes it as

> the impairment or loss of moral discernment; the incapacity to hear, though one has ears; or to see, though one has eyes (e.g., Mark 8:14–21). I refer, thus, not so much to an evil mind as to a paralyzed conscience; not so much to either personal or corporate immorality as to a social pathology possessing persons and institutions; not so much to malevolence, however incarnate, as to the literal *demoralization* of human life in society.[29]

Perhaps Stringfellow's explanation is a twentieth-century application of what St. Paul meant when he wrote to the Ephesians, "our battle is not against human forces but against the principalities and powers" (Eph. 6:12). It is not so much dealing with what we can see—the human forces of the individual and interpersonal levels—but with what is not seen—the environmental, the social, the institutionalized and systematized *manifestations of original sin*. This is the way the powers and principalities, the diabolical forces of our day, try to lead us into temptation.

One of the ways we can do battle with them and resist their effort to immobilize us into subservience and obeisance to ways that "are not my ways" (Isa. 55:8) is to call for social responsibility within economic and political institutions and so eliminate the isms of society. Yet any resistance, coming with our call for such responsibility, cannot be limited to a gospel addressed only to the economic and political institutions; it must be addressed to our religious institutions as well. They too stand in need of conversion. They too need evangelization: "While the Church is bound to give witness to justice," the 1971 Synod of Bishops declared, "she recognizes that anyone who ventures to speak to people about justice must first be just in their eyes. Hence we must undertake an examination of the modes of acting, and of the possessions and lifestyle found within the Church itself."[30]

Our lifestyle, then, becomes one of resistance, identified with that of Christ who resisted the temptation to be conformed to his world and who prayerfully determined that his ministry would enable people to be liberated from the sin of the world. Having been led out of temptation himself, he would give his life to deliver the world from evil.

10

. . . *Deliver Us from Evil*

To better understand this second part of the last petition of the Our Father, it might be good to recall the Latin version of the *Pater Noster*. During the liturgy, the priest would chant all but this last part of the Lord's Prayer. The people would conclude: *sed libera nos a malo*. If there is any prayer that should be on our lips, after our previous reflections on the other parts of the Lord's Prayer, it should be an ongoing plea to be delivered from seduction by our world of sin: *libera nos, Domine*, liberate us, Lord. These words, found only in Matthew's version of the Our Father, seem best understood in their direct relation to the petition immediately preceding it: "Lead us not into temptation."

Deliverance from evil, or liberation, is the opposite of being led into sin. Liberation, or deliverance, resulted from the Jews' being led out of temptation in the desert. Jesus began a ministry of liberation from every kind of sin, enslavement, and oppression when the Spirit who had led him into the desert brought him out. This same lifestyle of liberation reflected in prayer and ministry should mark our lives. It should flow naturally from our continual effort to promote the liberation of human beings, to resisting the effort of the powers and principalities to lead us into temptation. Deliverance from false kinds of enslavement—from freedom and happiness as defined by the powers and principalities—was what Christ prayed for his community: "I gave them your word, and the world has hated them for it; they do not belong to the world. I do not ask you to take them out of the world, but to guard them from the evil" (John 17:14–15).

If we reflect on the way God deals with his people throughout history, delivering them from evil, a pattern seems to evolve that requires the formation of basic communities whose style of life is based on a conscientization process. This process includes an ongoing reflection on any and all enslavements that affect the community as well as all those elements that can empower it. The other side of the conscientization process adds the element of faith wherein we "write history" by identifying how we can continue creation's purposes of sharing the earth's resources and realizing God's image in all people. The atmosphere in which the community continually goes through this conscientization process is one of prayerful conversion, not only for itself and its individual members, but on behalf of the entire world.

This pattern of liberation from evil seems to take place whenever people gather together to reflect on how they can be more closely identified with the Lord's purposes in history. It takes place in small discussion gatherings, basic communities, religious communities, priests' support groups, in classrooms and prayer groups—wherever people take seriously the effort to create a way of life reflective of that of the Trinity itself.

How can this pattern be outlined? Its three major dimensions of *community, conscientization,* and *conversion* include steps that are essential to the overall process. These steps, which are interdependent, include: (1) a gathering of people with unique gifts forming community; (2) a reflection on their individual, group, and environmental enslavements; and (3) a realization of their individual, group, and environmental empowerments. This reading of their reality enables them to see that they can (4) co-create history in the two ways that have been stressed throughout this book: by sharing resources of all kinds and by promoting the divine image in every person, approaching every person as a subject rather than an object. The atmosphere in which these steps are made involves (5) a continual conversion of minds, morals, and spirituality.

If this indicates the way God related to his people and continues to relate to us—always leading us out of evil—we must investigate these steps within themselves and determine how they relate to being led out of temptation. If we are to apply this pattern of liberation from evil as an ongoing lifestyle in our prayer and ministry, we can never forget that it results from living in a world marked by the grave sin that manifests the pervasive presence of our contemporary powers and principalities. The chart on p. 189 should help make the connection to show how "deliverance from evil" is an ongoing process of resistance to the ways we are "led into temptation" by the infrastructures. It becomes the outline for an action-reflection model that can be used to structure a new kind of movemental Christianity.

COMMUNITY: THE GATHERING OF GIFTS

The first element involved in liberation is the gathering of people for the formation of community. Not as the world interprets and forms community does the God of history form community. Since any community formed by God reflects its maker, all real community has to be participative. It is a gathering of people with unique gifts into a community existing to reflect the Godhead. True community is a "gathered" community of unique people, not a mere collection of isolated individuals. A gathered community identifies with a common purpose. Thus, "where two or three are gathered *in my name*, there am I in their midst" (Matt. 18:20). When any group of people come together in the name of the Lord of history, their individuality and their fragmented groups give way to the task with which the name of God has been identified in revelation: liberation. As Yahweh revealed his name in the process of liberation by forming a gathered community (cf. Exod. 4:11–14), Jesus' name reveals a God acting in history to liberate people from their sin (cf. Matt. 1:21) and a God who will form a community based on baptism in the name (cf. 28:19). Thus, whenever people gather together in his name, they gather to be identified with his reasons for revealing his name—for liberation from all that profanes that name, from sin and enslavement of any type.

Within each community gathered in the name there should exist a "liberated area in history." By being faithful to the meaning of his

HOW POWERS AND PRINCIPALITIES IN THE INFRASTRUCTURES "LEAD US INTO TEMPTATION"

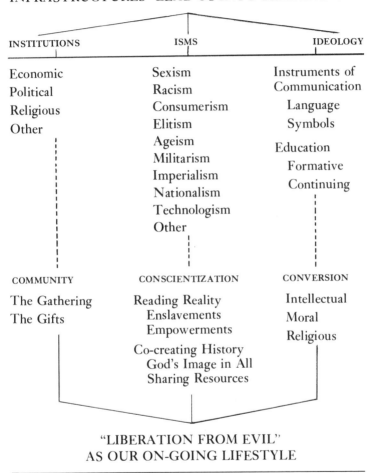

INSTITUTIONS	ISMS	IDEOLOGY
Economic	Sexism	Instruments of Communication
Political	Racism	
Religious	Consumerism	Language
Other	Elitism	Symbols
	Ageism	
	Militarism	Education
	Imperialism	Formative
	Nationalism	Continuing
	Technologism	
	Other	

COMMUNITY	CONSCIENTIZATION	CONVERSION
The Gathering	Reading Reality	Intellectual
The Gifts	Enslavements	Moral
	Empowerments	Religious
	Co-creating History	
	God's Image in All	
	Sharing Resources	

"LIBERATION FROM EVIL" AS OUR ON-GOING LIFESTYLE

name, people, Jesus declared, could come within his presence at any time and find their freedom. "Today [now] this Scripture passage is fulfilled in your hearing [here]" (Luke 4:21); this was the platform for his ministry. Thus, wherever and whenever we allow the Word of God to take root in our lives and to be revealed in us, we have the opportunity to create a liberated area in history.

God gathered the elders (cf. Exod. 4:16) that they might be instruments of the Hebrews' liberation. Jesus gathered his disciples (cf. Mark 1:15) that they might identify with his name (cf. Matt. 7:22) in freeing people from their enslavements and offering them good news. Those same disciples gathered together, reflecting on their fears and anxieties in the Upper Room, and were able to discover themselves as a community empowered by the Spirit to bring healing to the world through this name (cf. Acts 3:16). In light of this, it should be the goal of every gathering of our various communities to reflect on the ways God is calling us, here and now, to be instruments of our individual, communal, and global liberation.

In response, then, to the institutionalization that pervades our lives, we come together to experience ourselves as participative communities, as basic communities nourished by the support, values, and ideals as well as gifts of our individual members. We each come to our various gatherings in his name, to use our gifts for the service or freedom of our co-members, so that by the common sharing of our lives we may offer a larger, more significant gift of freedom to our world. Our individual gifts or charisms come to us from God's spirit to build up the community of the total body. "To each person the manifestation of the Spirit is given for the common good," Paul writes of our individual gifts (1 Cor. 12:7). Because of the gifts and ministries of its individual members, the body as community is able to offer a gift and ministry to institutions, to structures, to the world.

If through our prayer and ministry we are to exist as liberated communities, as participative support groups, then we begin to see that, precisely as communities, we have a gift and ministry to share with the world. We have a common gift and ministry that we exercise through our corporate charism and service. In the case of religious life, it itself becomes charism.[1]

The world of the thirteenth century experienced not only the gift and ministry of Francis, but of his followers as well. Celano tells us their individual charisms and service were united in basic communities existing in the world with a corporate charism for its liberation:

> Many of the people, both noble and ignoble, cleric and lay, impelled by divine inspiration, began to come to St. Francis, wanting to carry on the battle constantly under his discipline and under his leadership. All of these the holy man of God, like a plenteous river of heavenly grace, watered with streams of gifts; he enriched the field of their hearts with flowers of virtue, for he was an excellent craftsman; and, according to this plan, rule, and teaching, proclaimed before all, the Church is being renewed in both sexes, and the threefold army of those to be served is triumphing. To all he gave a norm of life, and he showed in truth the way of salvation in every walk of life.[2]

As communities we exist to evangelize the church, to humanize creation, and to preach the gospel to the whole world (cf. Matt. 28:16). We are able to be a sign to all of these by our prayer and ministry manifested in a realistic lifestyle so that, like the early community, we may live as "true followers of justice"[3] who have embraced "the delegation of peace."[4]

Thus, whenever (time) and wherever (place) we gather with others, we have the opportunity in the here and now to create a community that will be fruitful of freedom. The primacy of prayer and ministy that has freedom as its goal will have little or nothing to do with giving undue importance to structured times or physical places. In fact, we will try to be as free as possible from any temptations to "settle in" to norms and traditions that may frustrate our effort to continually pass over from institutions and structures that might lock us in, creating alienation. Community will be one of people, not one of place.

Because the formation of communities based on the equal sharing of our various resources and gifts is essential to our life, it becomes the gift we are best able to offer to others in our ministry. If by our gathering together in Jesus' name we are to reveal what creation should look like, it can be accomplished not by words, prayers, and symbols alone; it must be accompanied by our ministry as well. When we share with others the joy of membership in participative communities that are countersigns to the alienated and institutionalized collections of individuals about us, our ministry becomes "particularly sensitive to Christians who are confused about their faith, to men and women approaching faith, and to groups of Christians who, in different ways, wish to build and live in community."[5]

If in the here and now we are not attempting to create ourselves into participative communities and do not recognize that this should be the goal of whatever gatherings we enter, it will be difficult, if not impossible, to identify in prayer with God, exemplar of a true gathering of persons sharing all things in participative community. Further, as our ministry to the world is to be one of forming basic communities, of gathering together people to share all things in common (cf. Acts 2:42ff.), our prayer in the world must be formed by our experience of God. The community of God is constituted of unique persons who gather into themselves the reality of each other and reveal this to us. The participative community of the Trinity is composed of uniquely ingathered persons. This must be reflected in our ministry and prayer.

In our prayer we also become ingathered, or nearer to ourselves. By drawing nearer to myself, I am at the same time making it possible to participate more deeply in the reality of others and the world. According to Gabriel Marcel, I am a being-in-situation; my deeper contact with myself cannot be alienated from my deeper participation in my reality. To be ingathered in contemplation, one cannot be separated from a ministry aimed at ingathering all in Christ. "There can be no contemplation without a kind of inward regrouping of one's resources, or a kind of ingatheredness," Marcel wrote. This contemplation results from our effort to gather people into community and, in turn, reinforces this ministry: "To contemplate is to ingather oneself in the presence of whatever is being contemplated, and this in such a fashion that the reality, confronting which one ingathers oneself, itself becomes a factor in the ingathering."[6]

The result of contemplation and action is the same: to be liberated from alienation to participation, on a deeper level, in the community that is God and the world. This was the goal that Jesus prayed his followers would be able to achieve so that this result would become the real sign of God's presence in their lives and in the life of the world: "I do not pray for them alone," Jesus told the Father. "I pray also for those who will believe in me through their word, that all may be one as you, Father, are in me, and I in you; I pray that they may be [one] in us, that the world may believe you sent me" (John 17:20–21).

CONSCIENTIZATION: READING REALITY TO WRITE HISTORY

Jesus prayed for those who "through their word" would enable others to believe. We discover that the Word of God that has been addressed to our sin-marked world is essentially a liberating Word. Jesus entered his reality, controlled by the institutions, isms, and ideology of his day, and declared that it was his goal to take the world's sin away, to deliver it from those evils. He read his reality as needing liberation from all the enslavements of the powers and the principalities.

When people gather together, often the only thing they share in common is their fear, their alienation, their mistrust of each other and their reality, as well as their effort to protect themselves from manipulation or control from "the outside." As a result, the second task in being delivered from evil, after coming together as a gathering, is to become aware of common enslavements.

Whether people were suffering from physical enslavements that crippled them or made them blind, mental disturbances that alienated them from others, or psychological needs that limited them from truly discovering their real potential, Jesus realized that identification with God in prayer or ministry would be impossible if such pathologies controlled them. Jesus realized that his followers had to be healed from their pathologies and the pathology of the world if they were to unite with him in ministering God's liberation to history. Until people are willing to deal with their pathologies and enslavements, their sinful condition—be it self-inflicted or from one's community or environment—they cannot function effectively as a gathered people. Rather, they remain isolated bodies and mere collections of alienated beings, relating as individuals and as part of groups from a context of separation in all its various forms.

Even while stressing the effect of these enslavements on the levels of individuality and community, spirituality and asceticism have been ineffective to the degree that they have failed to take into account the "sin of the world": that is, the underlying pathology that infects both individuals and communities. Since this whole book has attempted to describe this form of sin and since the isms discussed in the previous chapter have a direct bearing on re-lationships among peoples that keep them separated, it should be our place here to lay greater stress on how we can be led out of these enslavements: *Libera nos a malo, Domine.*

Reading our reality, then, means becoming critical thinkers able to reflect on sin "in its individual and social manifestations."[7] At the same time this reading of reality should be done by people of faith, aware of grace "in its individual, group, and environmental manifestations" as well. Where sin abounds, grace—with all the new possibilities and hope that come with it—is able to abound the more (cf. Rom. 5:20). Both sin and grace elements were seen by Francis as contained in creative reality. Thus, Celano wrote, "with respect to *the world-rulers of this darkness*, he used it as a field of battle; with respect to God, he used it as a very bright *image* of his goodness."[8]

While an understanding of our enslavements (sin) is essential for any gathering, the third stage in God's delivering us from this evil involves an understanding of our empowerments (grace). In face of all the isms and alienations dividing people, the power of God's Spirit of love within us and all people calls us to a continued effort to achieve the breaking of all barriers that keep people unfree.

The two disciples walking with Jesus, burdened by the en-slavement that came with their sense of loss, powerlessness, and fear, were able to begin dealing with these alienations when he began to interpret for them those passages of Scripture that un-locked a sense of hope and power in their hearts (cf. Luke 24:25ff.). So too, the realization of the grace that is within us, in our com-munities, and in our world results from a faithful and critical reflection on our reality in light of the Scriptures. In read-

ing the Scriptures we discover that people controlled by their
enslavements who gathered to reflect on God's revelation—the
Hebrews under the Egyptians (cf. Exod. 3:16ff.) or the disciples in
the Upper Room (cf. Acts 1:13ff.)—were led to see themselves as
empowered to be free from their enslavements. They were led to
believe that God's freeing action in their histories meant he would
empower them to be free from any form of sin in order to be
identified with him through the grace of his Spirit. Belief in this
grace of God, supported in prayer and ministry, would make
possible a new creation, a new state of affairs.

To the enslaved Hebrews this new creation came in the form of
leaving Egypt and by praying and working for the promised land.
To the first disciples it came in the form of leaving all things that
they might pray and work for a new way of relating to each other
and the world. To the post-resurrection Christians it came in the
form of leaving the fear and isolation of the Upper Room, which
kept them separated from the world, that they might re-enter it
with good news. To Francis it meant leaving the militarism,
consumerism, and all the alienations of his day to begin a new way
of living, "daily filled with the consolation and the grace of the
Holy Spirit."[9]

Sin represents the effectiveness of the powers and principalities
to manipulate and control reality; through prayer we recognize its
futility in light of the primacy of God who brings about true
liberation from sin. As we recognize the powerlessness that is ours
before God, prayer enables us to discover our need to be totally
empowered by God.

Only through prayer did Francis realize how his community
would be empowered to enable all people to find access to God.
Celano writes:

> One day, when he was wondering over the mercy of the Lord with
> regard to the gifts bestowed upon him, he wished that the course of
> his own life and that of his brothers might be shown him by the
> Lord; he sought out a place of prayer, as he had done so often, and
> he persevered there for a long time *with fear and trembling* standing
> *before the Lord of the whole earth*, and he thought *in the bitterness of his*
> *soul* of the years he had spent wretchedly, frequently repeating this
> word: *O God, be merciful to me the sinner.*[10]

Francis's prayer, "O God be merciful to me the sinner," as well as his oft-repeated "My God and my All," were ways through which he established a creative rhythm in his life. This unique version of the "Jesus Prayer"[11] enabled him to become identified with the Lord of history and to be given over to the purposes the Lord wanted to accomplish in history through him. The fact that the Lord enabled him to have access to him as a resource forced Francis to share his prayer with others. As Celano writes, there was formed a *"partnership* between them in the *matter of giving and receiving"* such spiritual gifts.[12]

Francis's relation with the Lord of history gained through prayer empowered him to try to create in his community and in the world those conditions that reflected God's concerns. In a special way, poverty became as important an element in his ministry as it did in his prayer. He who could lay no claim to ownership of any spiritual resource could not claim ownership to resources of any other kind. As God intervened in history, empowering with his grace where there was enslavement, bringing liberation where there was oppression, reallocating resources where they were alienated, replacing idols with his image, so Francis envisioned the members of his community as committed to this good news. They could be committed—and effective—because the Holy Spirit was the source of their empowerment.[13] Whenever the former manifestations of sin existed, he and his followers tried to unite with God as co-creators of a new history, calling God's people to grace.

Our co-creation of history takes us, a spirit-gathered people, back to history's beginnings where we discover God's purposes for creation. In Genesis we discover that the original purpose of creation was to enable all people to have adequate access to the earth's resources. This was to enable all people to live in community as images of God. In God's participative community each person images the other. Each has equal access to the other's resources. The example of the Trinity becomes the fourth way we pattern our communities on the style the Lord has used in history: to become co-creators by the way we share resources and promote God's image.

By our share in the Spirit, given according to our need (cf. 1 Cor. 12), we become co-creators, called to work to make resources available to all others according to their need. Only if his followers would pray for this effect of the creative Spirit in their lives (cf. Rom. 8) and work to make it a reality, according to Francis, would they be able to share in God's resources as imaging God's Son. As a result of their prayer and ministry there had to be a better distribution of all their resources—from a mantle to the only Bible they might have in their possession—with those who had less, or else they could not image God to those made in God's image.

What Francis preached reflected what Jesus preached and what John the Baptizer and the prophets before them had preached: conversion from temptations and enslavements. Through conversion, a new way of living can begin. Conversion (along with community and conscientization) becomes the final step by which we can resist being led into temptation.

CONVERSION: INTELLECTUAL, MORAL, AND RELIGIOUS REFORM

All of us, in the here and now of our historical existence, have been formed by various individual, interpersonal, and environmental dimensions, creating each of us as unique persons. Inputs from these three dimensions of reality, in their varying degrees, have both enslaved and empowered us. They have contributed to a stance, the way we look at reality and live in reality, that indicates the degree of our identification with God as person in prayer and God's purposes in ministry. These experiences and inputs of our past and present both condition and limit our present and our future. They also condition and limit our openness to deciding to go beyond these boundaries to identify more closely with the Lord of history.

According to Bernard Lonergan, these boundaries indicate "horizons."[14] Horizons reflect each person's historical stance. These horizons are gained from knowledge and experience of the three dimensions of reality (the individual, the interpersonal, and the infrastructural). Within these horizons we try to be delivered from the evil of being objects enslaved to fit into the order created by others. We exercise our freedom as subjects empowered to co-create our own destiny.

If we choose to be objects, our freedom is going to be defined within the horizon or reality that has become ordered and institutionalized in various norms, traditions, laws, or cultural patterns. This kind of freedom is "horizontal" freedom. If, however, we choose to be subjects rather than objects, our freedom is going to find us in the process of being liberated from self-imposed horizons or horizons communally or environmentally imposed; we will be moving "from grace to grace."[15] This freedom offered by a "vertical" exercise of liberation results from a contemplative stance rooted in God's power. This freedom comes only to those willing to be converted and become as little children (cf. Matt. 18:3).

A childlike attitude enables us to be open, to go beyond the conditions and limits of old horizons to discover and create the new. Such an attitude comes from having a faith-base in the God who exceeds all boundaries. It enables us to expand our horizons, thinking, morality, and spirituality, to risk giving ourselves to enter into a higher viewpoint. We come to a way of looking at reality that previously was not part of our horizon. In leaving the old horizon and accepting the new, as the Hebrews left their enslavement and began a journey into the unknown (cf. Exod. 12ff.) and the disciples left their insecurities and fears to begin preaching a new message (cf. Acts 2:4ff.), we experience what Lonergan calls conversion.

As with the Hebrews and the first Christians, true conversion affects all three dimensions of reality—the individual, the interpersonal, and the infrastructural. Each of the three, which has had inputs that have helped create every person's horizon, will be rejected, reinforced, or refined.

Each conversion of an individual constitutes an invitation to one's community and society to go beyond the ordered horizon that can enslave. It invites to a new level of reality wherein people are empowered in their lives to determine the way their freedom will be exercised. Refusal of this invitation results from a continued dominance of the existing ideology that strives to reinforce a conditioning of humans, groups, and the infrastructures that limit them. This is sin. It manifests the presence of the powers and principalities. The conditioning that results from such an ideology, the Synod of Bishops stated in 1971, maintained "by the established order, allows the formation only of the man desired by that order, that is to say, man in its image—not a new man, but a copy of man as he is."[16] This ideology is primarily maintained through the media and education, as ways of leading us into the temptation to remain within our horizon, to remain within a sinful situation. Pope Paul VI offers conversion as the way to be delivered from this evil:

> Impelled by the need to keep in view both the personal and social aspects of the announcement of the Gospel, so that in it an answer may be given to men's most fundamental questions, the Church not only preaches conversion to God to individuals, but also, almost as society's conscience, she speaks as best she can to society itself and performs a prophetic function in this regard, always taking pains to effect her own renewal.[17]

As we see it, the conversion envisioned by Pope Paul involves three areas: intellectual, moral, and religious. "While each of the three is connected with the other two," Lonergan writes, "still each is a different type of event and has to be considered in itself before being related to the others."[18]

The three levels of maturity discussed earlier—the child (body), the adolescent (ego), and the adult (self)—correspond to the individual, the interpersonal, and the infrastructural. An understanding of these is very important if we are to grasp the nature of conversion in its intellectual, moral, and religious expressions. Such an understanding will help us become, like Francis, "an example to all of conversion."[19]

"*Intellectual conversion* is a radical clarification, and consequently the elimination of an exceedingly stubborn and misleading myth concerning reality, objectivity, and human knowledge,"[20] according to Lonergan. A myth that keeps so many well-meaning people locked into their horizon is precisely their belief that prayer and ministry can be effective on the first two levels—related to individuals and interpersonal groupings—without consideration of the third level of the environment of a world marked by sin. The radical clarification concerning reality, objectivity, and human knowledge goes beyond the child's level of immediacy. It goes beyond the adolescent's level of manipulation. It goes beyond all these mythical forms and enters the world of the adult, of the self; it enters the world of meaning. The world that now becomes understood and judged is the tri-level world, the real world that the Synod of Bishops calls a "network," or system, of domination. Yet to come to this understanding and judging itself demands a conversion of thinking, a new way of looking at reality. It demands transcendence to a new horizon:

> Only the critical realist can acknowledge the facts of human knowing and pronounce the world mediated by meaning to be the real world; and he can do so only inasmuch as he knows that the process of experiencing, understanding, and judging is a process of self-transcendence.[21]

Intellectual conversion, then, results from our resisting the effort of the powers and principalities to lead us into the temptation to remain under their control. It means we accept in our minds the fact that we can be delivered from their evil. This is what Lonergan means when he writes that we have "to be liberated." We become liberated in our minds when we discover that

> the self-transcendence proper to the human process of coming to know is to break often long-ingrained habits of thought and speech. It is to acquire the mastery in one's own house that is to be had only when one knows precisely what one is doing when one is knowing. It is a conversion, a new beginning, a fresh start. It opens the way to ever further clarifications and developments.[22]

Not until one can penetrate beyond the surface level to discover reality's infrastructures—with their institutions, isms, and ideologies—subtly operating to keep us on this surface level can "one know precisely what one is doing when one is knowing." Yet once my horizon includes this dimension I am not being controlled in my mind by surface perceptions. I am invited to "know" in a new way. I cannot look at my world in the old way again.

"*Moral conversion* changes the criterion of one's decisions and choices from satisfactions to values," Lonergan states, indicating that this change enables one to pass over from a child to an adolescent to an adult.[23] On the level of the child and adolescent, morality is often determined by the norms and traditions of those controlling one's horizons. The laws and sanctions become the conditioning and limiting factors in morality, defined by one's communities and environment. Yet as we pass over from these levels and are delivered from their evil

> we move to the existential moment when we discover for ourselves that our choosing affects ourselves no less than the chosen or rejected objects, and that it is up to each of us to decide for himself what he is to make of himself. Then is the time for the exercise of vertical freedom and then moral conversion consists in opting for the truly good, even for value against satisfaction when value and satisfaction conflict.[24]

To be faced with the fact that we may have to make such a moral conversion in favor of value, when it conflicts with the satisfaction that makes us secure, is one of the most difficult steps in the conversion process. It may mean we will have to forsake the horizons of the institutions, isms, and ideologies and their security in order to enter a different kind of freedom which no longer will offer us the individual, interpersonal, and environmental supports that come from settling into society's norms and traditions.

Individuals, communities, and institutions living in a world marked by sin have to face the possibility that their need to make moral conversion part of their style of living may "take them out" of their environments, literally or figuratively, in order to be saved. We live in a society where 65 percent of all managers questioned in a survey said they felt pressured to compromise their personal standards for their organizations.[25] We live in a society where "an honest politician" becomes an oasis to whom people go out of desperation, voting for him or her on that unique basis alone, even if other credentials are lacking.

Compromising individual morality with community or environmental morality is not limited to the economic and political spheres only. It is very much part of the institutional reality of the church as well, where we often find morality compromised by institutional horizons. Saul Alinsky wrote:

I've been asked, for example, why I never talk to a Catholic priest or a Protestant minister or a rabbi in terms of the Judaeo-Christian ethic or the Ten Commandments or the Sermon on the Mount. I never talk in those terms. Instead I approach them on the basis of their own self-interest, the welfare of their church, even its physical property.

If I approached them in a moralistic way, it would be outside their experience, because Christianity and Judaeo-Christianity are outside the experience of organized religion.[26]

There will be times when moral conversion may be demanded of institutions as well as individuals and communities, when institutions will have to look at other institutions and their environment and accept the fact that the security and satisfaction gained from accommodation to the horizons offered by the world are not equal to the resulting compromise that must be made with gospel values. An example is in order. Two institutions of religious women who had made a decision to incorporate principles of social responsibility in their investments discovered that a bank that helped them float loans, when no other bank would do so, came into conflict with the gospel values they wanted to advance through their investments. They had accepted the gospel strategy outlining the way to deal with someone with whom they differed: dialogue, coalition, litigation, and divestment.[27] When the bank refused to disclose what its hiring and lay-off practices and policies were for minorities and women, these two institutions of religious women were faced with a conflict. They received satisfaction by obtaining funds to meet their needs—which they hoped pertained to the gospel they had said they would follow. Yet these same banks that provided funding violated their values. While this particular conflict resolved itself through a subsequent disclosure of the bank's hiring practices, the future will present more conflicts between the security offered by the world and the values demanded by the gospel. In the future, more institutions supported by tax exemptions and contributions given as a result of a system based on unequal sharing of resources and responsibilities will face the possibility of the need to make moral conversion part of their ongoing response to the world as well.

Such a conversion will be possible, and people within institutions will be led out of the temptation and supports of their environment, only when we begin to take our theology seriously and practice what we preach. Only when we believe that in order to be delivered from evil we have to do battle with the powers and principalities (cf. Eph. 6:10ff.) will we be able to move to another horizon. This brings us to the third level of conversion.

"*Religious conversion* is being grasped by ultimate concern," Lonergan wrote.

> It is other-worldly falling in love. It is total and permanent self-surrender without conditions, qualifications, reservations. But it is such a surrender, not as an act, but as a dynamic state that is prior to and the principle of subsequent acts. It is revealed in retrospect as an under-tow of existential consciousness, as a fated acceptance of a vocation to holiness, as perhaps an increasing simplicity and passivity in prayer. It is interpreted differently in the context of different religious traditions. For Christians it is God's love flooding our hearts through the Holy Spirit given to us. It is the gift of grace.[28]

The person who lives out of a religious conversion has a new basis for all intellectual judgments and viewpoints and for all moral values and options. The person who lives out of a religious conversion has passed beyond the child need of relating by means of the rituals and recipes of false religiosity and the adolescent need of imitating the saints and other great heroes. A person who lives out of a religious conversion continually passes from grace to grace (cf. John 1:16), entering one horizon after another, growing into the fullness of the Godhead itself: "This means that if anyone is in Christ, he is a new creation. The old order has passed away; now all is new; . . . in him we become the very holiness of God" (2 Cor. 5:17,21).

An understanding of our share in the new creation comes to us through prayer when we experience the Spirit groaning in us for its realization (cf. Rom. 8:18ff.). In the ingatheredness of our contemplation, our faith creates a horizon, a stance opening us to be led by the Spirit into other horizons beyond our control and experience. In prayer, the Spirit enables us to be led to those horizons that indicate religious conversion (ecstasy). This fact should make us no less trusting that the Spirit will lead us to new and fuller horizons in our ministry and life as well.

The reason we often resist being led by the Spirit may have much to do with our unwillingness to be converted on an intellectual and moral level. But ultimately the reason we resist being given to the Spirit rests only with the measure of our faith. At the point of religious conversion we either accept the enslavement of our present horizons or the empowerment that comes from faith. Either we believe or we don't. By belief in the abiding presence of the Spirit of God we are enabled to transcend our horizons on all levels and begin to experience a new creation. We begin to experience and practice what we have talked about and professed. If our faith isn't deep enough, we remain where we are. There will be no conversion. There will be no growth.

During the Second Vatican Council, the bishops began realizing the implications of the intellectual and moral conversion that had begun an outline for a new horizon for the church. Seeing these as the beginnings of a freedom from former enslavements and of a new way of living for individuals, communities, and even the world, many began to fear the consequences and hesitated to go further. This point of transcending one horizon and leading into another was the point of religious conversion for the council itself. Yet here, as with the Hebrews in the desert, the security of enslavements seemed better for some bishops in the Vatican than the freedom of an unknown future beyond their control. At this point they needed to be reminded about the Holy Spirit. If they professed the Holy Spirit as the soul of the church, how could they believe that they could be led into error? How could they fear, since perfect love—the Spirit—drives out fear?

At this point Cardinal Suenens addressed the council, recalling that Pope John had opened a window toward a new horizon, against the wishes of the prophets of doom who could see things only from their limited, conditioned horizons. "Indeed, for him," Cardinal Suenens reminded the delegates, "the Council was not first of all a meeting of the bishops with the Pope, a horizontal coming together. It was the first and above all a collective gathering of the whole episcopal college with the Holy Spirit, a vertical coming together, an entire openness to an immense outpouring of the Holy Spirit, a kind of new Pentecost."[29] "O weak in faith!"

Jesus had said to his disciples, future bishops who were sometimes limited by their horizons, "Stop worrying, then . . . " (Matt. 6:30–31). "Do not let your hearts be troubled. I will ask the Father and he will give you another Paraclete—to be with you always, the Spirit of truth, whom the world cannot accept" (John 14:1, 16–17).

Only through the donation of ourselves to the Spirit of God who empowers us can our religious conversion be accomplished; otherwise the enslavements of our personal fears, our group alienation, and our world of sin will be too overpowering. We will remain within the horizons our reality defines for us "for our salvation."

Because he had given himself over to be guided by the Spirit, Francis was able to make religious conversion the very foundation of his prayer and ministry. In the words of Celano:

> Behold, when the blessed servant of the Most High was thus disposed and strengthened by the Holy Spirit, now that the opportune time had come, he followed the blessed impulse of his soul, by which he would come to the highest things, trampling worldly things under foot. He could not delay any longer, because a deadly disease had grown up everywhere to such an extent and had so taken hold of all the limbs of many that, were the physician to delay even a little, it would snatch away life, shutting off the life-giving spirit. He rose up, therefore, fortified himself with the sign of the cross . . . and, free of all luggage, he started back, wondering with a religious mind. . . . [30]

"Because a deadly disease had grown up everywhere," Francis knew he had to be converted from its influence and effort to control him in order to live. He had to put to death this deadly disease. In a similar way, we have seen, our world is marked by a deadly disease that is the grave, or mortal, sin of injustice. Our world is pathological. It is filled with a "deadly disease [that has] grown up everywhere." We need to be freed from this cultural addiction.

The only way we, the patients who are part of these infrastructures of death, can be healed will be if we "free ourselves of all luggage." We need a conversion. We need to wonder with "a religious mind." But, like all those suffering from a terminal disease, we must accept the fact that death is part of us and has invaded our lives on all three levels of our reality. We must accept this grave sin for the death-dealing reality that it represents to our life in Christ.

When we hear it said that we are dying, we, like all those suffering from forms of pathology, respond by an initial rejection—of both the reality itself and the bearer of the news.

Elisabeth Kubler-Ross notes: "Denial, at least partial denial, is used by almost all patients, not only during the first stages of illness or following confrontation, but also later on from time to time."[31] We, as members of our society who have accepted our present reality as life-giving, will hardly accept the news that it is, in fact, death-dealing. Others, as members of the same society who have accepted our present reality as life-giving, will hardly accept the news that it is in fact death-dealing when we begin to preach a gospel calling for conversion from this death in order to live (cf. John 16:1–4).

In many cases, for America to begin to live means that it must accept itself as dead. For Americans (especially white males) to begin to live means that they must accept the death that is theirs because they are denying access to resources to over 50 percent of society at home and over 65 percent of society abroad. Conversion is demanded. This conversion means we must leave death behind and work for life based on the incorporation of all those who are now on the margins of society.

Within the United States, between 1959 and 1974, there has been an increase of inequity between black and white family income despite rises in black income. During the same time the income gap between men and women has widened, although, again, there has been an increase in the income of women. The wealth of the United States in the world community is increasing at the expense of the developing nations, whose income is growing, but not in proportion. Since these inequities have resulted from the infrastructures, only a conversion of the infrastructures, of the system itself, can make the American reality (and those who are part of it) begin to square with God's will for the whole world and all its people.

Such a concentration of wealth has been due to unique, unrepeatable situations in the American context. Yet it continues to be interpreted as a God-given result of the independence and

freedom of the economic system itself, even though this independence and freedom have been limited to the powerful at the expense of the powerless, who continue to be blamed for the maldistribution. Thus we now face the reality that, although there is
equality of opportunity, there is no corresponding equality of
results. The consequences of this fact, and the resulting need for
conversion if there is to be both equality of opportunity and
results, has been made clear by Pope Paul VI when he stated in his
1977 Lenten message:

> Of course we find it hard to share our possessions in order to
> contribute to the disappearance of the inequalities of a world that
> has grown unjust. Yet statements of principles are not enough. That
> is why it is necessary and salutary for us to remember that we are
> stewards of God's gifts, and that "during Lent, penance would not
> be only internal and individual but external and social."[32]

In addition, Pope Paul showed his courage to call those in power
to such a conversion on their part when, within a few weeks of the
above words, he asked a group of business managers, "that your
Christian testimony may really contribute to spreading among
business circles the conviction of the universal purpose for which
created goods are meant. 'As all men follow justice and unite in
charity, created goods should abound for them on a reasonable
basis.' "[33]

While there are many areas where such an example will be
needed to be applied concretely to bring about the greatest amount
of freedom and equality for the greatest amount of people, two
present themselves at this time quite dramatically. These refer to
the relation of freedom and equality among the races and sexes
(image of God) and the relation of these two values to the use of this
earth's goods (access to resources). It is my conviction that only a
"religious mind" that judges reality in light of a religious conversion will be able to develop and call for a lifestyle in our nation that
will find these values of freedom and equality based on justice "for
all."

A person who recognized the gospel demand to apply this ethic
on all levels of reality with specificity to the employment of women
and minorities was my mother. After she died in 1974, we discov-

ered in her Bible a clipping from the Fond du Lac (Wisc.) *Reporter* that stated: "A spokesman for the University of Wisconsin said today the institution must discriminate against white males if it is to draw more women and minorities into its workforce."[34] Reading her reality in light of the Word of God (rather than reading the Word of God in light of her reality) brought her to accept the consequences of the fact that, on the infrastructural level, one group systemically has exercised its freedom (read "independence") at the expense of others' freedom—and, therefore, of their equality. As a result, this group might have to give up that freedom for a time in order that others might be more equal in practice as well as principle.

The reading of her reality in light of God's Word (part of what we have called the conscientization process) brought her to recognize two facts. First of all, the "freedom" of one group was being sustained—as results already noted show—by conditions that systemically restrain the freedom of other groups, even though the law says all should be treated equally. Secondly, she realized that the gospel value of justice and independence is to be more than words. This demands a certain giving up of freedom, or other resources (the "cross"), if the kind of community on earth that reflects the Trinity will be promoted.

Another area where freedom and equality must be judged in terms of the gospel's demand for conversion to build the total community relates to the earth's non-renewable resources. Because one group's lifestyle on this earth has reached a point where it "needs" almost one-third of the world's goods, even though it contains only 6 percent of the earth's people, how can it define as an expression of "freedom and equality" that situation which can be sustained only at the expense of others' freedom and equality? And if calls for voluntary restraints on the use of that freedom of access to resources continue to go unheeded, is it wrong—for the sake of the freedom of the wider community—to place restraints on the exercise of freedom if, by this act, others can have more equal access to the earth's resources?

This possibility seems to have been accepted in the area of energy by the Chairperson of Exxon, the world's largest corporation, when he noted in 1976 that "voluntary conservation programs seem to have had limited impact, and I think we should be looking at other means."[35] Yet this same possibility ought to be applied to the whole production-consumption pattern of our country in view of a global ethic. Clark Kerr recognizes that some kind of conversion will be necessary—either made freely or resultant from some kind of restraint:

> Freedom and equality both generally tend to increase, as compared with prior historical periods where inherited status and physical power were the determinant influences on the status of individuals, under the first two definitions of equality (equality before the law and equality of opportunity); freedom and these kinds of equality are mutually supportive. Under the last definition (equality of results), freedom clearly loses in favor of equality; freedom and this kind of equality are mutually exclusive. At the current stage of history in many industrial nations, points of conflict between freedom and equality are arising and being intensified, as movement is made in the direction of the two remaining definitions of equality (compensatory opportunity and compensatory results). Within this range of possibilities, greater equality may, depending upon the means, reduce freedom.[36]

Only a "religious mind" will accept what our intelligence shows us about our present reality and what our morals tell us about basic human rights, the sharing of resources, freedom, and equality. Only a person or community formed with such a religious mind will be able to accept that our environmental reality demands that we who have become so much a part of it must now accept death to this pathological condition in order that we may truly live (cf. Luke 18:18–30). As partakers of the wealth that represents the American reality, we are like the rich young man who must accept the necessity of conversion, the necessity to die a corporate death so that the whole may live (cf. John 11:50).

"Free of all luggage," Francis was able to "wonder with a religious mind." The wonder that always results from true prayer, from religious experience, freed Francis from all those things burdening him down and keeping him within set horizons. His religious mind enabled him to be converted, with all the consequences and risks that conversion entails. He was able to leave father and mother, wealth and honor, in the name of ministry toward a greater goal, a vision that prayer enabled him to work for in a new way.

Prayer enabled him to go beyond the horizon of reality as it had been defined by all the inputs of his young life. It offered him a new way of looking at his ministry. Whereas once, limited by his former horizon, he had interpreted "repair my church" in a literal sense,[37] when he grew in his conversion he came to discover that this would not be limited to his individual brick and mortaring. The repair of the church through his ministry would have effect on three communities, on a revitalized church, and on the world itself. Once, limited by his former horizon, he had thought the greatest thing he could be was a soldier. Yet the Spirit of the Lord enabled him to pass beyond an environment and horizon of militarism ("It seemed to Francis that his whole home was filled with the trappings of war."[38]). He changed his "carnal weapons into spiritual ones and in place of military glory"[39] he tried to offer a new basis—far removed from the fear of each other's armaments —on which people and even nations could relate to each other. This had its effect on an ism of his day (feudalism), for members of his communities resisted the bearing of arms.

It may have been true for Francis (as well as for ourselves) that such conversion "is existential, intensely personal, utterly intimate." But, Lonergan insists, it can go beyond:

> It is not so private as to be solitary. It can happen to many, and they can form a community to sustain one another in their self-transformation and to help one another in working out the implications and fulfilling the promise of their new life. Finally, what can become communal, can become historical. It can pass from generation to generation. It can spread from one cultural milieu to another. It can adapt to changing circumstances, control new situations, survive into a different age, flourish in another period or epoch.[40]

Conversion enabled Francis to become a different individual; it enabled a community of like-minded people to be formed and to have an effect on society. Our fidelity to this same conversion, based on a continual conscientization process, will find us gathering together as individuals into basic communities so that we may reflect on the way this conversion can be worked out in our world marked by sin. Living such a conversion by our prayer and ministry, by our reflection and action, Lonergan concludes, should affect

> all of a man's conscious and intentional operations. It directs his gaze, pervades his imagination, releases the symbols that penetrate to the depths of his psyche. It enriches his understanding, guides his judgments, reinforces his decision. But as communal and historical, as a movement with its own cultural, institutional, and doctrinal dimensions, conversion calls forth a reflection that makes the movement thematic, that explicitly explores its origins, developments, purposes, achievements, and failures.[41]

With these thoughts from Lonergan, we find ourselves concluding this chapter where we began this book. We started it by describing how people who want to be converted from the horizons offered them within the institutions of their environment begin living a new life which attracts others who share this common unwillingness to be controlled at that horizon. The result is the creation of a new movement. We went on to suggest that a deeper reflection on our world might enable all of us, mechanized into our monuments and institutions, to initiate a movement ourselves as basic communities. This will happen when we recognize the need to work together to resist the bigger reality of the sin of our world rather than remaining locked into the horizons of our individual adaptations and communal alienations. We tried, in succeeding chapters, to show how this sin of the world is an obstacle to the experience of God's presence on earth.

Having reflected on a way we can structure and process our communities, groups, and meetings to be "delivered from evil," we hope we are ready to begin a new movement, a religious movement based on a continual conversion, a continual effort to form a basic community out of a conscientization flowing from and into prayer and ministry. If we would be able to become such a movement for our age, as Francis's form of the movement was for his age, our common goal would be advanced: the creation on earth through our action of what we pray for to our Father in heaven. To him be the power, the honor, the glory. To us be the power, the honor, the glory as well.

11

Amen

In Scripture, "amen" indicates the fulfillment of whatever is stated, proclaimed, or promised. To say "amen" means that one declares his or her participation in the present event or words. This is true historically. Yet our era has unconsciously participated in the evolution of "amen" from meaning "so it is" (with its stress on participation in the present creation of reality) to "let it be" (with its stress on hope in the future creation of reality that seems beyond us).

This evolution seems to have its roots in the transformation of our understanding of faith itself. Although biblical faith implies participation (response to the third level of reality) through the Spirit of Jesus indwelling our prayer and ministry, we often live on a second level and even a first level of faith that makes us spectators to the working out of God's mystery in the world. According to Robert Aron:

> Ancient Hebrew, in Jesus' day the language of prayer, has no word to denote "belief" as we understand it today. There is, however, a word, *Emuna*, which implies certainty. It has for its root, *amn*, which can be pronounced *amen*. For Jews and Christians alike those three letters indicate the consent of the faithful to the will of God. Although the term is the same before and after Jesus, the meaning has changed. For the Jew of Jesus' time, *amen* traditionally expressed a statement of fact. For many believers today for whom religious experience is less immediate and direct, *amen* is a wish, a hope, an aspiration. In our day *amen* often means "so be it." To the ancient Jew, the syllables meant "so it is."[1]

Throughout this book it has been my attempt to outline a spirituality that reflects a faith based on the religious experience of those Jews of Jesus' time who found in him *the* Amen (Rev. 3:14), the meaning of their discipleship. Discipleship enabled them to leave secure patterns that they might participate more fully in the life of their leader. As a result of their mystical union with Jesus, they were enabled to be for their generation what Jesus was for his: signs of contradiction. "If we live by the Spirit," Paul reminded the Galatians, who had to battle with the tension between a religious mode that reflected their environment and a new way in conflict with it, "let us follow the Spirit's lead" (5:25).

The Spirit of Jesus in us enables us to say, "Amen," to affirm that the reality of Jesus and the pattern of his life are in us. Our goal, then, as followers of Jesus living in our present reality, is to make sure, by prayer and ministry, that the pattern of God's revelation of his kingdom that was in Jesus for his world be part of our spirituality as we relate to individuals, interpersonal groupings, and the infrastructures of our world. All reality has to share in this revelation, which demands passing over from death to life, from sin to grace, from oppression to liberation. The pattern of deliverance from evil (outlined earlier) must become the pattern of our individual lives, of the lives of our communities, and of the life of our environment and its infrastructures. Wherever this pattern is lacking, the call and possibility of conversion for fuller discipleship must be offered.

Just as transactional analysts have shown that our "personal scripts" are shaped by our "cultural scripts," so our personal biographies, which have been highly influenced by our cultural addictions and pathologies, must be shaped by the theological script that is God's plan for the world. Our biography must be our theology. Theology means bringing the Word of God to bear upon our reality. Judging reality by the Word (which is one word, "Amen") demands that the pattern of God's action in the world, which was made present in times past through the prophets and which has become incarnate in the Word, Jesus (cf. Heb. 1:1–2), must become the pattern of our lives. "Be imitators of me, my brothers. Take as your guide those who follow the example that we set" (3:17) was Paul's admonition to the early Christians living in the Philippian culture. "Imitate me as I imitate Christ" (1 Cor. 11:1).

The more we reflect on Jesus' life and on his spirituality expressed in prayer and ministry, the more we find that the specific pattern in his biography was that found in the theology of the prophets. Through Mary, Joseph, and the other members of his remnant community, Jesus was lead to Isaiah and Jeremiah in a special way. Their stress on a life of servanthood was the inspiration for him to bring healing and empowerment and hope to his contemporaries. As the prophets demanded, he lived to enable his contemporaries to have access to the resources they needed as individuals and communities. Yet, to accomplish this goal, Jesus had to pray it, preach it, and prepare his disciples for it in a society whose infrastructures depended on exactly the opposite. The message of Jesus fulfilled the theology of the prophets: reconciliation with God's will means irreconciliation with the will of the world.

Today, our biographies as individuals and communities should reflect the theology of the prophets and of Jesus in the same pattern. As those who have been born into the American reality (especially the white, male-dominated American environment), our biographies ought to be lived from the awareness that we are conditioned by the infrastructures of our nation to give our allegiance to its institutions, isms, and ideologies. Yet, into this very reality we are called to enter with our "Amen," saying to our generation, as Jesus did to his, "You justify yourselves in the eyes of men, but God reads your hearts. What man thinks important, God holds in contempt" (Luke 16:15).

These words of Jesus did not ingratiate him with the Pharisees, many of whom had developed a lifestyle supportive of the existing infrastructures, which, in turn, rewarded them with symbols and positions of prestige. They must be remembered as words of particular importance today, as we American Christians try to create spiritualities that will enable our biographies to become living theologies. These words are even more important to U.S. Catholic Christians, it seems to me, because we are heirs of this tradition that has done much to create a spirituality through institutions, isms, and ideologies that will "justify yourselves before men."

The "promised land" of America has attracted millions of Catholics oppressed by natural and societal afflictions in their European homelands. Coming *en masse* to an alien culture, with which, however, they shared similar goals, Catholics created schools, hospitals, and churches as alternatives to the culture of the day, but as supportive of the overall goal of becoming full partners in the American dream. The history of the American Catholic church is the history of a united effort of clergy, religious, and laity to enter the melting pot and a willingness to sacrifice personnel and resources to implement the meeting of that goal.

By 1975 it became clear that this goal was well-nigh achieved. A study by the National Opinion Research Center in Chicago showed that many Catholics, whose ancestors were immigrants to this once predominantly Protestant country, now outclass Protestants in wealth and education, having become "more successful than the American Protestants, which constitute the host culture."[2] The study, which did not include nonwhites and Spanish-speaking groups, indicated to what extent strong, ethnically supportive institutions were able to help meet the goal of participation in the American dream. The table on p. 216 from the study summarizes religio-ethnic origin and family-income data.[3]

American Catholics now face a situation that is quite different from the past. First, the need for support institutions of the type that were created around ethnic lines is fast diminishing. Catholics have become integrated into other institutions which now reinforce their true values and goals (cf. Luke 16:10–13) more adequately than the church does. They no longer "need the church," especially those levels of the church that appeal to child-level body needs of survival in an alien world and adolescent-level ego needs of acceptance and involvement with significant others. Second, as Andrew Greeley, head of the research group that prepared the statistics quoted above, notes, "financial success is no longer considered a good thing by many Americans. It used to be said of the ethnics that they were no good because they could not achieve educationally or economically. Now it will be said they are no good because they have achieved educationally and economically."[4] Whereas Catholics at one time created institutions to help integrate them into the American reality, they now are faced

DENOMINATIONS AND ETHNIC GROUPS	FAMILY INCOME
Jews	$13,340.00
Irish Catholics	12,426.00
Italian Catholics	11,748.00
German Catholics	11,632.00
Polish Catholics	11,298.00
Episcopalians	11,032.00
Presbyterians	10,976.00
Slavic Catholics	10,826.00
British Protestants	10,354.00
French Catholics	10,188.00
Methodists	10,103.00
German Protestants	9,758.00
Lutherans	9,702.00
Scandinavian Protestants	9,597.00
"American" Protestants	9,274.00
Irish Protestants	9,147.00
Baptists	8,693.00

with the need to create new institutions that are not conformed to the American reality, but to the gospel (when the two are in contradiction). Such new institutions will differ from the old because they will not reinforce the common goal of the average American Catholic (who often equates Catholic with America) in pew and school, nor many institutional goals of the nation itself.

Precisely at this point we must ask if what has been achieved has not, in fact if not by intention, created for us (and here I speak of all Christians, not just Catholics) new idols. Have we, in effect, identified God's will with the will of American free enterprise and manifest destiny? Might it be said of us that "their unbelieving minds have been blinded by the god of the present age so that they do not see the splendor of the gospel showing forth the glory of Christ, the image of God" (2 Cor. 4:4)?

Only a third-level Christian who looks at the present reality ("marked by the grave sin of injustice"[5]) can be an effective disciple in this world that is so influenced by American ways. True prayer enables us to transcend the gods of this world and of our own making to meet in transcendence the God who is beyond the experience of what can be seen and touched. And true ministry enables us to call people to conversion. This demands that we call the institutions, isms, and ideologies of our infrastructures to conversion. If we don't include this part of reality in our prayer and ministry, we will have failed to deal with that which is the base of all reality.

Prayer and ministry that try to bring the pattern of "amen" into our reality often will not be accepted among Christians who have become accustomed to other gods—many of whom have unconsciously been promoted by Christian preaching and institutions. But this is the consequence of participation in the Word that "came into his own home, and his own people received him not" (John 1:11). Anyone who would follow Christ must be prepared to be separated from nation, family, material goods, and even self. The consequence of letting the pattern of the "amen" become the theology that dictates the biography of our lives is the cross—the very reality our world refuses to embrace.

The consequence of living out our "amens" means that we will stand in society as those who say, by prayer and ministry, that everyone has the same right to exercise their "amens" as do we. Everyone has the right to image the Word of God in their lives; everyone has the right to say, "So I am." "So I am" and "So are you." And together we strive for the freedom, justice, and peace that result from each person being able to say, "I am," with no "I am" at the expense of other individuals, groups, or classes.

The kind of discipleship called for by Jesus is not American, but global. As soon as we understand our discipleship within its global context, we begin to see reality, prayer, and ministry in a new perspective. The North American perspective—from which we have too often tended to judge all reality, including our prayer and ministry—sees itself as an island untouched by the cries and miseries of the world. It is protective of our lifestyle and consumption patterns. The crumbs of bread we have shared through various governmental and voluntary programs, while having value in

13. Francis S. MacNutt, O.P. (reporter), *First Latin-American Charismatic Leadership Conference* (St. Louis: Thomas Merton House of Prayer, 1973), p. 4. We are in full agreement with the effort of Leon Joseph Cardinal Suenens to emphasize the charismatic renewal in the church as a deeper appreciation and experience of living our lives on the third level, under the influence of the Holy Spirit: "To grasp the meaning of the Charismatic Renewal and its true bearing in our lives, we have to avoid two tendencies. First, we should not apply to it ready made categories. Secondly, we should not see in this Renewal just one more movement to be set alongside many others in the Church today, or worse still, as in competition with them. Rather than a movement, Charismatic Renewal is a moving of the Holy Spirit which can reach all Christians, lay or cleric. It is comparable to a high voltage current of grace which is coursing through the Church. Every Christian is charismatic by definition; the difference lies in our degree of faith, our awareness of this fundamental and necessarily common reality.

"We are not speaking of a 'movement,' if by that we understand a structural organization with membership and fixed obligations. To benefit by this current, there is no need even to join a formal prayer group. Our Lord told us: 'Where two or three meet in my name, I shall be there with them' (Mt. 18:20). If there is only this modest number, there can be community prayer among Christians. The Spirit blows how and where he wills; he does not need the help of an organization to penetrate all classes of society: lay persons in every walk of life, members of religious congregations and orders, all are within his reach" *(A New Pentecost?* trans. Francis Martin [New York: Seabury Press, 1975], pp. 111–12).

2. OUR FATHER WHO ART IN HEAVEN

1. Joachim Jeremias, *Prayers of Jesus*, trans. Christoph Burchard (London: SCM Press, 1967), p. 76.

2. "Justice in the World," Introduction, *The Pope Speaks* 16 (1972), p. 377.

3. Ibid., II, p. 381.

4. David R. Griffin, *A Process Christology* (Philadelphia: Westminster Press, 1973), p. 155.

5. St. Cyprian, *The Lord's Prayer*, 8, trans. and ed. Roy J. Deferari, *The Fathers of the Church* 36 (New York: The Fathers of the Church, Inc., 1958), p. 132.

6. Gabriel Marcel, *Homo Viator*, trans. Emma Crauford (New York: Harper & Row, 1962), p. 12.

7. Mary Daly, *Beyond God the Father* (Boston: Beacon Press, 1973), p. 32.

8. Jacques Ellul, *The Technological Society*, trans. John Wilkinson (New York: Alfred A. Knopf, 1964), p. 415.

9. Abraham Heschel, *Man Is Not Alone* (New York: Farrar, Straus and Young, 1951), p. 69.

10. Claus Westermann, *Creation*, trans. John J. Scullion, S.J. (Philadelphia: Fortress Press, 1974), p. 11.

11. George W. Coats, "The God of Death: Power and Obedience in the Primeval History," *Interpretation* 29, no. 3 (July 1975), p. 228.

12. Walter Brueggemann, "The Kerygma of the Priestly Writers," *Zeitschrift für die Alttestamentliche Wissenschaft* 84, no. 4 (1972), pp. 400–01.

13. Ibid., p. 401.

14. George W. Coats, "God of Death," p. 229.

15. *Second Celano*, 12, p. 372.

16. Thomas of Celano, *The First Life of St. Francis*, 76, in Marion A. Habig (ed.), *St. Francis*, p. 292. Hereafter cited as *First Celano*.

17. Ibid., pp. 292–93.

18. *Second Celano*, 120, p. 461.

19. Raymond E. Brown, S.S., "The Pater Noster as an Eschatological Prayer," *New Testament Essays* (Garden City, N. Y.: Doubleday Image Books, 1965), pp. 287–88.

20. St. Francis of Assisi, "Letter to All the Faithful," in Marion A. Habig (ed.), *St. Francis*, p. 94.

3. MAY YOUR NAME BE HOLY ON EARTH AS IN HEAVEN

1. Raymond E. Brown, S. S., "The Pater Noster as an Eschatological Prayer," *New Testament Essays* (Garden City: Doubleday Image Books, 1965), p. 299.

2. Joachim Jeremias, *The Prayers of Jesus*, trans. John Reumann (London: SCM Press, 1967), p. 99.

3. Jürgen Moltmann, *The Gospel of Liberation*, trans. H. Wayne Pipkin (Waco, Texas: Word Books, 1973), pp. 18–19.

4. Walter Brueggemann, "The Kerygma of the Priestly Writers," *Zeitschrift für die Alttestamentliche Wissenschaft* 84, no. 4 (1972), p. 405.

5. Ibid., p. 406.

6. Richard Byrne, O.C.S.O., "Living the Contemplative Dimension of Everyday Life," unpublished dissertation (Pittsburgh: Duquesne University, 1973), p. 198. Later Father Richard shows that "my experience of Christian contemplation is thus a *participation* in the mystery of Jesus coming from the Father and returning to the Father" (p. 234).

7. Abraham Heschel, *The Prophets* (New York: Harper & Row, 1962), p. 231.

8. Richard Byrne, O.C.S.O., "Living the Contemplative Dimension," p. 63.

9. Rollo May, *Love and Will* (New York: W.W. Norton, 1969), pp. 29–30.

10. Abraham Heschel, *The Prophets*, p. 309.

11. Jacques Ellul, *False Presence of the Kingdom*, trans. C. Edward Hopkin (New York: Seabury Press, 1972), p. 68.

12. A Monk of the Eastern Church, *The Prayer of Jesus*, trans. A Monk of the Western Church (New York: Desclee Co., 1967), p. 14.

13. Leon Joseph Cardinal Suenens, *A New Pentecost?* trans. Francis Martin (New York: Seabury Press, 1975), p. 135.

14. Cardinal Jaime L. Sin, in Richard John Neuhaus, "Excursus III: Neither Guerrillas nor Patsies," *Worldview* (December 1974), p. 6.

15. Pope Paul VI, "On the Renewal of the Religious Life," no. 17, *The Pope Speaks* 16 (1971), p. 115.

16. Ibid., quoting "Pastoral Constitution on the Church in the World of Today," no. 63, *The Pope Speaks* 11 (1966), p. 302.

17. Ibid., no. 17, p. 115.

18. *Second Celano*, 165, p. 495. According to Francis, "it was a great reproach and a shame to withhold what was asked in the name" of Christ. Cf. *First Celano*, 17, p. 243.

utilization of scarce resources" (Eirik G. Furobotn and Svetozar Pejovich, "Property Rights and Economic Theory: A Survey of Recent Literature," *Journal of Economic Literature,* vol. 10, no. 4 [December 1972], p. 1139).

26. Ralph K. White, *Nobody Wanted War: Misperception in Vietnam and Other Wars* (Garden City, N.Y.: Doubleday Anchor Books, 1970), p. 14.

27. "Justice in the World," I, p. 378.

6. THY WILL BE DONE ON EARTH AS IN HEAVEN

1. "Israelite tradition was unanimous in ascribing the destruction of Sodom and Gomorrah to the wickedness of these cities, but traditions varied in regard to the nature of this wickedness. According to the present account of the Yahwist, the sin of Sodom was homosexuality (19, 4f.), which is therefore also known as sodomy; but according to Isaiah (1, 9f.; 3, 9), it was a lack of social justice; Ezekiel (16, 46–51) described it as a disregard for the poor, whereas Jeremiah (23, 14) saw it as general immorality" (footnote to Gen. 18:20 in *The New American Bible* [New York: P.J. Kenedy & Sons, 1970], p. 24).

2. *First Celano,* 92, p. 307. Celano continues, showing how Francis broke open the Word to reveal what God's will intended him to do: "One day therefore he went before the holy altar which was erected in the hermitage where he was staying, and taking the book in which the holy Gospel was written, he reverently placed it upon the altar. Then he prostrated himself in prayer to God, not less in heart than in body, and he asked in humble prayer that the good God, *the Father of mercies and the God of all comfort,* would deign to make known his will to him, and that he might be able to carry out what he had earlier begun simply and devoutly; and he prayed that it might be shown to him at the first opening of the book what was more fitting for him to do."

3. Hendrik Berkhof, *Christ and the Powers* (Scottdale: Herald, 1962), pp. 30ff.

4. "Declaration on Procured Abortion," nos. 10–11, *The Pope Speaks* 19 (1975), p. 256.

5. Pope John XXIII, *Pacem in Terris,* no. 11 (Washington, D.C.: National Catholic Welfare Conference, 1963), p. 5.

6. "Pastoral Message of the Administrative Committee," National Conference of Catholic Bishops, February 13, 1973 (Washington, D.C.: United States Catholic Conference, 1973), pp. 1–2.

7. Ibid., p. 2, quoting Pope John XXIII, *Pacem in Terris,* no. 61, p. 16.

8. "Declaration on Procured Abortion," nos. 22, 23, p. 260.

9. Ibid., no. 24, p. 261.

10. Ibid., no. 27, p. 262.

11. Ibid., no. 26, p. 261.

12. William H. Marshner, "A Theory for Political Action," *The Wanderer,* June 19, 1975.

13. Pope Paul VI, "On the Renewal of the Religious Life," no. 18, *The Pope Speaks* 17 (1972), p. 115.

14. Jürgen Moltmann, *The Gospel of Liberation,* trans. H. Wayne Pipkin (Waco, Texas: Word Books, 1973), pp. 38–39.

15. *First Celano,* 24, p. 248.

16. "The Vocation of the Order Today," no. 34, p. 79.

17. *Second Celano,* 193, p. 517.

18. Pope Paul VI, "On the Renewal of the Religious Life."
19. Pope John XXIII, *Pacem in Terris*, no. 61, p. 16.
20. "The Vocation of the Order Today," no. 35, p. 71.
21. *First Celano*, 22, p. 247.

7. GIVE US THIS DAY OUR DAILY BREAD

1. John T. Pawlikowski, "On Renewing the Revolution of the Pharisees: A New Approach to Theology and Politics," *Cross Currents* (Fall 1970), p. 417.
2. Raymond E. Brown, S.S., "The Pater Noster as an Eschatological Prayer," *New Testament Essays* (Garden City, N.Y.: Doubleday Image Books, 1965), p. 314.
3. *Second Celano*, 71, p. 423.
4. Francis MacNutt, O.P., *Healing* (Notre Dame: Ave Maria Press, 1974), p. 169.
5. Thomas Barrosse, "The Passover amid the Paschal Meal," *Concilium: Theology in the Age of Renewal*, vol. 40 (New York: Paulist Press, 1969), p. 23.
6. "The Right to Food," *Wall Street Journal*, April 8, 1976.
7. "Cereal's Big Four Questioned," *Milwaukee Sentinel*, April 8, 1976.
8. "Justice in the World," III, *The Pope Speaks* 16 (1972), p. 386.
9. Jacques Ellul, *False Presence of the Kingdom*, trans. C. Edward Hopkin (New York: Seabury Press, 1972), p. 10.

8. FORGIVE US OUR DEBTS AS WE FORGIVE THOSE INDEBTED TO US

1. Although Luke's theology is Jubilee, paradoxically, in his version of the Lord's Prayer, he uses the shorter and earlier form, which includes the word *amartia* for debt. However, his theology expands the notion of debt to the broader, literal meaning.
2. John Howard Yoder, *The Politics of Jesus* (Grand Rapids: W.B. Eerdmans Publishing Co., 1972), p. 66.
3. Ernst Lohmeyer, *Our Father*, trans. John Bowden (New York: Harper & Row, 1965), p. 163.
4. *Second Celano*, 87, pp. 434–35.
5. Francis MacNutt, O.P., *Healing* (Notre Dame: Ave Maria Press, 1974), p. 173. The Scriptures continually make a connection between healing of diseases and forgiveness of sins.
6. Pope Paul VI, "Holy Year 1975: Renewal and Reconciliation," *The Pope Speaks* 18 (1973), p. 5.
7. James H. Cone, *The Spirituals and the Blues* (New York: Seabury Press, 1972), p. 90.
8. Bishop of London, "Letter to Masters and Mistresses," May 19, 1727, in Peter G. Mode, *Source Book and Bibliography Guide for American Church Historians* (Boston: J.S. Canner & Co., 1964), p. 551.
9. Rights flowing from and to property must be considered beyond land-related notions but as a whole "bundle" of rights. Confer Eirik G. Furobotn and Svetozar Pejovich, "Property Rights and Economic Theory: A Survey of Recent Litera-

ture," *Journal of Economic Literature*, vol. 10, no. 4 (December 1972), pp. 1137–62.

10. Maurice Cardinal Roy, in Samuel Ruiz Garcia, "The Quest for Justice as Latin Americans Live It," unpublished paper delivered at Catholic Inter-American Cooperation Program (CICOP) (Washington, D.C.: United States Catholic Conference Division for Latin America), p. 4.

11. Denis Goulet, "Development—or Liberation," *Freedom and Unfreedom in the Americas: Toward a Theology of Liberation* (New York: IDOC, 1971), p. 6.

12. "Justice in the World," Introduction, *The Pope Speaks* 16 (1972), p. 377.

13. Dr. Hernan Santa Cruz, "UNCTAD III: Global Town Hall Meeting or Folkloric Carnival?" *IDOC* 53 (May 1973), p. 21.

14. Ibid.

15. Constantine V. Vaitsos, "Employment Problems and Transnational Enterprises in Developing Countries: Distortions and Inequality" (New York: Carnegie Center for Transnational Studies, 1976), p. 17.

16. Radomiro Tomic, "Poverty, Power, Environment: Issues of Justice in Latin America," *IDOC* 53 (May 1973), p. 11.

17. *Second Celano*, 59, p. 413.

18. Pope Paul VI, "On the Development of Peoples," no. 26 (Washington, D.C.: United States Catholic Conference, 1967), p. 12.

19. "Mexican Factories Continue to Spread along the U.S. Border," *Wall Street Journal*, April 14, 1975.

20. Pope Paul VI, "Apostolic Letter to Cardinal Maurice Roy," no. 44 (Washington, D.C.: United States Catholic Conference, 1971), p. 24.

21. Report, in possession of the authors, quoted in Ralph Nader, Mark Green, Joel Seligman, *Constitutionalizing the Corporation: The Case for the Federal Chartering of Giant Corporations* (Washington, D.C.: The Corporate Accountability Research Group, 1976), p. 352.

22. William Comanor and Robert Smiley, "Monopoly and the Distribution of Wealth," Research Paper No. 16 (Stanford University, 1973), p. 19 and passim.

23. Phillip I. Blumberg, *The Megacorporation in American Society: The Scope of Corporate Power* (Englewood Cliffs: Prentice Hall, 1975), p. 24.

24. Cf. James D. Smith and Stephen D. Franklin, "The Concentration of Personal Wealth, 1922–1969," unpublished report presented to the American Economic Association, New York, December 1973. According to Smith, "The most serious thing about concentration is . . . in *the ability to set the pace for what appropriate thought behavior is*. The great concentration of wealth allows the people who have it to shape the nation's priorities. It's not that these people are necessarily badly motivated, but their perceptions of the world almost inevitably are different from those of the great masses of people. For example, the wealthy have a tendency to believe that persons who need welfare have something wrong with them" (James D. Smith, quoted in "Very Rich Keep Share of US Worth," *Milwaukee Journal*, January 18, 1974; emphasis my own). The insight of Smith—that the rich are able to determine "what appropriate thought behavior is"—indicates the influence wealth has over the formation of ideology. Such ideology keeps us from having a true, open discussion related to the need for a redistribution of wealth in America. As long as those who call for such a redistribution, based on principles of distributive justice and the gospel, can be considered "radical," the average people who do the name-calling will be effective instruments in the perpetuation of the ideology by their "thought behavior."

Given an objective reading of our reality, however, it seems evident that the reality itself will demand such a change, which, in turn, will affect the ideology. A survey taken of primarily top- and middle-management people by William F. Martin and George Cabot Lodge entitled "Our Society in 1985—Business May Not Like It" *(Harvard Business Review* 53 [November-December 1975]:143–52) indicates a reluctant acceptance of the fact that present realities are working to bring about a change in the kind of economy that will predominate in America in the future. More importantly, the authors discuss the kind of economy presently in operation and expected in the future in terms of an *ideology.* Showing that the majority of respondents believe events will bring about a more communitarian economy with property rights "regulated according to the community's needs, which often differ from individual consumer desires," the authors note that the perception of this reality (ideology) "requires an awareness of whole systems and of the inter-relationships between and among the wholes."

The importance of ideology in their approach underscores the importance we give to it throughout this book. In their words, "ideology serves as a bridge by which a community translates timeless, universal values such as survival, justice, and self-fulfillment into real-world application. It is the framework of ideas that integrates and synthesizes all aspects of a community's being—political, social, economic, cultural, ecological, and others. Ideology legitimizes a community's institutions—business, government, universities, or whatever—and thus it under-lies the authority and the rights of those who manage the institutions. It is a particularly useful concept in the United States today because, as the survey shows, many believe we are in the midst of an ideological transition.

"When a traditional ideology becomes incoherent and loses acceptance, the community loses direction. Its institutions are no longer legitimate and the power-ful are suddenly drained of authority. A community that is unmindful of its ideology is apt to be misled by it. This is a problem for Americans. Most of us would deny that the United States has ever had an ideology; we prefer to think that we came from 'the old country,' leaving ideology and all its troubles behind, and then in the American wilderness we proceeded to build a great nation by pragmatically doing what seemed to work. Americans have believed that what is described here as the Lockean ideology is not a transitory bridge between values and reality, but the law of God and Nature. . . .

"Pretending to lack an ideology, we have ignored it. Still, as the survey results make plain, the respondents subscribe to the old myths with nearly religious fervor, even as they know they are vanishing. This ideological unconsciousness becomes serious when we contemplate the ominous possibilities that can accompany the communitarian way, as George Orwell speculated in *1984* and Aldous Huxley did in *Brave New World.* A society that ignores ideological change may promote the anarchy that inevitably leads to totalitarian temptations; history is replete with examples of active, planning states that *imprison* as well as *plan"* (pp. 149–50).

25. Bishops of the West Indies, "Joint Pastoral on Justice and Peace," in *Mission Intercom* (Washington, D.C.: United States Catholic Mission Council, May 1976), p. 2.

26. *Second Celano,* 81, pp. 429–30.

27. *First Celano,* 25, p. 249. The realization that the earth is the Lord's and that the goal of the Friars Minor is to witness to this by sharing the earth's resources as equally as possible as a Jubilee community is further reinforced in Celano's account of Bernard's conversion: "A certain Bernard of the city of Assisi, who was after-wards a son of perfection, since he was planning to perfectly despise the world, after the example of the man of God, humbly sought his advice. He therefore consulted him, saying, 'If someone, father, possessed for a long time *the goods of some lord* and

did not want to keep them any longer, what would be the more perfect thing to do with them?' " (*Second Celano*, 15, pp. 374–75; emphasis mine).

28. P. Cameron, "Social Stereotypes: Three Faces of Happiness: Effects of Income," *Psychology Today*, August 1974, pp. 62–64.

29. *Second Celano*, 99, pp. 443–44.

30. José Marins, unpublished paper discussing the formation of basic communities, trans. William Calhoun (Milwaukee: Justice and Peace Center, 1975).

31. Pope Paul VI, General Audience of May 16, 1973, *L'Osservatore Romano*, May 23, 1973.

9. LEAD US NOT INTO TEMPTATION . . .

1. "Justice in the World," II, *The Pope Speaks* 16 (1972), p. 381.

2. Ibid., Introduction, p. 377.

3. Gregory Baum, "The Dynamic Conscience," *The Ecumenist*, vol. 12, no. 4 (May–June 1974), p. 63.

4. Ibid.

5. Michele Cardinal Pellegrino, in "Cardinal Agrees with Abbot's Rap at Church," *Catholic Herald Citizen*, October 7, 1973.

6. Cardinal Stephen Kim, in "Justice Linked to Evangelization," *National Catholic Reporter*, October 25, 1975.

7. *Second Celano*, 31, p. 389.

8. Ibid., 148, pp. 481–82. Also cf. *First Celano*, 37, p. 260.

9. Pope Paul VI, "Universal Day of Peace," *The Pope Speaks* 17 (1973), p. 342.

10. Amitai W. Etzioni, in James P. Gannon, "Getting Off the Treadmill," *Wall Street Journal*, April 12, 1974.

11. Ibid.

12. Donald Gaudion, "Business and the World," *Milwaukee Journal*, January 27, 1974.

13. "Justice in the World," III, p. 385.

14. "Soviet Orders Dissident into Mental Home," *New York Daily News*, November 27, 1973.

15. "Three South Africans Burn Black," *Milwaukee Journal*, January 27, 1974.

16. "Statement on the Family Viewing Policy of the Television Networks," Administrative Board, United States Catholic Conference (Washington, D.C., 1975), p. 10; emphasis mine.

17. Phillip H. Dougherty, "How I.T.T. Improved Its Image," *New York Times*, April 18, 1975.

18. Richard Barnet and Ronald Müller, *Global Reach: The Power of the Multinational Corporations* (New York: Simon and Schuster, 1975), pp. 244–45.

19. See chap. 5, note 4, above.

20. For further discussion of research into IBM, cf. Michael H. Crosby, O.F.M. Cap., "A Primer for Shareholder Responsibility at the IBM 1975 Annual Meeting" (Milwaukee: Justice and Peace Center, 1975), pp. 4–5. In 1977 the Midwest Capuchins presented a shareholder resolution in which they discussed the connection of IBM's directors to Carter's cabinet and called for IBM to disclose the voting power behind its top thirty owners; the resolution was withdrawn after IBM agreed to seek this information and make it available. Its example, I hope, will be followed by other companies as an important step in overcoming the secrecy that has

surrounded concentrated ownership in large corporations.

21. Leslie H. Gelb, "The New American Establishment is Called the Community," *New York Times*, December 19, 1976.

22. Ibid.

23. "Jimmy Carter's Computer Connection," *Forbes*, January 15, 1977, p. 27.

24. *General Constitutions*, p. 93.

25. "Justice in the World," III, p. 385.

26. Ibid.

27. Ibid., p. 384.

28. *Second Celano*, 125, p. 466.

29. William Stringfellow, *An Ethic for Christians and Other Aliens in a Strange Land* (Waco, Texas: Word Books, 1973), p. 29.

30. "Justice in the World," p. 383.

10. . . . DELIVER US FROM EVIL

1. Cf. "Gaudium et Spes," no. 38, in Walter M. Abbott, S.J. (ed.), *The Documents of Vatican II* (New York: Guild Press, 1966), p. 236. Also "Lumen Gentium," no. 43, ibid., p. 73.

2. *First Celano*, 37, p. 260.

3. Ibid., 35, p. 258.

4. Ibid., 24, p. 248.

5. "The Vocation of the Order Today," 32, *General Chapter Documents—Madrid, 1973* (Cincinnati: St. Anthony Messenger, 1974), pp. 70–71.

6. Gabriel Marcel, *The Mystery of Being*, trans. Rene Hague (Chicago: Henry Regnery Company, 1960), pp. 156, 158.

7. "Justice in the World," II, *The Pope Speaks* 16 (1972), p. 381.

8. *Second Celano*, 165, p. 494.

9. *First Celano*, 26, p. 249.

10. Ibid., p. 250.

11. For a background on this form of prayer, cf. A Monk of the Eastern Church, *The Prayer of Jesus*, trans. A Monk of the Western Church (New York: Desclee Company, 1967).

12. *Second Celano*, 101, p. 445.

13. Ibid., 193, p. 517.

14. Bernard Lonergan, *Method in Theology* (New York: Herder and Herder, 1972), pp. 235–37.

15. John 1:16 emphasizes the relation of grace and love as they draw us into a deeper participation in the Godhead.

16. "Justice in the World," III, p. 385.

17. Pope Paul VI, "The Ministerial Priesthood," *The Pope Speaks* 16 (1972), p. 368.

18. Lonergan, *Method in Theology*, p. 238.

19. *First Celano*, 2, p. 231, and 24, p. 249.

20. Lonergan, *Method in Theology*; emphasis mine.

21. Ibid., p. 239.

22. Ibid., p. 239–40.

23. Ibid., p. 240; emphasis mine.

24. Ibid.

25. Archie B. Carroll, "A Survey of Managerial Ethics: Is Business Morality Watergate Morality?" *Business and Society Review 13* (Summer 1975): 58–59.

26. Saul Alinsky, *Rules for Radicals* (New York: Random House, 1971), p. 88.

27. Cf. Michael H. Crosby, O.F.M. Cap., *Catholic Church Investments for Corporate Social Responsibility* (Milwaukee: Justice and Peace Center, 1973), pp. 37–39.

28. Lonergan, *Method in Theology*, pp. 240–41; emphasis mine.

29. Cardinal Leon Joseph Suenens, "Pope John XXIII," *The Furrow* 15 (July 1964): 435.

30. *First Celano*, 8, pp. 235–36.

31. Elisabeth Kubler-Ross, *On Death and Dying* (New York: Macmillan Company, 1970), p. 35.

32. Pope Paul VI, 1977 Lenten Message, *L'Osservatore Romano*, March 3, 1977; quote from "Constitution on the Sacred Liturgy," no. 10.

33. Pope Paul VI, Address to Business Managers, *L'Osservatore Romano*, March 3, 1977; quote from "Church in the Modern World," no. 69, 1.

34. "Discrimination Reported Necessary to Draw Women, Minorities into Jobs," *Fond du Lac Reporter*, June 11, 1976.

35. C.C. Garvin, Jr., in "Energy-Tax Boost is Exxon Suggestion to Aid Conservation," *Wall Street Journal*, October 19, 1976.

36. Clark Kerr, "Does Freedom Make Might Right?" *PHP: A Forum for a Better World*, March 1976, p. 22.

37. *Second Celano*, 10–11, pp. 370–71.

38. *First Celano*, 5, p. 233.

39. *Second Celano*, 6, p. 366.

40. Lonergan, *Method in Theology*, pp. 130–31.

41. Ibid., p. 131.

11. AMEN

1. Robert Aron, *The Jewish Jesus*, trans. Agnes H. Forsyth and Anne-Marie de Commaille (Maryknoll: Orbis Books, 1971), p. 3.

2. "Protestant Lead Over, Study Says," *Milwaukee Journal*, October 19, 1975.

3. Ibid.

4. Andrew Greeley, quoted in ibid.

5. "Justice in the World," II, *The Pope Speaks* 16 (1972), p. 381.

Acknowledgements

Aldine Publishing Company: From *Social Interaction: Process and Products* by Musafer Sherif. Copyright 1967 by Aldine Publishing Company. Reprinted with permission of Aldine Publishing Company.

American Economic Association: From "Property Rights and Economic Theory: A Survey of Recent Literature" by Eirik G. Furobotn and Svetozar Pejovich. Copyright December 1972 by *Journal of Economic Literature*. Rep:inted by permission of the authors and American Economic Association.

Associated Press: From "Discrimination Reported Necessary to Draw Women, Minorities into Jobs." *Fond du Lac Reporter*, June 11, 1974. Reprinted with permission of the Associated Press.

Ave Maria Press: From *Healing* by Francis MacNutt, O.P. Copyright 1974 by Ave Maria Press. Reprinted by permission of Ave Maria Press.

Beacon Press: From *Beyond God the Father* by Mary Daly. Copyright 1973 by Mary Daly. Reprinted by permission of Beacon Press.

Benziger Bruce & Glencoe, Inc.: From *New Testament Essays* by Raymond E. Brown, S.S. Copyright 1965 by The Bruce Publishing Company. Reprinted by permission of Benziger Bruce & Glencoe, Inc.

Richard Byrne, O.C.S.O. From *Living the Contemplative Dimension of Everyday Life* by Richard Byrne, O.C.S.O. Copyright and permission given by author.

J.S. Canner & Company: From *Source Book and Guide for American Church History* by Peter G. Mode. Copyright 1964 by J.S. Canner & Company Inc. Reprinted by permission of J.S. Canner & Company.

The Catholic University of America Press: From *The Fathers of the Church* by St. Cyprian, tr. and ed. by Roy J. Deferrari. Copyright 1958 by Fathers of the Church, Inc. Reprinted by permission of The Catholic University of America Press.

Cistercian Publications: From *The Climate of Monastic Prayer* by Thomas Merton. Copyright 1969 by Cistercian Publications. Reprinted by permission of Cistercian Publications.

Confraternity of Christian Doctrine: From *The New American Bible*. Copyright 1970, by the Confraternity of Christian Doctrine. Reprinted by permission of the Confraternity of Christian Doctrine.

Council on Religion and International Affairs: From "Excursus III: Neither Guerillas Nor Patsies" by Richard John Neuhaus, *Worldview*, December 1974. From "Employment Problems and Transnational Enterprises in Developing Countries: Distortions and Inequality" by Constantine V. Vaitsos, Carnegie Center for Transnational Studies, July 1976. Copyright 1974, 1976 by Council on Religion and International Affairs. Reprinted with permission of *Worldview* and Michael Sloan.

Cross Currents: From "On Renewing the Revolution of the Pharisees: A New Approach to Theology and Politics" by John T. Pawlikowski. Copyright Fall 1970 by *Cross Currents.* Reprinted by permission of *Cross Currents.*

Doubleday & Company, Inc.: From *Nobody Wanted War: Misperception in Vietnam and Other Wars* by Ralph K. White. Copyright 1968, 1970 by Ralph K. White. Reprinted by permission of Doubleday & Company, Inc.

Phillip H. Dougherty: From "How I.T.T. Improved Its Image" by Phillip H. Dougherty, April 18, 1975. Copyright 1975 by *The New York Times.* Reprinted by permission of Phillip H. Dougherty.

Dow Jones & Company, Inc.: From "The Right to Food" April 8, 1976. From "The Environmentalist Crusade" by Irving Kristol, December 16, 1974. From "Mobil's Advocacy Ads Lead a Growing Trend, Draw Praise, Criticism" by Michael J. Connor, May 14, 1975. From "Mexican Factories Continue to Spread Along the U.S. Border," April 14, 1975. From "Getting Off the Treadmill" by James P. Gannon, April 12, 1974. Reprinted with permission of *The Wall Street Journal.* Copyright 1974, 1975, 1976 by Dow Jones & Company, Inc. All rights reserved.

William B. Eerdmans Publishing Co.: From *The Politics of Jesus* by John Howard Yoder. Copyright 1972 by William B. Eerdmans Publishing Company. Reprinted by permission of William B. Eerdmans Publishing Company.

English-Speaking Conference of the Order of Friars Minor: From "The Vocation of the Order Today" in General Chapter Documents—Madrid, 1973. Reprinted by permission.

Farrar, Straus & Giroux, Inc.: From *Man Is Not Alone* by Abraham Heschel. Copyright 1951 by Abraham Joshua Heschel. Reprinted by permission.

Forbes, Inc.: From "Jimmy Carter's Computer Connection," *Forbes,* January 15, 1977. Copyright Forbes, Inc. 1977.

Fortress Press: From *Creation* by Claus Westermann, tr. by John J. Scuillion, S.J. Copyright 1974 by SPCK and Fortress Press. Reprinted by permission of Fortress Press.

Franciscan Herald Press: From *St. Francis of Assisi: Writings and Early Biographies*, ed. by Marion A. Habig. Copyright 1972 by Franciscan Herald Press. Reprinted with permission.

The Furrow: From "Pope John XXIII" by Cardinal Joseph Suenens. Copyright July 1964 by *The Furrow.* Reprinted by permission of *The Furrow.*

C. C. Garvin, Jr.: From "Recognizing Today's Realities" by C.C. Garvin, Jr., October 18, 1976. Reprinted with permission of C.C. Garvin, Jr.

Andrew M. Greeley: From "Protestant Lead Over, Study Says," *The Milwaukee Journal,* October 19, 1975. Reprinted with permission of Rev. Andrew Greeley of the National Opinion Research Center.

Harper & Row, Publishers, Inc.: From *The Lord's Prayer* by Ernst Lohmeyer, tr. by John Bowden. Copyright 1965 by Harper & Row. From *The Prophets* by Abraham Heschel. Copyright 1962 by Abraham Heschel. Reprinted by permission of Harper & Row, Publisher, Inc.

Harvard Business Review: From "Our Society in 1985—Business May Not Like It" by George Cabot Lodge and William F. Martin, *Harvard Business Review,* November-December 1975. Copyright 1975 by the President and Fellows of

Harvard College; all rights reserved. Reprinted by permission of *Harvard Business Review*.

Herald Press: From *Christ and the Powers* by Hendrik Berkhof. Copyright 1962 by Herald Press. Reprinted by permission of Herald Press.

IDOC/North America: From "Development or Liberation" by Denis Goulet, *Freedom and Unfreedom in the Americas: Toward a Theology of Liberation*, 1971. From "Unctad III: Global Town Meeting or Folkloric Carnival?" by Dr. Herman Santa Cruz and "Poverty, Power, Environment: Issues of Justice in Latin America" by Radomiro Tomic. Copyright 1971, 1973 by IDOC/North America. Reprinted by permission of IDOC/North America.

Interpretation: From "The God of Death: Power and Obedience in the Primeval History" by George W. Coats, July 1975. Copyright 1975 by Interpretation. Reprinted by permission of Interpretation.

Alfred A. Knopf, Inc.: From *The Technological Society* by Jacques Ellul, tr. by John Wilkinson. Copyright 1964 by Alfred A. Knopf, Inc. Reprinted by permission of Alfred A. Knopf, Inc.

John Knox Press: From *The Vitality of Old Testament Traditions* by Walter Brueggemann and Hans Walter Wolff. Copyright John Knox Press 1975. Used by permission of the publisher.

Macmillan Publishing Co., Inc.: From *On Death and Dying* by Elisabeth Kubler-Ross. Copyright 1969 by Elisabeth Kubler-Ross. From *Social Theory and Social Structure* by Robert K. Merton. Copyright 1957 by The Free Press. Reprinted by permission of Macmillan Publishing Co., Inc.

Francis S. MacNutt, O.P.: From notes taken by Rev. MacNutt of the First Latin American Charismatic Conference. Reprinted by permission of Francis S. Mac-Nutt, O.P.

Ralph Nader: From *Constitutionalizing the Corporation: The Case for the Federal Chartering of Giant Corporations* by Ralph Nader, Mark Green, and Joel Seligman. Copyright 1976 by Ralph Nader. Reprinted by permission of the Corporate Accountability Research Group.

The New York Times: From "The New American Establishment Is Called the Community" by Leslie H. Gelb, December 19, 1976, Business Section. Copyright 1976 by The New York Times Company. Reprinted by permission.

W.W. Norton & Company, Inc.: From *Civilization and Its Discontents* by Sigmund Freud. Copyright 1958 by W.W. Norton & Co. From *Love and Will* by Rollo May. Copyright 1969 by W.W. Norton & Company, Inc. Reprinted by permission of W.W. Norton & Company, Inc.

PHP Institute, Incorporated: From "Does Freedom Make Might Right?" by Clark Kerr. Reprinted by permission of Clark Kerr.

Paulist Press: From *Contemplation* by James Carroll. Copyright 1972. From "The Dynamic Conscience" by Gregory Baum. Copyright May-June 1974 by *The Ecumenist*. From "Francis of Assisi" by Giulio Basetti-Sani, O.F.M., tr. Michael Tully, O.S.B. in *Concilium: Theology in the Age of Renewal* 37. Copyright 1968 by Paulist Fathers, Inc. and Stichting Concilium. From *Jesus and the Eucharist* by Tad Guzie, S.J. Copyright 1974 by Tad W. Guzie, S.J. From "The Passover Amid the Paschal Meal" by Thomas Barrosse in *Concilium: Theology in the Age of Renewal* 40.

Copyright 1969 by Paulist Fathers, Inc. and Stichting Concilium; all reprinted with permission of The Paulist Press.

Prentice-Hall: From *The Megacorporation in American Society: The Scope of Corporate Power* by Phillip I. Blumberg. Copyright 1976 by Prentice-Hall, Inc. Reprinted by permission of Prentice-Hall, Inc.

Random House, Inc.: From *The Federalist: A Commentary on the Constitution of the United States* by James Madison. From *Rules for Radicals* by Saul Alinsky. Copyright 1971 by Saul Alinsky. Reprinted by permission of Random House, Inc.

Henry Regnery Company: From *The Mystery of Being* by Gabriel Marcel, tr. by Rene Hague. Copyright 1960 by Gabriel Marcel. Reprinted by permission of Henry Regnery Company.

SCM Press Ltd.: From *Prayers of Jesus* by Joachim Jeremias, Copyright by Dr. Christoph Burchard. Reprinted by permission of SCM Press Ltd.

Seabury Press: From *False Presence of the Kingdom* by Jacques Ellul, tr. by C. Edward Hopkin. Copyright 1972 by The Seabury Press, Inc. From *Method in Theology* by Bernard Lonergan. Copyright 1972 by Bernard Lonergan. From *A New Pentecost?* by Leon Joseph Cardinal Suenens, tr. by Francis Martin. Copyright 1975 by The Seabury Press, Inc. From *The Prayer of Jesus* by a Monk of the Eastern Church. Copyright 1967 Desclee and Company. From *The Spirituals and the Blues: An Interpretation* by James H. Cone. Copyright 1972 by James H. Cone. All used and reprinted by permission of The Seabury Press.

Simon & Schuster, Inc.: From *Global Reach: The Power of the Multinational Corporations* by Richard Barnet and Ronald Müller. Copyright 1974 by Richard J. Barnet and Ronald E. Müller. Reprinted by permission of Simon & Schuster, Inc.

James D. Smith and Stephen D. Franklin: From *The Concentration of Personal Wealth, 1922–1969* by James D. Smith and Stephen D. Franklin, 1973. From "Very Rich Keep Share of US Worth" by James D. Smith, *Milwaukee Journal*, January 18, 1974. Reprinted with permission of James D. Smith and Stephen D. Franklin.

Sojourners: From "The Politics of Worship" by Robert Sabath. Copyright 1972 by *Post-American*. Reprinted by permission of *Sojourners*.

United Press International: From "Cereal's Big Four Questioned," April, 1976. Copyright 1976 by United Press International. Reprinted by permission of United Press International.

United States Catholic Conference: From "Apostolic Letter to Cardinal Maurice Roy" by Pope Paul VI, 1971. From "On the Development of Peoples" by Pope Paul VI, 1967. From "Pastoral Message of the Administrative Committee," February 1973. From "The Quest for Justice as Latin Americans Live It," unpublished. Copyright 1967, 1971, 1973 by United States Catholic Conference. Reprinted by permission of United States Catholic Conference.

U.S. News & World Report: From "Sizing Up the Nation's Most Powerful Institutions," April 18, 1977. Copyright 1977 by U.S. News & World Report, Inc. Reprinted with permission.

Verlag Herder: From *Principalities and Powers in the New Testament* by Heinrich Schlier. Used by permission of Verlag Herder in Freiburg, Germany.

The Wanderer: From "A Theory for Political Action" by William H. Marshner. Copyright June 1975 by *The Wanderer*. Reprinted by permission of *The Wanderer*.

The Washingtonian Magazine: From "God and Man in Washington: How Religion is Used and Abused in the Eternal City of Politics" by Laurence Leamer. Copyright 1975 by Laurence Leamer. Reprinted by permission of *The Washingtonian Magazine.*

The Washington Post: From "Live Not by Lies" by Alexander Solzhenitsyn. Copyright February 1974 by *The Washington Post.* Reprinted by permission of *The Washington Post.*

The Westminster Press: From *A Process Christology* by David R. Griffin. Copyright 1973 by the Westminster Press. Used by permission.

Word Books: From *An Ethic for Christians and Other Aliens in a Strange Land* by William Stringfellow. Copyright 1973 by Word, Incorporated. From *The Gospel of Liberation* by Jürgen Moltmann, tr. by H. Wayne Pipkin. Copyright 1973 by Word, Incorporated. Reprinted by permission of Word Books, Publisher, Waco, Texas.

Ziff-Davis Publishing Company: From "Social Stereotypes: Three Faces of Happiness: Effects of Income" by P. Cameron. Copyright 1974 Ziff-Davis Publishing Company. Reprinted by permission of *Psychology Today* Magazine.

Scriptural Index

Genesis

1:26	40
1:26–28	27
1:29	29–30
2:7	56
2:19–20	38
3:9	31
3:10	38
4:9	31
8:17	40
9:7	40
12:3	98
17:20–25	40
18:17–19	98
18:20	224
18:21	98
19:4f	224
28:1–4	40
31:54	130
48:3–4	40

Exodus

3:4f	39
3:7	39, 41, 91
3:7–8	119
3:8	40, 41, 63, 91
3:12	119, 133
3:13–14	40
3:15	40
3:16f	195
4:11–14	188
4:16	190
6:1f	39
12f	198
15:35b	87
16:3	72
16:18	156
17:1–7	119
17:3	72

18:13–27	87
19:8	88
21:1	87
24:3	130

Leviticus

24:1f	137
25	137
25:23–24	151
25:50	144
25:55	137

Numbers

21:8–9	98

Deuteronomy

15:1–11	138
15:2	139

Tobit

7:11–15	130

Psalms

8:6–8	31
24:1	94, 150
33:11	184
34:9	35
41:10	130
78:13	134
119:172	87
137:1	144

Proverbs

19:21	184
21:13	55

Wisdom

9:13	184
9:17	184

Isaiah

1:1f	131
1:2	120
1:2–17	46–47
1:9f	224
1:11–17	121
1:16–19	140
1:21	120
3:9	224
9:5	50
10:1–4	88
13:9	87
13:11	87
42:1	102
42:5–8	102
42:6	43, 129
53:10–11	102
55:8	185
55:8–9	38
58:5–9	143
61:1	102

Jeremiah

22:13–16	45
22:15–16	121
23:6	41
23:14	224
31	184
31:13–34	124

Ezekiel

9:4	58, 115
16:46–51	224
36:23–28	125

Daniel

11:2   60

Hosea

2:19   50
4:1–7   89
4:7   89
6:6   46, 119,
        120
6:6–7   89
6:7   119

Matthew

1:20   125
1:21   48, 103,
        188
2:1–8   3
2:16–18 3
3:15   102
4:1   163
4:10   166
5:1f   155
5:3   30
5:6   164
5:13   9
5:17   22
5:20   86
5:23–24 140
5:48   33, 110
6:9   36
6:30–31 205
7:9   125
7:21   67
7:22   190, 124
7:23   67
8:7–10 119
8:11–12 118
8:20   69
9:10–13 118
10:12   96
11:3f   102
11:4   9
11:6   49
12:41   113
15:3   165
15:6   165
15:13–21 129
15:24   10
16:6   165
16:24–28 71

18:3   25, 198
18:20   51, 188,
        220
18:27   139
18:34–35 139
19:29   37
20:22–23 129
20:25–28 164–65
21:31   67, 118
21:38   103
21:42–43 104
21:43   118
22:2f   122
25:31–41 123
25:34   123
25:52   77
26:53   67, 164
28:16   191
28:18   164
28:19   50, 115,
        188

Mark

1:15   17, 49,
        137, 190
2:22   8
2:23f   87
3:15   164
7:6   91
7:6–7   86
7:7   114
7:8   88
7:9   87
7:13   88
8:14–21 184
8:31   103
8:31f   72
9:30f   72
10:32f 72
14:36   103

Luke

1:51–53 160
2:51   160
4:1–2   163
4:3   163
4:5–7   164
4:9–11 165
4:16f   143
4:16–19 136
4:18   141

4:18f   102
4:20–21 137
4:21   190
5:12f   141
6:34–36 138
7:22–23 141
7:27   168
9:1   17
9:1–2   181
10:3   135
10:17–25 181
11:3   125
11:11–13 125
12:13–21 176
12:19f 157, 176
12:22–31 176
12:30   176
12:32–34 176
14:12–14 117
14:28   72
14:35   12
16:10–13 215
16:15   214
17:11–19 141
18:1f   57
18:7–8 57
18:18–30 209
18:28–30 37
19:2f   49
19:45–46 141
22:19   133
22:29–30 34
23:2   69
23:47   104
24:21   133
24:25f 194
24:35   130
24:47   19

John

1:11   217
1:16   198, 203,
        229
1:29   48
1:38–39 25
2:19   165
3:13–21 99
3:17   44, 103
4:34   101, 164
5:18   21
5:30   101

6:12–15	164	2:45	156	5:17	203	
6:15	164	3:6	50	5:17–21	112	
6:35	117	3:16	190	5:20	113	
6:38	97	4:12	50	5:21	51, 129,	
6:38–39	37	4:17–18	52		203	
6:39–40	97	4:29–30	52	8:9	156	
6:40	104	5:29	109	8:12–15	156	
6:51	117, 164	5:38–42	52			
6:53	125	17:7	60, 109			
6:63	125			*Galatians*		
6:68–69	8, 77	*Romans*				
7:37–38	24			5:25	213	
7:39	24	1:17	47			
11:45f	77, 100	1:18–23	85	*Ephesians*		
11:47–48	100	1:19–25	177			
11:48	69, 129	1:25	85, 89	2:12–18	126	
11:49–53	101	4:7	47	2:18	26	
11:50f	69, 209	5:5	125	6	174–75	
11:52	98, 104	5:20	194	6:5	144	
12:32	97	8	126, 158,	6:10	90	
14:1	205		197	6:10f	203	
14:16–17	205	8:14–16	33–34	6:10–12	166	
15:18f	134	8:18f	203	6:10–17	77	
15:18–19	5	8:19–22	33–34	6:12	185	
15:20	5	8:26–27	33–34	6:14	174	
16:1–3	106	12:1	16	6:16	78	
16:1–4	206	13:8	140			
16:2	108	14:17	67	*Phillipians*		
16:8	106					
17:6	37	*1 Corinthians*		2:8f	104	
17:14–15	186			2:10–11	50	
17:14–19	79	1:18–19	70, 104	3:17	213	
17:17	85	1:21–25	104			
17:20	65	1:23	165	*Colossians*		
17:20–21	193	2:8	105			
17:25–26	91	10:3	119	1:20	110	
18:37	37	11:1	214	2:9–10	70	
19:11	106, 164	11:17–22	127	2:12–15	70	
19:12	59, 69	11:18	128	2:15	105, 166	
19:12–16	3	11:22	127			
19:15	69	11:24	129	*1 Thessalonians*		
		11:26–29	128			
Acts		11:29–32	128	2	60	
		12	16, 173,			
1:8	181		196	*Hebrews*		
1:13f	195	12:7	190			
2:4f	198	12:12–13	125	1:1–2	213	
2:38	51			3–4	158	
2:40	51	*2 Corinthians*		4:1–3	83	
2:42	51			4:7–11	83	
2:42f	77, 192	4:4	216	10:5–7	101	
2:44	51	5:16–21	127			

James			1 John			13	60
						13f	3
1:26–27	47		2:29	55		13:8	55
4:1–2	94		3:12–18	99–100		14:1–12	116
			3:14	58		18:1	61
1 Peter			3:17	160		18:1–18	61–62
						18:2	65
1:12–22	33		*Revelation*			18:19	65
3:8–12	33					18:21	61
			1:5	61		18:23–24	61
2 Peter			1:6	61		19:11–16	58
			3:14	213		19:16	60
2:3	153		7:3	58		22:20	61

Celano Index

First Celano

Number	Page
2	199
5	210
8	205
22	115
24	92, 112, 119
25	157
26	195
35	90, 191
37	172, 191
39	84
76	32, 32–33
92	103, 224

Second Celano

Number	Page
6	210
10–11	210
12	5, 32
15	228
30	73
31	172
47	93
59	151
71	123
81	156–57
87	139
99	159
101	196
120	33
125	184
148	172
165	55, 92, 194
193	114, 196

General Index

ABC, 179
Abortion, 82, 108, 110, 170
Abraham, 98, 104, 118
Action-reflection, 39, 55, 77, 183, 188
Adaptation, 12–13, 14, 183, 211
Addiction, 18, 53, 72, 193, 194, 205f, 213
Adolescent level, 14–15, 24, 49, 199, 200, 201, 215
Adult, see Self
Adultery, 88–89, 132
Advertising, 80–81, 133, 158, 176, 178
Advertising agencies, 11
Affluence, 157; see also Blessing, Wealth
Africa, 146
Ageism, 66, 167, 173, 189
Agribusiness, 152
Aid, 147f
Airstrikes, 82
Alexian Brothers, 112
Alienation, 69, 70, 72, 118, 128, 139, 173–74, 192, 194, passim
  adaptation to, 8, 11–12, 144–45, 169
  environmental, 18, 29, 50, 68f, 98–99, 126, 142, 174, 183, 195, 211
  as expression of sin, 18–19, 38, 43, 68, 128, 145, 193
  and infrastructures, 26, 28f, 84, 146f
Alinsky, Saul, 201–02
Allende, Salvador, 178
Ambassador, see Shaliach
Amen, 65, 131, 132, 212f
America, see United States of America
Amnesty, 143; see also Indulgence
Amorites, 63
Amos, 117
Andean Pact Nations, 149
Anger, 15, 83, 87
Anti-Americanism, 64, 66
Anti-Christ, 33; see also Powers and Principalities

Anxiety, 38, 176, 190, 193, 194, 195, 198, 204, 205
Apathy, 43–45, 109, 114, 139, 184
Appalachia, 58
Aquinas, St. Thomas, 1, 5, 158
Aristotle, 144, 146, 148, 150
Arms, 93, 95, 96, 175, 210
Aron, Robert, 212
Asia, 146
Aspen, Colorado, 149
Astrodome, 71
Atlanta, Georgia, 181
Attica, New York, 68
Auden, W.H., 84
Augustine, St., 1, 5
Authority, 87, 110, 113, 164–165
Awe, 27, 35, 39; see also Contemplation

Babylon, 59, 61, 65, 67, 116, 144, 184
Bankers Trust, 81
Banks, 11, 148, 152, 179f, 202, 223
  New York, 81, 179
Baptism
  sacrament, 50f, 70, 79, 125, 145, 172, 188
  in the Spirit, 20, 195, 220
Basic communities, 13, 113, 160, 187, 190f, 210–11, passim
  conflicts in, 94–96
  participative, 20, 93; see also Participative community
  as reflective of the Trinity, 23–27, 93, 96; see also Trinity
Basseti-Sani, Giulio, 78
Baum, Gregory, 166–68
Beast, 58–60
Beatitudes, 123
Bell, Griffin, 181
Berger, Peter L., 219
Berkhof, Hendrik, 105–6
Bernard, Brother, 92, 227–28
Bernard, St., 78, 156–57

Berrigan, Daniel, 69
Big Business, *see* Transnational corporations
Biography as theology, 213–15, 217; *see also* Spirituality
Bishops, 19, 108, 155, 169, 172, 204
Blessing, 27, 64, 128, 157–58, 176
  in Genesis, 27, 29f, 40–41, 98
  as participation in God's plan, 40–41, 49, 98, 122–24, 155
  as sharing resources and rights, 40–41, 123, 155
Blood, 125, 126
Blumenthal, W. Michael, 180
Body Level, 14–15, 24, 58, 199
Boldness, 53
Bonaventure, St., 150
Boycott, 162
Brand names, 49, 50
Branscomb, Dr. Louis, 181
Bread, 125, 131, 163–64, 217
Britain, 62
Brokenness, 129f; *see also* Alienation
Brown, Harold, 181
Brown, Raymond, 8, 34, 37, 123
Business, *see* Corporations
Brueggemann, Walter, 29, 40–41
Brzezinski, Zbigniew, 180
Budget, 174
Bureaucracy, U.S., 11
Byrne, Richard, 42, 44

CBS, 179
CIA, 79
Cabinet, U.S., 11, 181–82, 227
Caesar, 3, 60, 69, 71, 103
Caiaphas, 100–01, 104
Call of God, 41f
Campus Ministry, 172–73
Canaanites, 63
Canada, 145
Capitalism, 26, 71, 147, 151f
Capuchin Franciscans, Midwest Province, 81, 112, 179, 228–29
Caring, 41–42, 131, 203
  as creative of justice, 43f, 121
  as fundamental for contemplation and ministry, 43–45
  God's pathos, 43f, 50, 121
Carroll, James, 68–69
Carter, Jimmy, 180, 181, 227
Catechism, 124
Catholic Theological Union, 120

Catholics, 214–16, passim
Celano, Thomas of, *see* Celano Index
Celibacy, *see* Purity of Heart, Sexuality
Cereal, 132–33
Chaos, *see* Alienation, Exile, Sin
Chancery, 172–73
Change, 54, 77; *see also* Conversion
de Chardin, Teilhard, 68–69
Charismatic Renewal, 20, 220
Charisms, 49, 50, 124, 141, 172, 187, 188, 189, 190–91
Charity, *see* Love
Chase Manhattan, 80
Chicago, Illinois, 68, 120, 215
Child, 24, 36
  discipleship, 24–25, 198
  level, 15, 24, 49, 199, 201, 215; *see also* Body level
Chile, 150, 178
Christ, *see* Jesus Christ
Christopher, Warren, 181
Chrysostom, St. John, 94
Church, 6, 67, 127f, 140, 161–62, passim
  as God's kingdom, 66f, 222
  as institution, 7f, 66, 68, 163, 188, 189, passim; *see also* Institution
  as liberated zone in history, 51, 188
Cicero, Illinois, 113, 136
Civil disobedience, 60–61, 87, 108; *see also* Disobedience
Civil religion, 62f, 74
  and liturgy, 4, 64
Civil rights, 11, 96, 170
Civil War, 64
Class, 10, 96, 147, 220
Classism, *see* Clerics, Elitism, Priests
Clerics, 10, 113–14; *see also* Priests
Coats, George W., 29, 30–31
Cohen, Jerry S., 17
Coleman, William T., Jr., 181
Colonialism, 146, 149
Columbia University, 175
Commodities, 155
Communications
  instruments of, 167, 189
  media, 177, 178f; *see also* Ideology, Radio, Television
Communism, 64
Community, 91, 119, 137, 187, 188f, 197, 201–2, 210–11, passim; *see also* Gathering

Compassion, 119, 121, 129; *see also* Empathy, Pathos, Sympathy
Competition, 151, 179
Compromise, *see* Neutrality
Concern, *see* Care, Plan of God
Cone, James H., 144–45
Confirmation, 79, 172
Congregation for the Doctrine of the Faith, 107, 108, 109
Conscience, 80, 109; *see also* Ethics, Morality
Conscientization process, 187f, 197, 208, 210–11
Consecration, 48, 79, 84
Conspiracy, 180, 181, 182
Constitution, U.S., 107, 145
Consumer, 81, 152, 178, 227
Consumerism, 65, 66, 82, 167, 171, 174, 175–76, 189, 195, 217; *see also* Production-Consumption
Contemplation, 15, 16, 18, 20, 41–42, 92, 101, 158f, 192–93, 221
  and care, 42–44, 203–4; *see also* Awe, Prayer
Control, 26, 27, 49, 158, 195, 199, 204, 223; *see also* Enslavement, Language
  and power, 146, 172–73, 179
Conversion, 6, 10, 12, 17f, 51, 68, 73, 88, 101, 118, 187, 197f, 217–18; *passim*
  based on critique, 54–55, 182–183; *see also* Critical reflection
  intellectual, 54, 187, 197, 199–200; *see also* Mind-sets
  moral, 187, 197, 199, 200–03; *see also* Ethics
  movement of reform, 77, 108, 197
  religious, 187, 197, 199, 203
  systemic, 137f, 140, 148, 161, 168, 169–70, 178, 184, 206
  on three levels of reality, 140, 158, 189, 198, 199
Corporate responsibility, 132, 179, 185, 202, 227–28
Corporation, 80, 162, 179f, 207, 208, 223, 227, 228; *see also* Transnational corporation
Council of the Americas, 181
Council on Foreign Relations, 180, 181
Counselling, 141
Covenant, 43, 50, 89, 137, 191; *see also* Creation

Creation, 26f, 43f, 92, 97, 191, 194, 195
  and God's plan, 27f, 119f, 148, 196–97
  purpose of, 28f, 40f, 207
  restoration of, 92, 101–2, 111–12, 123, 137
Credibility Gap, 9, 10, 67, 79, 182; *see also* Truth
Credit, 152, 155
Crime, 174
Crisis, 96
Critical reflection, 10, 12, 13, 65, 67, 102, 158–62, 183, 187, 194, 199f; *see also* Action-Reflection, Conversion, Deliverance
Crosby, Blanche, 207–8
Crosby, Michael, 75
Cross, 70f, 79, 86, 115, 126, 132, 165, 208
  as instrument of insurrection, 59, 69, 111f, 166
  and will of God, 97, 103, 217–18
Crucifixion of Jesus, 70f
  as response of religio-politico-economic forces, 69, 85, 101, 104f, 110–11
Crusader, 72f, 77, 80
Cultural addiction, *see* Addiction, Ideology, Infrastructure, Environmental alienation, Social sin
Culture, 171, 227; *see also* Language, Reality
Cumulative voting, 179
Curia, Roman, 171
Cyprian, St., 1, 23
Cyril of Jerusalem, St., 1

Dallas, Texas, 68
Daly, Mary, 25, 57
Datsun, 49
Day of Atonement, 138
Death, 16, 205–6, 213; *see also* Pathology
Debts, 137, 138f, 225
Deception, 81, 85, 105; *see also* Credibility, Truth
Declaration of Independence, 63–64
Decree on Ecumenism, 10
Decrees, 124, 141
Dedication, *see* Consecration
Delano, California, 113
"Delegation of Peace," 92, 112, 191

Deliverance, 18, 52–53, 141, 178, 186f, 213; *see also* Liberation, Name, Holy Spirit
Democracy, 50, 64
Democratic Party, 11
Denial, 80, 82, 205–6
Denominations, 216
Deodorant, 82
Department, U.S.,
  of Commerce, 181
  of Defense, 82, 181
  of Housing and Urban Development, 181
  of Justice, 112, 181
  of State, 149, 173, 180, 181
  of Transportation, 181
  of Treasury, 181
Dependency, 146, 148, 149
Desert, 136, 163–66, 186, 204; *see also* Alienation
Detergents, 82
Developing Nations, 145–50, 173
Development, 147–48, 149, 151
Devil, 78, 163–66; *see also* Powers and Principalities
Dichotomy between prayer and ministry, 6, 35, passim
Diocese, 113; *see also* Bishops
Discipleship, 7, 24–25, 49, 69, 72, 77, 78, 108, 113, 190, 194–95, 213–14, 216, passim
Discipline of the Secret, 2–3
Disclosure, 79
Discrimination, 173–74, 208; *see also* Enslavement, Isms, Oppression
Disease, *see* Pathology
Disobedience to oppressive government, 87, 108–10, 114; *see also* Resistance
Disponibilité, 24f
Distribution, 96; *see also* Power, Property, Wealth
Distributive justice, 150, 154–55, 156, 178f, 226; *see also* Ethics, Equality
Doctrine, 10
Documents, 124
Domestication, 144–45, 173; *see also* Enslavement
Domination, 30, 137; *see also* Enslavement, Exploitation, Oppression
Domitian, 60, 62

Doublespeak, 82
Dulles, Avery, 6, 222
DuPont, 181

Eagles Club, 162
Eastern Europe, 180
Eckhart, Meister, 1
Ecological balance, 82, 146, 152, 175, 227; *see also* Resources
Economic institution, 145, 163–64, 177, 189, 227; *see also* Corporation
Ecstasy, 48, 56, 203
Education, 134, 167, 177, 182–83, 189
Educational institutions, 177, 180f, 227; *see also* Schools
Ego level, 14–15, 24, 58, 199; *see also* Adolescent level
Eliot, T.S., 44
Elitism, 113–14, 167, 171–73, 179, 180, 189
Ellul, Jacques, 26, 49, 135
Emancipation Proclamation, 144
Emotion, 48
Empathy, 44, 45f, 95, 139; *see also* Care
Emperor, 2, 59f
Employment, 58; *see also* Equality, Work
Empowerment, 57, 187, 190, 194–95, 197, 198, 204, 214; *see also* Basic Community, Grace, Power, Participative community, Social grace
Enemies List, 60, 95f
Energy, 152; *see also* Resources
Enslavement, 84, 98, 104, 111, 133, 142, 144f, 178, 186, 188, 189, 193, 197, 198, 204, 227; *see also* Oppression, Sin
  chattel slavery, 144–46, 150
  de facto slavery, 144, 146–50
Environment, 67, 126; *see also* Alienation, Exploitation, Infrastructures, Resources, World
Equality, 119, 155–56, 166, 172, 202, 207f
  of opportunity, 173, 174, 207f
  of result, 173, 174
Eschatological fulfilment, 34, 66, 117–18
Ethics, 60, 147; *see also* Morality, Conversion
  founded on information, 79–80

and lifestyle, 61–62, 85, 209; *see also* Lifestyle
relationship to individual, interpersonal, and infrastructural levels, 88f, 108, 200f
Ethnics, 161, 215, 216
Etzioni, Amitai, W., 175
Eucharist, 117f, 133
Evangelization, 161, 169, 185, 191; *see also* Conversion
Evil, *see* Sin, Powers and Principalities
Exegesis, 6, 87
Exile, 28f, 40–41, 68–69; *see also* Alienation
Exodus, 39–42, 163f, 188f
Exorcism, 67, 124; *see also* Healing, Deliverance
Exploitation, *see* Resources, Oppression
of the earth, 31, 50, 82, 152
of people, 30f, 59, 61, 158; *see also* Rights
Exxon, 208

Faith, 1, 3, 8, 9, 15–16, 57, 68, 78, 97, 98, 100, 104, 116, 132, 187, 192, 204, 212, 220
foundation for renewal, 14, 47
Faith Tours, 142
Family, 11, 20, 95, 154, 178, 215, 216; *see also* Basic community
Farmers, 131, 132, 158
Farmworkers, 132
Fasting, 67, 142, 143
Father, God the, 20, 36, 50, 97, 106, 110, 135, 171, 193, 211, 221, passim
Abba, meaning of, 21, 34, 38
Favella, 58
Federal Trade Commission, 132–33, 153
Feudalism, 210
Finance, 179, 215; *see also* Credit, Business
Finkelstein, Rabbi Louis, 65
First Latin American Charismatic Conference, 20
Fond du Lac Reporter, 208
Food Day, 132
Food for Peace, 174
Ford, Gerald, 181

Forgiveness, passim; *see also* Reconciliation
of debts, 137, 138f, 144; *see also* Healing
of sins, 138f, 144; *see also* Indulgence
Formula for Prayers, 8–9, 15; *see also* Ritual
Fort Worth, Texas, 174
Fortune, 8, 154
Francis of Assisi, St., 26, 34–35, 69, 78, 96, 114, 209–10; *see also* Celano Index
Franciscans, 2, 123; *see also* "Delegation of Peace," "True Followers of Justice"
Free Enterprise, 132, 153, 216
Freedom, 8, 36, 50, 56–57, 64, 111, 119, 133, 166, 191, 197, 198, 201, 207f, 217; *see also* Grace, Holy Spirit
and control, 36, 63, 139, 145
Freud, Sigmund, 18
Frontier, 146, 147

Garbage collection, 9
Garvin, E.C., 208–9
Gathering, 51, 77, 97–98, 104, 133, 187, 188–93, 194, 203, 210, 220; *see also* Church, Name
Gaudion, Donald, 177
Gelb, Leslie H., 180, 182
General Electric, 74–76
Genesis, *see* Biblical Index
blessing in, 29f
God's goal for creation, 27f, 196
written in context of chaos and exile, 28–29
Genocide, 175
George III, King, 62
Germany, Federal Republic of, 148
Gettysburg Address, 64
Gifts, *see* Charisms
Glory, *see* Praise
Gospel, 110, 132, 157, 158, 191, 202, 216, 224, passim
essential elements of, 90–91; *see also* Plan of God
Goulet, Denis, 147
Government, 132, 177, 179f, 217, 227; *see also* Institution, Society
purpose of, 63, 94, 107, 108, 114
state and local, 11

Grace, 203–4, 213; see also Freedom, Love, Holy Spirit, Social Grace
Graham, Dr. Billy, 65
Grain, 93, 131–32
Grave sin of social injustice, 1, 2, 19, 22, 36, 53, 80, 85, 90, 166, 182, 206, 216
Greeley, Andrew, 215
Gregory of Nyssa, St., 1
Gresham, Wisconsin, 112, 113
Griffin, David R., 22
Gross National Product, 147
Ground of Being, 56; see also Self, Father
Groups, see Interpersonal level
Guilt, 15; see also Anxiety
Guzie, Tad, 219

Half truths, 80–81, 85
Happiness, 157–58, see also Blessing
Harris, Patricia Roberts, 181
Harris Poll, 9
Hate, 44–45; see also Alienation
Hatfield, Mark, 62
Healing, 51, 52, 127f, 141, 190, 214, 225; see also Deliverance, Pathology, Charism
    essential to Jesus' ministry, 141, 193
    kinds of, 141, 193
    movement of the Spirit, 20, 141, 190
    on three levels, 141, 193
Heart, 91, 124, 184
    prayer of, 56–57, 91, 176
    purity of, 36, 56, 184
Hecker, Isaac, 69
Heralds of the Great King, 67, 73
Herod, King, 3
Heschel, Abraham, 27, 43, 47–48
Hills, Carla Anderson, 181
Hispanics, 173
Hittites, 63
Hivites, 63
Holiness, 86, 112, 124–25, 127, 203; see also Justice, Perfection
Holy Name Province, O.F.M., 2, 4
Holy Year, 141–42; see also Jubilee
Homosexuality, 224
Hope, 10, 25, 29, 35, 126, 144, 194, 214
Horizons, 24, 197f
Hosea, 45
Hospital, 58
House of Representatives, U.S., 11

Human Rights, 82, 96, 107, 118, 148, 169, 170, 209; see also Image of God, Rights
Hunger, 132, 160, 163–64
Huxley, Aldous, 227

IBM, 179–81, 227–28
ITT, 113, 178
Iconoclasm, 111; see also Subversion
Ideals, 8–13, 63, 77, 86, 89, 110, 140, 182, 190
Ideas, 109, 182; see also Information, Language, Mind-sets
Identification, 15, 16, 20, 99, 195
Ideology, 6, 72, 133, 166, 176–84, 189, 193, 200, 201, 213; see also Idol Worship, Language, Communication, Education
    described, 226–27
    in education, 177, 182–83, 199
    in institutions, 2, 6, 59, 61, 74–75, 85, 151, 166, 171, 198
    in instruments of communication, 6, 177, 178–82, 199
Idol worship, 30, 38, 49f, 59–60, 61, 62, 67, 86, 102, 115, 120, 125, 171, 176, 196, 216; see also Ideology, Powers and Principalities
    and brand names, 49–50, 176
    and powers and principalities, 53, 54, 85, 105, passim
Illusion, 106; see also Language
Image of God, 23, 27f, 72, 119, 127, 196, passim; see also Rights, Person, Isms, Word of God
    in all, 66, 137, 177, 189
    basis of spirituality, 31–32, 122–23
    relation to resources, 95, 166, 189, 207f
    relation to rights, 63, 87, 95, 207f
Imperialism, 167, 189
Income, 154, 206
Individual, 14, 15, 20, 31, passim; see also Person, Reality
Indochinese War, 82, 143; see also Vietnam
Indulgence, 141–42; 143; see also Debt
Inequity, 206; see also Distribution, Equality
Inflation, 132–33, 154

Information, 79–80; *see also* Truth, Ideology
controlled by institutions, 80, 182
necessary for ethical decisions, 80
Infrastructure, 10, 31, 37–38, 59, 112, 145f, 168f, 186f, 200, 201, 214, passim; *see also* Alienation, Social Sin
description of, 13, 17–18, 166
and ideology, 74–75, 133
level, 14–15, 17, 186f
relation to individuals and groups, 14, 59, 100–01
Injustice, 20, 87–88, 101, passim; *see also* Grave sin, Oppression, Exloitation
Insanity, 73f; *see also* Pathology
Insecurity, 15, 182, 198
Institution, 66, 90, 108, 166–70, 178, 182, 184, 189, 193, 200, 201, 213, 215, 217, 219
control over information, 80; *see also* Information, Language
evolution of political, 62f
evolution of religious, 8f, 68, 186f
Jesus' ministry to, 10
Insurrection, 69, 71, 72; *see also* Subversion
Interest, 140
Interfaith Center on Corporate Responsibility, 179; *see also* Corporate Responsibility
International Monetary Fund, 147
Interpersonal Level, 14, 20, 31, 140, 158, 189f; *see also* Reality, Community

Iroquois, 63
Isaac, 118
Isaiah, 45, 117, 213; *see* Biblical Index
Isms, 166, 167, 169, 170–76, 178, 179, 189, 193, 194, 200, 201, 213, 217, passim; *see also* Rights, Resources, Image of God

Jacob, 118
Japan, 146, 148, 180
Jebusites, 63
Jefferson, Thomas, 68
Jeremiah, 45, 117, 213; *see also* Biblical Index
Jeremias, Joachim, 21, 37–38

Jesus Christ, *see also* Word, Lord
and Eucharist, 118
as fulfillment of God's Plan, 9, 22, 48f, 97f, 136; *see also* Plan of God
ministry of, 48f, 136–37, 156, 163–66
name of, 48–58, 103, 188f
prayer of, 21–22, 91f, 193
as subversive, 5, 21, 88
as Way to the Father, 9, 20, 203–4, 221
Jesus Prayer, 56, 196
John the Baptist, St., 8, 197
John Chrysostom, St., 94
John XXIII, Pope, 68, 107
Jones, Reginald, 75
Joseph, St., 213
Joy, 56, 67
Jubilee, 136f, 225, 227–28
elements of, 137f; *see also* Deliverance
purpose of, 137, 155
sacred time, 136–37; *see also* Kairos
Judgment, 38
July Fourth, 64
Justice, 6, 55–57, 58, 67, 70, 78, 86–92, 98, 103, 106, 109, 113, 119f, 139, 217, 224, passim; *see also* Plan of God, Word of God
foundation for law, 87–88, 105–6, 120, 123–24
founded on care, 43f; *see also* Care
and God's pathos, 43–44
and knowing God, 41, 45–46, 48, 50–51, 67, 85, 86f, 120–21
and name of the Lord, 41, 48, 50–51
and restoration of creation, 43, 55, 58, 101–2, 40

Kairos, 136–37, 191
Kennedy, John, 68
Kennedy, Robert, 68
Kerr, Clark, 209
Kierkegaard, Soren, 68
Kim, Cardinal Stephen, 169
King, Martin Luther, 68
Kingdom, 6, 34, 62, 110, 118f, 155–56, 165, passim; *see also* Presence
church and, 66f
economic concept, 163–64
political concept, 59–60, 164–65
relation to name and will, 37–38, 97
relation to powers and principalities, 59–60, 103–4, 164–65, passim

Kirbo, Charles, 181
Knowing God/Known by God, 26, 31,
    39, 67, passim; *see also* Justice,
    Sacrifice
Korban, 86–87
Korff, Rabbi, 65
Kubler-Ross, Elisabeth, 206
Küng, Hans, 68

Labor Unions, 11, 132, 162
Land, 40–41, 119, 137, 140, 144, 146,
    147, 150f; *see also* Private Prop-
    erty, Property, Resources
Language, 130–31, 144–45, 167, 189
    conditioned by environment, 7,
        21–22, 57, 182, 201, 205
    control and, 7, 11, 45–46, 49, 50, 57,
        72, 74f, 80–83, 86–87, 104,
        117–18
    instrument of oppression, 57, 63, 72,
        88, 114, 171
    Jesus', 21–22
    as salvific, 65, 72, 74, 86–87
Last Judgment, 122–24, 128
Lateran Council IV, 114
Latin America, 146, 149
Law, 15, 16, 108, 117, 126, 152, 198,
    201
    and justice, 38, 87–88, 105–6, 120,
        123–24
Leadership, 90, 113, 118, 170, 171
Leamer, Lawrence, 64–65
Learson, T. Vincent, 181
Legal profession, 11
Leisure, 175; *see also* Rest
Lepers, 173
Liberation, 39–40, 49, 53, 85, 90–91,
    132, 133, 144–45, 185f, 200,
    213; *see also* Deliverance, Jesus,
    Name
    goal of, 40, 160
    revelation of the Name, 40f
Lies, 84–85, 89; *see also* Truth
Life, 100, passim
    as process of seeking our name, 38
Lifestyle, 69, 71, 77, 85, 102, 137, 176,
    185, 186f, 207, 214; *see also*
    Deliverance, Resistance
Light, 99, 102
Lincoln, Abraham, 64, 68
Liturgy, 4, 64, 122f
Lobbies, 11

Lohmeyer, Ernst, 138–39
Loneliness, 15; *see also* Alienation
Lonergan, Bernard, 197–203, 210, 211
Lord, Jesus as, 50, 104, 158, passim
Lord's Prayer, 3, 20, 22, 174
    discipline of the Secret, 2–3
    eschatological elements, 9, 34, 123
    and liturgical prayer, 2, 21
    and Sermon on the Mount, 8, 123
    and Sister Janet Mead, 1, 3
    as subversive, 2–3, 6, 16, 20–21, 53,
        59, passim
    as summary of the Beatitudes,
        123–24
    and third level of reality, 14, 16
    writings on, 1, 8, 23, 34, 123, 138,
        225
Los Angeles, California, 68
Love, 46, 49, 99–100, 106, 111, 140,
    141, 194, 203
    as care, 44, 46, 119
    and pathos, 42f
Luckmann, Thomas, 219
Luther, Martin, 1, 5

Macarius, St., 56
MacNutt, Francis S., 128, 141
Madison, James, 93–94
Madison Avenue, 49
Magazines, 11; *see also* Communications
Management, 206, 207, 227
Manifest Destiny, 216
Manipulation, 7, 26, 27, 36, 142, 158,
    182, 195, 200; *see also* Control,
    Language
Marcel, Gabriel, 24, 192
Marins, José, 160–61
Market, 131, 132, 153
Marschner, William H., 110
Martyrdom, 53; *see also* Witness
Mary, Blessed Virgin, 48, 102, 160, 213
Mary Magdalen, St., 49
Materialism, 65; *see also* Production-
    Consumption
Maturity dimension, 14f
May, Rollo, 44–45
McCarthy, Eugene, 68
McLaughlin, Dr. John, 65
Mead, Sister Janet, 2, 3
Meal, 117f, 130
Mechanization, 66f, 120, 211; *see also*
    Institution

Media, 152, 171, 177, 180f; *see also*
    Communications, Ideology, In-
    formation
    control of, 79, 178
Medical profession, 9, 11
Memorial Day, 64
Memphis, Tennessee, 68
Men, 57, 63, 171, 192, 206
Menominee Indians, 112
Merton, Thomas, 56
Mexico, 152
Middle Class, 80–81, 154–55
Miles Christi, 77
Militarism, 73, 167, 169, 171, 174–75,
    180, 189, 195, 210
Military, 9, 11, 78, 87–88, 90, 145
Milwaukee, Wisconsin, 170
Milwaukee Journal, 75
Milwaukee Sentinel, 132, 133
Mind-sets, 17f, 31, 42, 150, 178, 226; *see*
    also Conversion, Intellectual
Minister, 202
Ministry, 92, 126, 172–73, 190,
    191–92, 210, passim
    and care, 31, 44–45
    as mission of Jesus, 48f, 101f,
        136–37, 163–66
    relation to prayer, 17, 54–55, 159,
        passim
    three elements of, 35, 39–40, 192–93
    as will of God, 101f
    and work, 158–62; *see also* Work
Minorities, 179, 206; *see also* Isms
Mintz, Morton, 17
Miracles, 124
Miranda, José, 87
Mission, *see* Ministry
Mistrust, 95–96
Mobil Corporation, 80–82
Mohicans, 63
Moltmann, Jürgen, 38–39, 56, 70, 111
Mondale, Walter F., 180
Monopoly, 131, 132–33
Montgomery, Alabama, 170
Monument, *see* Infrastructure, Institu-
    tion
Morality, 109, 183, 184, 200f, 224; *see*
    also Ethics, Conversion
Mortgage, 58
Moses, 39–41, 62, 98–99, passim
Movement, Evolution of, 120, 166,
    210–11; *see also* Institution

political, 62f
religious, 7f, 66, 68, 163, 188, 210–11
Movies, 9, 11
Müller, Ronald, 179, 182
Multinational Corporation; *see*
    Corporation, Transnational
    Corporation
Mystery, *see* Blessing, Care, Plan of
    God
Myth, 15, 18, 147, 165, 199–200, 227;
    see also Ideology, Ritual

NBC, 179
Name, 37f, 112, 113
    baptism in, 49f, 188, passim
    and empowerment, 49, 80, 190; *see*
        also Empowerment, Grace
    and insurrection, 38, 51–52, 60–62
    of Jesus, 48f, 127, 188, 191–92, 221
    liberation and fidelity to, 39f, 91–92,
        102, 103, 188
    relation to control, power, 30, 36,
        37–39, 57
    relation to kingdom, will, 37–38, 97
    sharing in God's creative activity,
        28–29, 40, 188f
    sin as profanation of, 38, 50, 188; *see*
        also Alienation, Sin
Narragansetts, 63
Nation, 62; *see also* Society, United
    States
National Association of Manufacturers,
    177
National Conference of Catholic
    Bishops, 107
National Council of Teachers of Eng-
    lish, 82
National Defense, 82–83; *see also*
    Security
National Opinion Research Center,
    215, 216
National Security, 82–83; *see also*
    Security
Nationalism, 167, 189
Native Americans, 63, 112, 145
Needs, 156, 208, passim
    creative intervention of God, 41, 43
    determining of, 82, 140
    first element of prayer and ministry,
        35, 39, 40
Neighborhood, 20, 162

Network of domination, 14, 17, 19, 22, 74–75, 148, 166, 200
Neutrality, 43–45, 54, 80, 90, 109, 114, 182, 202
New International Economic Order, 146, 149
Newspapers, 11, 171; see also Communications
Nixon, Richard Milhaus, 64, 65, 82
Nonviolence, 60, 73
Norms, 8–13, 62, 63, 72, 77, 86, 87, 106, 108, 120, 124, 182, 198, 201
North-South configuration, 145–50, 173
Northern Cheyenne Indians, 173
Notre Dame University, 132
Nuclear Power, 74–75

OPEC, 180
Obedience, 13, passim; see also Disobedience
  defined by institutions, 12, 60, 84, 108, 114
Observant Franciscans, 2, 113
Ohio River, 145
Oil Companies, 80–81
Oligopoly, 150, 153–54, 179
Oppression, 20, 29, 41, 59, 63, 87–88, 107, 109, 113, 130, 132, 142, 145, 186, 213; see also Alienation, Enslavement
Organization for Economic Cooperation and Development, 147
Organized religion, 66f, 202, passim
  adaptation to other institutions, 10, 68, 168
  evolution of, 7f
  influence of, 9, 11
Origin, 1, 5
Original sin, 185; see also Alienation, Infrastructures, Sin, Social Sin
Orwell, George, 227

Parents, 157; see also Family
Parish structures, 112–13, 158, 160–61, 170, 172–73
Park Avenue, 71
Participative Community, 23f, 52, 118, 158, 190, 192, 221; see also Basic Community
  basis of spirituality, 15, 16, 18, 35, 96, 122–23, 156, 188; see also

Discipleship
  goal of creation, 25, 31
  through Holy Spirit, 16, 212, passim
  and Trinity, 23f, 34, 96, 156, 188
Patents, 155
Pathology, 16, 17f, 213
  freed by the Spirit, 20, 205–6; passim
  and normalcy, 72f, 177–78
  and sickness, 46, 225
  and sin, 17, 18–19, 46, 141, 184, 193, 194; see also Grave Sin of Social Injustice
  of world, 18, 44, 184; see also Sin
Pathos, 43f, 139
  and God's justice, 43, 109, 110
Paul VI, Pope, 53–54, 108, 141, 151–53, 162, 174–75, 199, 207
Pawlikowski, John T., 120
Payoffs, 79
Peace, 3, 67, 70, 78, 92–96, 112–13, 126, 130, 174, 217, passim
  based on just sharing, 92f, 119, 174
  relation to property, 112–13; see also Property, Resources
Peace and Justice Commission, Pontifical, 147
Pellegrino, Cardinal Michelle, 168
Penance, see Conversion, Reconciliation
Pentagon, 80, 113
Perfection, 15, 33–34, 110; see also Holiness, Justice
Perizites, 63
Persecution, 52, 72, 102–03, 170; see also Insurrection, Subversion
Person, 24f, 28, passim; see also Subject, Self
Pfeiffer, Jane Cahill, 181
Pharisees, 8, 86f, 100, 103, 105, 117, 165, 214, passim
Philippine Islands, 53
Piety, 105; see also Spirituality
Pilate, Pontius, 3, 103, 105
Pilgrims and strangers, 10, 68f, 86, 142, 150, 151, 158, 162, 166
Plan of God, 27f, 55, 63, 66, 85, 97f, 111, 127–28, 176, passim; see also Creation, Will of God
Pliny, 2, 3
Police, Local, 9
Political contributions, 79
Political institutions, see Government
Polls, 11, 219

Pollution, 152; *see also* Ecological Balance, Resources
Poor, 61, 65, 88, 92, 107, 127, 136, 142, 148, 155–57, 224; *see also* Poverty, Resources
cry of, 31, 39f, 53f, 67, 98, 110, 118
as image of Christ, 32–33, 221, passim
Poverty, 26, 27, 72, 91, 129–30, 148, 155–56, 157, 158, 196, passim; *see also* Poor, Resources, Oppression, Distribution
described, 155, 158
Power, 25, 27, 57, 63, 65, 96, 106, 110, 111, 119, 157, 161, 164–65, 211; *see also* Wealth
distribution of, 146f, 179f; *see also* Distribution
God's, 25, 27f, 106; *see also* Plan of God
Powerlessness, 63, 65; *see also* Enslavement, Oppression, Poor
Powers and Principalities, 38, 90, 102, 213; *see also* Alienation, Social Sin, Grave Sin of Social Injustice, Subversion
conquered on Cross, 85, 104–6
goal of, 80, 85–86, 198
infrastructures and, 2, 70, 71, 141; *see also* Infrastructures
Jesus and, 163–66, 186
resistance to, 2, 59–60, 62, 77–78, 102f, 186f
Powhatans, 63
Praise, 3, 51–52, 211, passim
Prayer, 7, 13, 16–17, 31, 56–57, 92, 101, 129, 158–62, 190f, 195–96, 203–4, 212f, passim; *see also* Contemplation
as effort to name God, 38–39
groups, 187; *see also* Basic communities
having access to God as ultimate resource, 31, 142
Jesus', 21–22, 91f, 136, 193
levels of, 14f, passim
relation to ministry, 54–55, 159, 196
in the Spirit, passim
three elements of, 35, 39–40, 192–93
Preaching, 34, 52, 53, 73, 85, 90, 106, 115, 157, 171, 199; *see also* Conversion, Ministry, Charisms

Prejudice, 173–74; *see also* Isms
Presence, 35f, 39, 48, 192; *see also* Self
and name of God, 41, 92
second level of prayer and ministry, 35, 39
Price-fixing, 131, 132–33
Priesthood of the Faithful, 172–73
Priestly version
Genesis, 27, 28, 31, 40–41
Exodus, 39
Priests, 46, 47, 89–90, 102, 169, 171, 173, 187, 202, 215; *see also* Clerics, Class
Prison(ers), 136, 142
Privilege, 168–69
Production-Consumption, 3, 4, 30, 158, 175–76, 209; *see also* Capitalism, Consumerism
Profit, 81, 132–33, 151, 152–53, 154
Propaganda, 86; *see also* Ideology, Language
Property, 51, 103, 144
"Bundle of Rights," 146, 148, 151, 202, 223–24, 225; *see also* Rights, Human Rights
Jubilee, 144f, 227–28
and land, 63, 93, 148, 150f
private, 151, 156–57, 223–24
relation to security, 84, 93
relation to state (society), 94
relation to war, 93–94, 151
Prophecy, 124, 199
Prophet, 45–48, 78, 134, 204, 213; *see also* Biblical Index
false, 89–90
identification with plan of God through prayer and ministry, 47, 118f, 214
primary mission to own institutions, 45, 47
Proposition, 15, 75
Protestants, 214–16, passim
Psychology, 14, 18; *see also* Pathology
Purity of Heart, 36, 56, 184

Rabbi, 202
Racism, 63, 65, 96, 144, 145f, 162, 166, 169, 171, 179, 180, 189, 207f, 213
analysis of, 173; *see also* Isms
in development patterns, 146
Radio, 11, 133, 177; *see also* Communications

Reality, 20, 63, 95, 182–83, 187, 189
  levels of, 14f, 213, passim; see also
    World
  and prayer, 7, 43–44
  and ritual, 119f
Reconciliation, 110f, 125f, 213; see also
    Conversion
Recruits, 72, 155, 156–57
Redlining, 58
Religion, 120, 158, 161–62, 165, 177,
    215, 216, passim; see also Church,
    Institution
  as instrument of oppression, 144–45;
    see also Domestication
Religious experience, 23, 41–42, 47f,
    159, 160, 176; see also Faith, Grace
Religious life, 187, 190, 202, 215, 220;
    see also Basic communities
Religious movement, 7f; see also
    Institution, Movement
Reparation, 127; see also Reconciliation
Republican Party, 11
Resistance, 60–62, 67, 70, 77, 78, 96,
    102, 107–9, 110f, 132, 133, 211; see
    also Insurrection, Lifestyle
  as Jesus' response to sin, 163–66, 168,
    185
  as lifestyle, 166–68, 183, 185, 188
Resources, access to, 28, 31, 63, 72, 87,
    95, 101, 106f, 114, 146, 148,
    155–56, 158, 170, 174–76, 183,
    189, 196, 207f, 227–28, passim; see
    also Basic communities
  basis of spirituality, 23f, 31–32, 166,
    187
  described, 31, 66, 100, 102, 117, 118,
    119, 122–23, 223–24.
  Eucharist and, 117f; see also Eucharist
  and Trinity, 23, 93, passim
Response, 41–42
Rest, 83–84, 158–62; see also Security
Resurrection, 52, 104, 105–6, 111, 115;
    see also Cross
Revelation, 5–6; see also Word of God
  and creation, 43f
  God's pathos, 39f
Revolutionary War, 64
Right to food, 132–33
Right to life, 106f, 170
Right to privacy, 107
Right to property, 94, 151, 156–57,
    223–24, 225; see also Property, Re-
sources
Rights, 63, 88, 93–94, 96, 109, 183; see
    also Image, Human Rights
Ritual, 15, 21, 26, 46f, 67, 118f
Rochester, New York, 63
Rockefeller, David, 180
Rome, Italy, 142
Roy, Cardinal Maurice, 147

Sabath, Robert, 61, 69
Sabbath, 83, 138–39
  Jubilee Year, 138f; see also Jubilee
  rest, 158–62; see also Rest
Sacred Congregation for the Doctrine
    of the Faith, 107, 108, 109
Sacrifice, 46–47, 101, 118f, passim
Sadducees, 165
Sahel, 131
Saint Louis, Missouri, 174
Salvation, 48, 50, 56, 78, passim
  through Cross, 70, 104
  linked to institution, 66, 70, 104, 161
"Sanctification of the Name," 52
Sanity, 73f, 178–79; see also Pathology
Santa Cruz, Dr. Hernan, 148, 149
São Paulo, Brazil, 58
Satan, see Powers and Principalities
Schlier, Heinrich, 59–60
Schlotterbeck, Walter, 75
Schools, 158, 162, 169, 172–73, 183,
    187; see also Education, Ideology
Scribes, 86f, 100, 102, 105
Scripts, 213–14
Seattle, Washington, 174
Secrecy, 79, 182, 228; see also Truth
Security, 82–84, 180, 201, 202
  and biblical rest, 83–84, 158–62
  and consumerism, 82, 158, 176
  and militarism, 82–83, 94f
  relation to property, 83–84, 94; see
    also Property, Resources
Seeing God, 41–42, passim; see also
    Knowledge
Selective inattention, 95
Self, 15, 18, 20, 24f, 39, 49, 55–56, 199,
    200, 201, passim; see also Person
Selma, Alabama, 68, 113, 170
Senate, U.S., 11
Seoul, Korea, 169
Sermon, see Preaching
Sermon on the Mount, 202
Servant, 52, 101–2, 129, 134, 137

Sexism, 22, 25, 66, 167, 169, 171, 173, 179, 189, 207f, 213; *see also* Isms, Women
Sexuality, 13
Shaliach, 111–13, 126f
Shapiro, Irving, 181
Shareholders, 74–75, 80–81, 179, 223, 227–28
Sign, 100, 104, 129, 133–34, 135, 155
Silence, 59, 65, 95, 96, 145, 158f, 168
Simplicity, 91; *see also* Poverty
Sin, *see also* Alienation, Infrastructure, Powers and Principalities
  individual, 17, 91, 185, passim
  interpersonal, 17, 185, passim
  as profanation of the Name, 39
  of the world, 17, 48, 72, 91, 103, 163f, 193, passim; *see also* Infrastructure, Grave Sin of Social Injustice, Social Sin, Powers and Principalities
Sin, Cardinal Jaime, 53
Slaves, 61, 63, 137, 139, 144f; *see also* Enslavement, Oppression
Small business, 11, 152
Smith, Adam, 152
Social grace, 134, 187, 194–95, passim; *see also* Empowerment
Social sin, 18, 134, 163, 185, passim; *see also* Alienation, Addiction, Infrastructures, Grave Sin of Social Injustice, Powers and Principalities
  in ideology, 166, 170, 176–84
  in infrastructures, 18, 134, 163f, 167
  in institutions, 166, 167–70, 177, 178
  in isms, 166, 170–76, 178
Socialism, 152
Society, 20, 51, 124, 158, 160, 175–76, 179, 183, 184, 199, 201, 214, 227, passim; *see also* Government, Reality
  purpose of, 107, 148
Sociology, 6
Sodom and Gomorrah, 98, 224
Soldier of Jesus Christ, 77f
Solzhenitsyn, Alexander, 84–85
South Africa, 173, 177–78, 180
Spirit, Holy, 15, 16, 50, 56, 78, 91, 103, 114, 125, 163f, 195, 203–4, 213, 218
  giving access to Father, 20, 22, 24, 124, 125–27

liberating role of, 20, 133, 141, 186f
  and restoration on levels of reality, 20, 33–34, 141, 203–4, 212
Spirituality, 5–6, 194, 213f, passim
  biography as theology, 213–15
  lived in environment, 4f
  expression of Trinity, 33f; *see also* Trinity
  founded in Genesis 1:26, 27f
  levels of, 15, passim
Sport, 4, 70
State, *see* Government, Society
Stringfellow, William, 80, 184, 185
Subject, 25, 48, 55, 58, 187, 197, 217; *see also* Image, Person, Self
Subversion, 4, 53, 64, 86, 103; *see also* Cross, Insurrection, Lord's Prayer
  description of, 72, 102, 110–11
  early Christians and, 2–3, 50f
  Jesus as, 69, 100–01, 129; *see also* Jesus
  use of titles, 61, 69
Suenens, Cardinal Leo, 53, 204, 220
Suetonius, 60
Suffering, 47, 71, 101, 111; *see also* Pathology
  as inability to have access to resource of healing, 39, 51–52, 128–30; *see also* Healing, Deliverance
Supreme Court, U.S., 11, 107, 108, 170
Surface level, 15–16, 26, 200–01, passim; *see also* Reality
Symbols, 81, 167, 189
Sympathy, 44, 45f, 58, 109, 110, 139
Synod of Bishops
  1971, 1, 19, 90, 91, 96, 134, 148, 166, 177, 185, 198–99
  1974, 169
System, 143, 158; *see also* Infrastructure, Reality

Tau, 58, 114–15
Tax, 58, 81, 154–55, 168, 169
Teaching, *see* Education, Schools
Technology, 25–26, 145, 148, 155, 167, 177, 179, 181, 189
Television, 9, 11, 132, 177, 178; *see also* Communications, Media
Temple, 24, 165, 168
Temptation, 163f, passim; *see also* Powers and Principalities

Tertullian, 1
Third World, 148, 173, 180; see also Development, North-South Configuration
Thomas of Celano, Brother, see Celano Index
Tide, 50
Time, 158–60; see also Kairos
Tomic, Radomiro, 150
Trade, 146, 155
Tradition, 8–13, 62, 63, 72, 77, 86, 106, 108, 117, 120, 124, 126, 165, 182, 198, 201, passim
Trajan, 2
Transactional analysts, 213, 219
Transnational corporation, 11, 81, 146, 149–50, 152–54, 173; see also Corporation
Trilateral Commission, 146, 180, 181
Trinity, 23f, 35, 196, 208, passim
    as participative community, 23f, 187, 192
    Procter and Gamble's, 49–50
    Richard Nixon's, 65
"True Followers of Justice," 90, 191
Truth, 79, 80–86, 89, 95, 99, 105, 158, 177, 178; see also Morality, Ethics
    foundation for ethics, 79, 109
    language and manipulation, 80–82, 84
Tubman, Harriet, 145
Turin, Italy, 168

Union, 122, see also Contemplation, Identification, Prayer
Union of Soviet Socialist Republics, 177
United Kingdom, 148
United Nations, 173
    Development Decades, 147
    International Covenant on Human Rights, 148
    New International Economic Order, 146, 149
United States, 62f, 81, 93, 106f, 139, 145f, 148, 150, 152, 173, 178f, 206f, 213f, 227, passim
United States Catholic Conference, 178
Unity, 130, 193; see also Reconciliation
Usery, 140

Vaitsos, Constantine V., 149
Values, 8, 13, 63, 77, 78, 86, 110, 140, 182, 190, 200, 201, 202, passim

Van Kamm, Adrian, 219
Vance, Cyrus, 180, 181
Vatican City, 171
Vatican Council II, 10, 69, 204
Vietnam, 65, 68; see also Indochinese War
Violence, 77, 112; see also Apathy
    founded in property, 93, 112
    of institutions, 18, 72f, 171, 175
    of language, 84–85
Voluntarism, 208–9, 217
Vow, 79; see also Consecration, Discipleship

Wall Street, 11
Wall Street Journal, 73, 132–33, 175–76
The Wanderer, 110
War, 77, 78, 93, 143; see also Violence
    steps leading to, 94, 95–96
Warnke, Paul, 180
Washington, D.C., 62
Washington, George, 64
Watergate, 65, 79
Wealth, Concentration/Distribution of, 80–81, 88, 94, 96, 146f, 150f, 169, 179f, 206f, 215, 226, 228, passim
    described, 154; see also Resources
    effects of, 151, 155
Westermann, Claus, 28
West Indies, 155
Western Europe, 146, 180
White, Ralph K., 94–95, 112
White House, 11, 65, 80
Will, see Love
Will of God, 128, 130, 206, 216, passim
    identity with God's plan, 67, 87, 97f, 119–20, 164, 184; see also Plan of God
    relation to name and kingdom, 37–38, 97, 123
Wisconsin, 131, 208
Wisdom, 53, 70, 104; see also Genesis
Witness, 52–53, 55, 183
Women, 57, 58, 63, 147, 171, 179, 192, 206, 207f; see also Isms, Sexism
Wonder, see Awe, Contemplation
Word of God, 6, 10, 17, 19, 25, 32, 78, 79, 97, 125, 133, 160, 161, 165, 168, 183, 190, 193, 208, 213, 217, 224; see also Gospel, Jesus Christ, Plan of God
    giving access to the Father, 23, 193
    image of God, 23, 28, passim

Words, *see* Language
Work, 158–62, 175; *see also* Ministry
Workers, 152–53, 154; *see also* Labor
  Unions
World, 99, 100, 111, 158, 161–62, 166;
  see also Reality
World Bank, 147

Worship, 120f, 139; *see also* Liturgy
Wounded Knee, South Dakota, 113

Yoder, John Howard, 71, 138

Zacchaeus, 49
Zealots, 69, 71